501 Budget Meals RECIPES

Edited by
Susan O'Loughlan

OCTOPUS
BOOKS

Notes

All measurements in this book are given in metric, imperial and American. Follow one set only because they are not interchangeable.

Standard spoon measurements are used in all recipes
1 tablespoon = one 15 ml spoon
1 teaspoon = one 5 ml spoon
All spoon measurements are level

Ovens and grills (broilers) should be preheated to the specified temperature or heat setting.

All recipes serve 4 people, unless otherwise stated.

First published 1984 by
Octopus Books Limited
59 Grosvenor Street
London W1

© 1984 Octopus Books Limited

ISBN 0 7064 1932 4

Printed in Czechoslovakia
50538

Contents

BUDGET

Soups

MEALS

Carrot and Orange Soup

METRIC/IMPERIAL
25 g/1 oz butter
1 clove of garlic, crushed
1 medium onion, peeled and
  chopped
500 g/1 lb carrots, peeled and
  coarsely grated
900 ml/1½ pints water
2 tablespoons orange juice and
  finely grated zest of 1 orange
1 teaspoon tomato purée
1 chicken stock cube, crumbled
salt and freshly ground black
  pepper
1 teaspoon cornflour
2 tablespoons cold water
150 ml/¼ pint milk
1 teaspoon chopped parsley to
  garnish (optional)

AMERICAN
2 tablespoons butter
1 clove of garlic, crushed
1 medium-size onion, peeled and
  chopped
1 lb carrots, peeled and coarsely
  grated
3¾ cups water
2 tablespoons orange juice and
  finely grated zest of 1 orange
1 teaspoon tomato paste
1 chicken bouillon cube, crumbled
salt and freshly ground black
  pepper
1 teaspoon cornstarch
2 tablespoons cold water
⅔ cup milk
1 teaspoon chopped parsley for
  garnish (optional)

Melt the butter in a saucepan, add the crushed garlic, chopped onion and
grated carrot. Stir and cook, covered, for 5 minutes over a low heat. Add
the water, orange juice and zest, tomato purée and stock (bouillon) cube.
Season to taste. Simmer, covered, for 30 minutes. Moisten the cornflour
(cornstarch) with the cold water, stir into the soup and simmer for another
5 minutes. Liquidize the soup in an electric blender or pass through a
sieve. Stir in the milk and chill in the refrigerator. Before serving taste and
adjust the seasoning and, if liked, sprinkle with the chopped parsley.

Minestrone

METRIC/IMPERIAL	AMERICAN
1 medium leek, finely shredded	1 medium-size leek, finely shredded
1 medium carrot, thinly sliced	1 medium-size carrot, thinly sliced
175 g/6 oz cabbage, cored and finely shredded	1½ cups finely shredded cabbage
1 large onion, thinly sliced	1 large onion, thinly sliced
2 large celery stalks, thinly sliced	2 large celery stalks, thinly sliced
1 x 100 g/4 oz packet frozen green beans	1 cup frozen green beans
50 g/2 oz dried white haricot beans, soaked overnight and drained	⅓ cup dried navy beans, soaked overnight and drained
1 x 400 g/14 oz can tomatoes	1 x 1 lb can tomatoes
2 teaspoons chopped parsley	2 teaspoons chopped parsley
1 teaspoon dried basil	1 teaspoon dried basil
1 teaspoon sugar	1 teaspoon sugar
900 ml/1½ pints water	1 quart water
salt and pepper	salt and pepper
50 g/2 oz broken macaroni	½ cup broken macaroni
75 g/3 oz Cheddar cheese, finely grated	¾ cup finely grated Cheddar cheese

Put the leek, carrot, cabbage, onion and celery into a large saucepan. Add the green beans, haricot (navy) beans, tomatoes with their juice, parsley, basil, sugar, water and salt and pepper to taste. Bring to the boil, then lower the heat and cover the pan. Simmer gently for 1 hour.

Add the macaroni and simmer for a further 15 minutes.

Sprinkle with the cheese and serve.

Creamy Carrot Soup

METRIC/IMPERIAL	AMERICAN
25 g/1 oz butter	2 tablespoons butter
1 medium onion, coarsely grated	1 medium-size onion, shredded
225 g/8 oz carrots, coarsely grated	4 carrots (about ½ lb), shredded
1 large potato, coarsely grated	1 large potato, shredded
450 ml/¾ pint water	2 cups water
300 ml/½ pint milk	1¼ cups milk
25 g/1 oz long-grain rice	2½ tablespoons long-grain rice
large pinch of grated nutmeg	large pinch of grated nutmeg
½–1 teaspoon salt	½–1 teaspoon salt
2 teaspoons lemon juice	2 teaspoons lemon juice

Melt the butter in a large saucepan. Add the onion, carrots and potato and fry gently for 5 minutes. Add the water, milk, rice, nutmeg and salt and bring to the boil. Cover and simmer gently for 45 minutes to 1 hour. Stir in the lemon juice and serve.

Split Pea Soup with Frankfurters

METRIC/IMPERIAL

225 g/8 oz salt belly of pork, cubed
500 g/1 lb dried green peas,
    soaked overnight in cold water to
    cover
4 medium carrots, peeled and
    chopped
4 medium onions, peeled and
    chopped
2 medium leaks, white and pale
    green part, washed and chopped
4 stalks celery, scrubbed and
    chopped
1 small cooking apple, peeled,
    cored and chopped
1 tablespoon soft brown sugar or
    treacle
sprig of mint
sprig of parsley
salt and freshly ground black
    pepper
TO FINISH:
25 g/1 oz butter
2 or 3 frankfurters, cut into 1 cm/
    ½ inch lengths

AMERICAN

½ lb salt pork sides, cubed
2 cups dried split peas, soaked
    overnight in cold water to cover
4 medium-size carrots, peeled and
    chopped
4 medium-size onions, peeled and
    chopped
2 medium-size leeks, white and
    pale green part, washed and
    chopped
4 celery sticks, scrubbed and
    chopped
1 small cooking apple, peeled,
    cored and chopped
1 tablespoon firmly packed light
    brown sugar or molasses
sprig of mint
sprig of parsley
salt and freshly ground black
    pepper
TO FINISH:
2 tablespoons butter
2 or 3 frankfurters, cut into ½ inch
    lengths

Put the cubes of pork into a large saucepan. Cover them with water and bring slowly to the boil. Drain off the water and cover the meat with 2½ litres/4½ pints (11 cups) of fresh cold water.

Rinse the soaked peas under cold running water. Add the peas, vegetables, apple, sugar or treacle (molasses), herbs and seasoning to the saucepan and bring to the boil. Remove any scum with a slotted draining spoon. Reduce the heat, cover and simmer gently, stirring occasionally, for about 2 hours or until the peas are soft and pulpy. The time will depend upon the quality and freshness of the dried split peas.

Taste and adjust the seasoning. Remove the herbs and stir in the butter and frankfurters. Reheat and serve very hot with wholemeal bread.
Serves 8

French Onion Soup

METRIC/IMPERIAL
40 g/1½ oz butter
350 g/12 oz onions, thinly sliced
900 ml/1½ pints beef stock
salt and pepper
4 slices of French bread, 2.5 cm/
  1 inch thick
50 g/2 oz Cheddar cheese, finely
  grated

AMERICAN
3 tablespoons butter
2 large onions (about ¾ lb), thinly
  sliced
1 quart beef broth
salt and pepper
4 slices of French bread, 1 inch
  thick
½ cup finely grated Cheddar
  cheese

Melt the butter in a saucepan. Add the onions and fry very gently until golden brown. Pour in the stock (broth), season to taste with salt and pepper and bring to the boil. Cover and simmer for 45 minutes.

Preheat the grill (broiler) to high.

Pour the soup into a flameproof tureen or bowl. Float the bread on top and sprinkle with the cheese. Brown under the grill (broiler) and serve immediately.

Cold Cucumber and Prawn Soup

METRIC/IMPERIAL
1 large cucumber, peeled and
  halved
6 spring onions, trimmed
900 ml/1½ pints chicken stock
1 teaspoon dried dill
25 g/1 oz cornflour
3 tablespoons water
salt and freshly ground black
  pepper
few drops of green food colouring
50 g/2 oz peeled prawns
4 tablespoons single cream to
  garnish

AMERICAN
1 large cucumber, peeled and
  halved
6 scallions, trimmed
3¾ cups chicken stock
1 teaspoon dried dill
¼ cup cornstarch
3 tablespoons water
salt and freshly ground black
  pepper
few drops of green food coloring
2 oz shelled shrimp
¼ cup light cream for garnish

Deseed the cucumber and slice. Chop the spring onions (scallions), including as much of the green parts as possible, and simmer in the stock with the cucumber and dill until quite tender. Liquidize in an electric blender or pass through a sieve.

Reheat the soup. Moisten the cornflour (cornstarch) with the water, add to the soup, stir until boiling and simmer gently for 3 minutes. Remove from the heat and add the seasoning to taste. When cool stir in a few drops of food colouring, and the prawns (shrimp).

Chill well before serving with a spoonful of cream swirled into each portion.

Sweetcorn Soup

METRIC/IMPERIAL
25 g/1 oz butter
1 streaky bacon rasher, derinded
   and chopped
1 small onion, finely chopped
2 large potatoes, sliced
2 celery stalks, sliced
300 ml/½ pint chicken stock
salt and pepper
1 x 200 g/7 oz can sweetcorn
   kernels, drained
1 tablespoon cornflour
600 ml/1 pint milk
croûtons to garnish

AMERICAN
2 tablespoons butter
1 bacon slice, chopped
1 small onion, finely chopped
2 large potatoes, sliced
2 celery stalks, sliced
1¼ cups chicken broth
salt and pepper
1 x 8 oz can whole kernel corn,
   drained
1 tablespoon cornstarch
2½ cups milk
croûtons for garnish

Melt the butter in a saucepan. Add the bacon and onion and fry until the onion is softened. Stir in the potatoes and celery. Add the stock (broth), and salt and pepper to taste. Bring to the boil and simmer until all the vegetables are soft.

Stir in the corn kernels. Blend the cornflour (cornstarch) with some of the cold milk. Add to the soup with the remaining milk. Bring to the boil again and simmer for 5 minutes.

Rub the soup through a sieve, or purée in a blender or food processor. Reheat if necessary and serve garnished with croûtons.

Vegetable Soup

METRIC/IMPERIAL
25 g/1 oz butter
1 medium carrot, diced
1 small parsnip, diced
½ small turnip, diced
2 large celery stalks, chopped
1 medium onion, chopped
1 large leek, finely shredded
900 ml/1½ pints water
1 tablespoon well-washed pearl
   barley
1–1½ teaspoons salt
chopped parsley to garnish

AMERICAN
2 tablespoons butter
1 medium-size carrot, diced
1 small parsnip, diced
½ small turnip, diced
2 large celery stalks, chopped
1 medium-size onion, chopped
1 large leek, finely shredded
1 quart water
1 tablespoon well-washed pearl
   barley
1–1½ teaspoons salt
chopped parsley for garnish

Melt the butter in a saucepan. Add the vegetables and cover the pan. Fry gently for 7 minutes without browning, shaking the pan often.

Add the water, barley and salt and bring to the boil. Lower the heat, cover the pan and simmer for 1½ hours or until the barley is soft.

Sprinkle with chopped parsley and serve.

Cheese Soup with Dumplings

METRIC/IMPERIAL
50 g/2 oz butter
1 medium onion, peeled and finely
    chopped
25 g/1 oz flour
½ teaspoon dry mustard
900 ml/1½ pints chicken stock
300 ml/½ pint milk
½ teaspoon salt
¼ teaspoon freshly ground white
    pepper
¼ teaspoon grated nutmeg
75 g/3 oz Cheddar cheese, grated
FOR THE DUMPLINGS:
50 g/2 oz quick cook oats
25 g/1 oz shredded beef suet
1 tablespoon grated onion
1 tablespoon chopped parsley
salt and freshly ground white
    pepper
1 egg

AMERICAN
¼ cup butter
1 medium-size onion, peeled and
    finely chopped
¼ cup flour
½ teaspoon dry mustard
3¾ cups chicken broth
1¼ cups milk
½ teaspoon salt
¼ teaspoon freshly ground white
    pepper
¼ teaspoon grated nutmeg
¾ cup grated Cheddar cheese
FOR THE DUMPLINGS:
2 oz quick cook oats
3 tablespoons shredded beef suet
1 tablespoon grated onion
1 tablespoon chopped parsley
salt and freshly ground white
    pepper
1 egg

Melt the butter in a fairly large saucepan. Add the onion and fry gently until soft but not brown. Stir in the flour and the dry mustard and cook for 1 minute. Gradually add the stock and milk and bring to the boil, stirring constantly. Add the salt, pepper and grated nutmeg, stir well, cover and simmer for 10 minutes.

Meanwhile, make the dumplings. Place the oats, suet, grated onion and chopped parsley in a bowl and season to taste. Beat the egg until fluffy and use to bind the dry ingredients. Divide the mixture into 16 pieces and roll each one into a ball. Drop the balls into boiling salted water and cook gently for 10 to 15 minutes. Remove with a slotted draining spoon and keep warm.

Liquidize the soup in an electric blender, or pass through a sieve, and return to the rinsed-out saucepan. Stir in the cheese and reheat without boiling. Taste and adjust the seasoning, and serve topped with the brown dumplings.

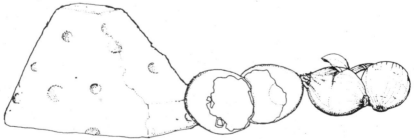

Curried Chicken Soup

METRIC/IMPERIAL
25 g/1 oz butter
2 teaspoons curry powder
1 teaspoon cornflour
450 ml/¾ pint chicken stock or
  water
½ teaspoon paprika
2 teaspoons chutney
50 g/2 oz cooked chicken meat,
  diced
1 egg yolk
salt and pepper

AMERICAN
2 tablespoons butter
2 teaspoons curry powder
1 teaspoon cornstarch
2 cups chicken broth or water
½ teaspoon paprika
2 teaspoons chutney
⅓ cup diced cooked chicken
1 egg yolk
salt and pepper

Melt the butter in a large saucepan. Stir in the curry powder and cornflour (cornstarch) and cook gently for 2 minutes. Gradually stir in the stock (broth) or water, then add the paprika. Cook, stirring, until the mixture comes to the boil and thickens slightly.

Add the chutney and chicken. Cover and simmer for 7 minutes.

Remove from the heat and stir in the egg yolk. Season to taste with salt and pepper and serve.

Beef Broth

METRIC/IMPERIAL
25 g/1 oz butter
1 medium carrot, diced
1 small parsnip, diced
½ small turnip, diced
1 medium onion, chopped
2 large celery stalks, chopped
1 large leek, chopped
100 g/4 oz lean stewing steak, cut
  into small strips
900 ml/1½ pints water
1 teaspoon well-washed pearl
  barley
1 teaspoon salt
chopped parsley to garnish

AMERICAN
2 tablespoons butter
1 medium-size carrot, diced
1 small parsnip, diced
½ small white turnip, diced
1 medium-size onion, chopped
2 large celery stalks, chopped
1 large leek, chopped
¼ lb beef for stew, cut into small
  strips
1 quart water
1 teaspoon well-washed pearl
  barley
1 teaspoon salt
chopped parsley for garnish

Melt the butter in a large saucepan. Add the vegetables and meat and cover. Fry gently, without allowing the vegetables to brown, for 7 minutes. Shake the pan often to prevent sticking.

Pour in the water, and add the barley and salt. Bring to the boil. Lower the heat and simmer gently for 1½ hours or until the meat is tender.

Garnish with parsley and serve.

Chicken Soup

METRIC/IMPERIAL
1 chicken carcass
1 medium onion, chopped
1 bay leaf
1 clove
600 ml/1 pint milk
1 chicken stock cube
4 tablespoons boiling water
1 tablespoon cornflour
4 tablespoons cold water
¼ teaspoon grated nutmeg
100 g/4 oz cooked chicken meat,
 chopped
salt and pepper

AMERICAN
1 chicken carcass
1 medium-size onion, chopped
1 bay leaf
1 clove
2½ cups milk
1 chicken bouillon cube
¼ cup boiling water
1 tablespoon cornstarch
¼ cup cold water
¼ teaspoon grated nutmeg
¾ cup chopped cooked chicken
 meat
salt and pepper

Break up the chicken carcass and put it in a large saucepan. Add the onion, bay leaf, clove and milk. Dissolve the stock (bouillon) cube in the boiling water and add. Bring to the boil and simmer very gently for 20 minutes.

Strain and return the liquid to the pan. Dissolve the cornflour (cornstarch) to a smooth paste in the cold water and add to the liquid. Cook, stirring, until it comes to the boil and thickens slightly.

Add the nutmeg and chicken, and season to taste with salt and pepper. Cover and simmer for 15 minutes. Serve hot.

Cabbage Soup

METRIC/IMPERIAL
25 g/1 oz butter
1 medium onion, coarsely grated
1 small cabbage (about 225 g/
 8 oz), cored and shredded
600 ml/1 pint beef stock
salt and pepper
chopped parsley to garnish

AMERICAN
2 tablespoons butter
1 medium-size onion, shredded
1 small head of cabbage (about
 ½ lb), cored and shredded
2½ cups beef broth
salt and pepper
chopped parsley for garnish

Melt the butter in a large saucepan. Add the onion and fry gently until softened and golden brown. Stir in the cabbage and stock (broth) and bring to the boil. Season to taste with salt and pepper. Cover the pan and simmer gently for 15 minutes.

Sprinkle with parsley and serve very hot.

Cauliflower and Green Pea Soup

METRIC/IMPERIAL
1 small cauliflower, trimmed and
   leaves removed
600 ml/1 pint water
1 medium onion, peeled and grated
salt and freshly ground white
   pepper
1 teaspoon grated nutmeg
50 g/2 oz butter
2 tablespoons flour
600 ml/1 pint milk
100 g/4 oz frozen green peas
1 egg yolk

AMERICAN
1 small cauliflower, trimmed and
   leaves removed
2½ cups water
1 medium-size onion, peeled and
   grated
salt and freshly ground white
   pepper
1 teaspoon grated nutmeg
¼ cup butter
2 tablespoons flour
2½ cups milk
¾ cup frozen green peas
1 egg yolk

Break the cauliflower into florets. Put them into a saucepan with the water, grated onion and seasonings. Bring to the boil and simmer, covered, for about 20 minutes or until the cauliflower is just tender. Remove the cauliflower florets with a slotted draining spoon and mash to make into a purée.

Melt the butter in a clean saucepan, stir in the flour and cook for 1 minute. Gradually stir in the water in which the cauliflower florets were cooked, add the milk and bring to the boil, stirring all the time. Reduce the heat, add the cauliflower purée and the frozen green peas and simmer for 10 minutes. Remove from the heat, adjust the seasoning if necessary and stir in the lightly beaten egg yolk. Return to the heat for 1 minute, stirring constantly, but do not allow to boil.

Lamb and Vegetable Broth

METRIC/IMPERIAL
500 g/1 lb scrag end neck lamb,
    trimmed of excess fat and cut
    into bite-size pieces
1 litre/1¾ pints cold water
1 large onion, chopped
2 medium celery stalks, chopped
1 medium carrot, diced
½ small turnip, diced
25 g/1 oz well-washed pearl barley
1½–2 teaspoons salt

AMERICAN
1 lb lamb neck slices, trimmed of
    excess fat and cut into bite-size
    pieces
1 quart cold water
1 large onion, chopped
2 medium-size celery stalks,
    chopped
1 medium-size carrot, diced
½ small turnip, diced
3 tablespoons well-washed pearl
    barley
1½–2 teaspoons salt

Put the lamb into a large saucepan with the water and bring to the boil, skimming off any scum. Cover and leave to simmer very gently for 10 minutes.

Add the vegetables, barley and salt to taste. Bring back to the boil, then cover again and simmer gently for 2 hours. Remove from the heat and leave until completely cold.

Remove and discard any fat from the surface, then bring the soup to the boil and serve.

Leek and Potato Cream

METRIC/IMPERIAL
25 g/1 oz butter
500 g/1 lb leeks, washed and sliced
500 g/1 lb potatoes, peeled and
    sliced
1 large onion, peeled and chopped
600 ml/1 pint water
salt and freshly ground black
    pepper
1 teaspoon grated nutmeg
1 bay leaf
300 ml/½ pint milk

AMERICAN
2 tablespoons butter
1 lb leeks, washed and sliced
1 lb potatoes, peeled and sliced
1 large onion, peeled and chopped
2½ cups water
salt and freshly ground black
    pepper
1 teaspoon grated nutmeg
1 bay leaf
1¼ cups milk

Heat the butter in a large saucepan. Add the leek, potato and onion and cook gently, covered, for about 5 minutes. Shake the pan occasionally to prevent the vegetables from sticking. Add the water, seasoning, grated nutmeg and bay leaf and bring to the boil. Simmer, covered, for 30 minutes. Remove the bay leaf. Liquidize in an electric blender or pass through a sieve.

Return the soup to the saucepan, add the milk and reheat. Taste and adjust the seasoning.

Paprika Beef Soup

METRIC/IMPERIAL
25 g/1 oz butter
1 medium onion, chopped
1 small red or green pepper, cored,
    seeded and chopped
350 g/12 oz shin of beef, cubed
1 tablespoon paprika
1 teaspoon tomato purée
½ teaspoon sugar
1 teaspoon salt
½ teaspoon caraway seeds
1 large potato, coarsely grated
1 litre/1¾ pints cold water
150 ml/¼ pint natural yogurt

AMERICAN
2 tablespoons butter
1 medium-size onion, chopped
1 small red or green pepper, cored,
    seeded and chopped
¾ lb beef for stew, cubed
1 tablespoon paprika
1 teaspoon tomato paste
½ teaspoon sugar
1 teaspoon salt
½ teaspoon caraway seeds
1 large potato, coarsely grated
1 quart cold water
¾ cup plain yogurt

Melt the butter in a saucepan. Add the onion and red or green pepper and fry gently for 5 minutes. Add the beef cubes and fry for a further 5 minutes, turning all the time.

Stir in the paprika, tomato purée (paste), sugar, salt, caraway seeds, potato and water. Bring to the boil, then lower the heat and cover. Simmer for 2 hours.

Remove from the heat, stir in the yogurt and serve.

Potato Soup

METRIC/IMPERIAL
40 g/1½ oz butter
500 g/1 lb potatoes, diced
1 large onion, thinly sliced
2 medium celery stalks, thinly
    sliced
450 ml/¾ pint water
salt and white pepper
25 g/1 oz cornflour
300 ml/½ pint milk

AMERICAN
3 tablespoons butter
1 lb potatoes, diced
1 large onion, thinly sliced
2 medium-size celery stalks, thinly
    sliced
2 cups water
salt and white pepper
¼ cup cornstarch
1½ cups milk

Melt the butter in a saucepan. Add the potatoes, onion and celery and fry gently until softened but not brown. Add the water, and salt and pepper to taste. Bring to the boil, then cover and simmer for 45 minutes.

Rub through a sieve or purée in a blender or food processor. Return to the saucepan.

Mix the cornflour (cornstarch) to a smooth paste with some of the cold milk and stir into the remainder. Add to the soup and bring to the boil, stirring all the time. Simmer for 5 minutes and serve.

Oaty Vegetable Soup

METRIC/IMPERIAL
15 g/½ oz butter
1 medium onion, peeled and
  chopped
1 medium carrot, peeled and
  chopped
1 small turnip, peeled and chopped
1 leek, white and pale green part,
  washed and chopped
25 g/1 oz medium oatmeal
600 ml/1 pint stock
salt and freshly ground black
  pepper
1 teaspoon chopped parsley
450 ml/¾ pint milk

AMERICAN
1 tablespoon butter
1 medium-size onion, peeled and
  chopped
1 medium-size carrot, peeled and
  chopped
1 small turnip, peeled and chopped
1 leek, white and pale green part,
  washed and chopped
¼ cup rolled oats
2½ cups stock
salt and freshly ground black
  pepper
1 teaspoon chopped parsley
2 cups milk

Melt the butter in a saucepan. Add the prepared vegetables and stir over gentle heat until all the butter is absorbed. Cover the pan and 'sweat' the vegetables for 2 to 3 minutes. Add the oatmeal and stir over moderate heat for a further 3 to 4 minutes. Pour on the stock, stir well and bring to the boil. Reduce the heat and simmer, covered, for 45 minutes. Season to taste and add the parsley.

Heat the milk in another saucepan until almost boiling. Stir into the soup and adjust the seasoning if necessary. Serve piping hot.

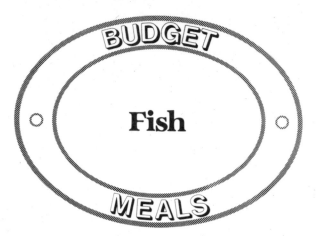

Cheese and Fish Pie

METRIC/IMPERIAL
1 kg/2 lb potatoes, chopped
salt and pepper
100 g/4 oz butter
milk
500 g/1 lb smoked haddock,
    chopped
40 g/1½ oz flour
175 g/6 oz cheese, grated

AMERICAN
2 lb potatoes, chopped
salt and pepper
½ cup butter
milk
1 lb smoked haddock (finnan
    haddie), chopped
6 tablespoons flour
1½ cups grated cheese

Put the potatoes in a saucepan of cold salted water. Bring to the boil and simmer for about 20 minutes. Drain and toss over a low heat to dry. Beat in 65 g/2½ oz (5 tablespoons) of the butter and a little milk until smooth.

Put the mashed potatoes into a piping (pastry) bag with a large star nozzle (tube). Pipe the potato over the bottom and sides of a greased shallow 20 cm/8 inch round casserole or pie dish. Put the dish under a preheated grill (broiler) and grill (broil) until the potato is just golden. Remove from the heat.

Put the fish in a saucepan and cover with milk. Bring to the boil, then cover and simmer for 7 to 10 minutes or until the fish is tender.

Drain the fish, reserving the milk. Make the milk up to 300 ml/½ pint (1¼ cups) with more milk, if necessary, and set aside. Remove any bones from the fish and flake.

Melt the remaining butter in a saucepan, stir in the flour and cook for 2 minutes without browning. Add the reserved milk from the fish and bring to the boil, stirring. Cook for 2 minutes. Add 100 g/4 oz (1 cup) of the cheese and the fish to the sauce and stir gently until the cheese has melted. Season to taste with salt and pepper.

Pour into the potato case and sprinkle the rest of the cheese on top. Grill (broil) until the cheese is bubbling.

Fish Cakes

METRIC/IMPERIAL

METRIC/IMPERIAL
350 g/12 oz white fish fillet, cooked
   and flaked
750 g/1½ lb potatoes, cooked and
   mashed
15 g/½ oz butter, melted
salt and pepper
1 egg, beaten
1 teaspoon chopped parsley
oil for shallow frying

AMERICAN
¾ lb white fish fillet, cooked and
   flaked
1½ lb potatoes, cooked and
   mashed
1 tablespoon butter, melted
salt and pepper
1 egg, beaten
1 teaspoon chopped parsley
oil for shallow frying

Mix the fish with the mashed potatoes, butter and salt and pepper to taste. Add as much of the egg as needed to bind the mixture, then add the parsley and beat well.

   Divide into eight portions, roll into balls and flatten into cakes. Fry in very hot fat until golden brown. Drain well on paper towels and serve.

Fish Croquettes

METRIC/IMPERIAL
225 g/8 oz cod fillet, cooked and
   flaked
1 teaspoon dried mixed herbs
1 tablespoon minced onion
25 g/1 oz butter, melted
225 g/8 oz dry breadcrumbs
1 teaspoon chopped parsley
1 egg, beaten
salt and pepper
oil for deep frying
TO COAT:
beaten egg
golden breadcrumbs

AMERICAN
½ lb cod fillet, cooked and flaked
1 teaspoon dried Italian seasoning
   herbs
1 tablespoon minced onion
2 tablespoons butter, melted
2⅔ cups dry bread crumbs
1 teaspoon chopped parsley
1 egg, beaten
salt and pepper
oil for deep frying
TO COAT:
beaten egg
golden bread crumbs

Mix the fish with the herbs, onion, butter, breadcrumbs, parsley, egg and salt and pepper to taste.

   Divide into eight portions and roll into small balls. Dip in beaten egg and coat with golden breadcrumbs. Deep fry in hot oil until golden. Drain on paper towels and serve hot.

VARIATION:
Fish Puffs – make the fish mixture as above. Roll out 225 g/8 oz (2 cup) quantity shortcrust (pie) pastry (page 246) very thinly and cut out 7.5 cm/3 inch rounds. Put the fish mixture on the dough rounds, fold over and press dampened edges together to seal. Brush with a little beaten egg, then shallow fry in hot oil until golden brown on both sides.

Creamy Herrings

METRIC/IMPERIAL
1 tablespoon made mustard
2 teaspoons milk
2 tablespoons cream
pinch of grated lemon rind
1 teaspoon brown sugar
1 tablespoon tomato purée
salt and pepper
4 large herrings, cleaned and
   filleted
juice of 1 lemon
finely chopped parsley to garnish

AMERICAN
1 tablespoon prepared mustard
2 teaspoons milk
2 tablespoons cream
pinch of grated lemon rind
1 teaspoon brown sugar
1 tablespoon tomato paste
salt and pepper
4 large herrings, cleaned and
   filleted
juice of 1 lemon
finely chopped parsley for garnish

Mix the mustard and milk together to make a creamy paste. Add the cream, lemon rind, brown sugar, tomato purée (paste) and salt and pepper to taste.

Lay the herrings flat and spread the mustard mixture over them. Roll up the herrings, starting at the tail end. Pack tightly into a 1.2 litre/2 pint (5 cup) casserole dish and pour the lemon juice over the top.

Cover and cook in a preheated moderate oven (180°C/350°F, Gas Mark 4) for 30 minutes. Sprinkle chopped parsley on top before serving.

Curried Cod Balls

METRIC/IMPERIAL
275 g/10 oz salt cod, flaked
4–6 potatoes, diced
2 eggs, beaten
pinch of pepper
25 g/1 oz butter
4 tablespoons milk
1 teaspoon curry powder
pinch of celery salt
pinch of paprika
oil for deep frying

AMERICAN
10 oz (about 1½ cups) flaked salt
   cod
4–6 potatoes, diced
2 eggs, beaten
pinch of pepper
2 tablespoons butter
¼ cup milk
1 teaspoon curry powder
pinch of celery salt
pinch of paprika
oil for deep frying

Put the fish into a saucepan, cover with cold water and heat slowly to boiling point. Drain and repeat, using fresh water.

Add the potatoes to the fish. Cover and cook until the potatoes are tender. Drain well and return to the pan. Mash, adding the eggs, pepper, butter, milk, curry powder, celery, salt and paprika. Beat with a spoon until light and fluffy. Chill.

Shape into balls, and deep fry in hot oil until brown. Drain well on paper towels and serve hot.

Fish Loaf

METRIC/IMPERIAL
40 g/1½ oz butter
4 tablespoons chopped onion
1½ tablespoons flour
350 ml/12 fl oz tomato juice
1 tablespoon lemon juice
¼ teaspoon dried marjoram
350 g/12 oz cod fillet, cooked and
   flaked
100 g/4 oz fresh white
   breadcrumbs
2 eggs, beaten

AMERICAN
3 tablespoons butter
¼ cup chopped onion
1½ tablespoons flour
1½ cups tomato juice
1 tablespoon lemon juice
¼ teaspoon dried marjoram
¾ lb cod fillet, cooked and flaked
2 cups soft white bread crumbs
2 eggs, beaten

Melt the butter in a frying pan, add the onion and fry until softened. Stir in the flour, then slowly add the tomato juice, stirring. Cook for 2 to 3 minutes, stirring. Add the lemon juice and marjoram and cook for 4 minutes longer. Mix in the fish, breadcrumbs and eggs and beat well together.

Put into a well-greased 1 kg/2 lb (9 x 5 inch) loaf pan that has been dusted with breadcrumbs. Cook in a preheated moderate oven (180°C/350°F, Gas Mark 4) for 35 to 45 minutes. Leave to cool in the pan for 5 minutes, then turn onto a warmed serving plate and serve.

Corn and Haddock Casserole

METRIC/IMPERIAL
2 medium potatoes, peeled
salt and pepper
500 g/1 lb haddock fillets, cut into
   8 pieces
50 g/2 oz butter, melted
1 tablespoon chopped parsley
1 x 225 g/8 oz can sweetcorn
   kernels, drained

AMERICAN
2 medium-size potatoes, peeled
salt and pepper
1 lb haddock fillets, cut into
   8 pieces
¼ cup butter, melted
1 tablespoon chopped parsley
1 x 8 oz can whole kernel corn,
   drained

Cook the potatoes in boiling salted water until just tender. Drain and leave to cool.

Brush the fish pieces with half of the melted butter, and season to taste with salt and pepper. Sprinkle the chopped parsley over the fish and roll up tightly. Hold in place with wooden cocktail sticks.

Pack the fish rolls tightly in a 1.2 litre/2 pint (5 cup) casserole dish. Slice the potatoes thickly and arrange around the top edge of the dish. Pour the corn between the fish and potatoes. Brush the potatoes and fish with the rest of the melted butter. Cover and cook in a preheated moderately hot oven (200°C/400°F, Gas Mark 6) for 35 to 45 minutes.

Tuna Pie

METRIC/IMPERIAL
450 ml/¾ pint water
175 g/6 oz long-grain rice
1 teaspoon turmeric
1 chicken stock cube
2 teaspoons oil
salt and pepper
1 medium onion, finely chopped
1 egg, beaten
FILLING:
1 x 200 g/7 oz can tuna fish,
   drained and flaked
2 eggs, beaten
1 small can evaporated milk
50 g/2 oz Cheddar cheese, grated
1 chicken stock cube
TO GARNISH:
tomato slices
parsley sprigs

AMERICAN
2 cups water
1 cup long-grain rice
1 teaspoon turmeric
1 chicken bouillon cube
2 teaspoons oil
salt and pepper
1 medium-size onion, finely
   chopped
1 egg, beaten
FILLING:
1 x 7 oz can tuna fish, drained and
   flaked
2 eggs, beaten
1 small can evaporated milk
½ cup grated Cheddar cheese
1 chicken bouillon cube
FOR GARNISH:
tomato slices
parsley sprigs

Bring the water to the boil in a saucepan. Add the rice, turmeric, crumbled stock (bouillon) cube, oil and salt and pepper to taste. Return to the boil, then cover and simmer gently for 15 minutes or until the rice has absorbed all the liquid.

Stir in one-quarter of the onion. Turn out into a mixing bowl, fluff up with a fork and leave to cool.

Mix in the beaten egg. Press the rice mixture over the bottom and up the sides of a greased 20 to 23 cm/8 to 9 inch shallow baking dish to form a shell.

Arrange the tuna on the bottom of the rice shell. Beat together the remaining filling ingredients with the rest of the onion and pour carefully over the tuna.

Bake in a preheated moderate oven (180°C/350°F, Gas Mark 4) for 30 to 40 minutes or until a knife inserted in the centre of the filling comes out cleanly. Garnish with tomato slices and parsley sprigs and serve hot or cold.

Fish Pie

METRIC/IMPERIAL
500 g/1 lb potatoes, cooked and
mashed
milk
50 g/2 oz cheese, grated
1 egg yolk
salt and pepper
dry mustard
225 g/8 oz cod fillet, cooked and
flaked
1 quantity parsley sauce (page
242)
pinch of grated nutmeg
15 g/½ oz butter

AMERICAN
1 lb potatoes, cooked and mashed
milk
½ cup grated cheese
1 egg yolk
salt and pepper
dry mustard
½ lb cod fillet, cooked and flaked
1 quantity parsley sauce (page
242)
pinch of grated nutmeg
1 tablespoon butter

Heat the potatoes in a saucepan with enough milk to moisten. Stir in half the cheese, the egg yolk and salt, pepper and mustard to taste. Use two-thirds of the mixture to line a buttered 1.8 litre/3 pint (2 quart) casserole dish.

Mix the fish with the parsley sauce and season with the nutmeg. Pile into the centre of the dish. Cover with the rest of the potato mixture and decorate with a fork. Sprinkle on the rest of the cheese and dot with the butter.

Bake in a preheated moderate oven (180°C/350°F, Gas Mark 4) for 30 minutes.

St Abbs Casserole

METRIC/IMPERIAL
750 g/1½ lb cod fillet, cut into
bite-size pieces
grated rind and juice of 1 lemon
225 g/8 oz tomatoes, skinned and
chopped
100 g/4 oz mushrooms, chopped
1 onion, finely chopped
2 leeks, thickly sliced
1 tablespoon brown sugar
25 g/1 oz butter

AMERICAN
1½ lb cod fillet, cut into bite-size
pieces
grated rind and juice of 1 lemon
½ lb tomatoes, peeled and
chopped
1 cup chopped mushrooms
1 onion, finely chopped
2 leeks, thickly sliced
1 tablespoon brown sugar
2 tablespoons butter

Put the fish into a buttered 1.8 litre/3 pint (2 quart) casserole dish. Sprinkle over the lemon rind and juice. Add the vegetables, scatter the sugar over the top and dot with the butter.

Cover and cook in a preheated moderate oven (160°C/325°F, Gas Mark 3) for 45 minutes.

Mushroom and Fish Halfmoons

METRIC/IMPERIAL
500 g/1 lb quantity shortcrust pastry
   (page 246)
350 g/12 oz cod fillet, cooked and
   flaked
½ x 298 g/10½ oz can condensed
   mushroom soup
1 egg, beaten
1½ teaspoons chopped parsley
1 hard-boiled egg, chopped
1 teaspoon lemon juice
salt and pepper
beaten egg yolk for brushing

AMERICAN
4 cup quantity pie pastry (page
   246)
¾ lb cod fillet, cooked and flaked
½ x 10½ oz can condensed
   mushroom soup
1 egg, beaten
1½ teaspoons chopped parsley
1 hard-cooked egg, chopped
1 teaspoon lemon juice
salt and pepper
beaten egg yolk for brushing

Roll out the dough to 3 mm/⅛ inch thick and cut into 12 equal rounds. Mix the fish, soup, beaten egg, parsley, hard-boiled egg and lemon juice together and season to taste with salt and pepper. Put a tablespoon of the mixture on the middle of each dough round. Dampen the edges, fold over and press well down using a fork.

   Brush with beaten egg yolk and place on a lightly buttered baking sheet. Bake in a preheated moderately hot oven (190°C/375°F, Gas Mark 5) for 25 minutes.

Haddock in Cider

METRIC/IMPERIAL
500 g/1 lb haddock fillet, cut into
   2.5 cm/1 inch cubes
225 g/8 oz tomatoes, skinned and
   sliced
50 g/2 oz button mushrooms, sliced
1 tablespoon chopped parsley
salt and pepper
150 ml/¼ pint cider
2 tablespoons grated cheese
2 tablespoons fresh white
   breadcrumbs

AMERICAN
1 lb haddock fillet, cut into 1 inch
   cubes
½ lb tomatoes, peeled and sliced
½ cup sliced mushrooms
1 tablespoon chopped parsley
salt and pepper
¾ cup apple cider
2 tablespoons grated cheese
2 tablespoons soft white bread
   crumbs

Put the fish cubes in a greased 1.8 litre/3 pint (2 quart) casserole dish. Cover with the tomatoes, mushrooms and parsley and season to taste with salt and pepper. Pour the cider over.

   Cover and cook in a preheated moderate oven (180°C/350°F, Gas Mark 4) for 25 minutes. Remove from the oven, uncover and sprinkle the cheese and breadcrumbs on top. Brown under a hot grill (broiler).

Herbed Herrings

METRIC/IMPERIAL
4 large herrings, cleaned and
  trimmed
salt and pepper
65 g/2½ oz butter
4 medium potatoes, thinly sliced
2 large onions, sliced
4 tomatoes, sliced
½ teaspoon dried chervil
¼ teaspoon fennel seed

AMERICAN
4 large herrings, cleaned and
  trimmed
salt and pepper
5 tablespoons butter
4 medium-size potatoes, thinly
  sliced
2 large onions, sliced
4 tomatoes, sliced
½ teaspoon dried chervil
¼ teaspoon fennel seed

Season the fish with salt and pepper and roll up from head to tail. Grease a 1.2 litre/2 pint (5 cup) casserole dish with half of the butter and put half the potatoes, onions and tomatoes in it. Top with the rest of the potatoes, place the rolled fish on top and cover with the rest of the tomatoes and onions. Season to taste with salt and pepper and sprinkle the herbs over. Dot with the rest of the butter.

Cover and cook in a preheated hot oven (220°C/425°F, Gas Mark 7) for 30 to 40 minutes. Remove the lid and cook for a further 10 minutes.

Tomato and Mackerel Parcels

METRIC/IMPERIAL
4 fresh mackerel (about 350 g/
  12 oz each)
salt and freshly ground black
  pepper
4 spring onions, trimmed and sliced
4 large tomatoes, sliced
1 lemon, quartered
1 bay leaf, quartered
1 teaspoon chopped parsley

AMERICAN
4 fresh mackerel (about ¾ lb each)
salt and freshly ground black
  pepper
4 scallions, trimmed and sliced
4 large tomatoes, sliced
1 lemon, quartered
1 bay leaf, quartered
1 teaspoon chopped parsley

Slit the mackerel from head to tail and clean them thoroughly. Remove the tails, fins, gills and eyes. The heads may also be removed if desired. Wash the fish well and dry on absorbent kitchen paper. Season the cavities.

Butter well 4 pieces of foil, each large enough to completely enclose a fish. Put on each square a layer of sliced onion and tomato, one mackerel, a lemon quarter and a piece of bay leaf. Season well, sprinkle with a little chopped parsley and fold up the foil, crimping the edges well together so that no juices can escape.

Place the 4 foil parcels on a baking sheet and bake in a moderate oven (180°C/350°F, Gas Mark 4) for 20 minutes. Serve individually in the foil parcels.

Crispy Corned Tuna

METRIC/IMPERIAL
25 g/1 oz butter
25 g/1 oz flour
300 ml/½ pint milk
50 g/2 oz Cheddar cheese, grated
salt and freshly ground black
  pepper
1 x 200 g/7 oz can tuna fish
1 x 326 g/11½ oz can sweetcorn
2 large tomatoes, finely sliced
1 x 71 g/2½ oz packet salted potato
  crisps

AMERICAN
2 tablespoons butter
¼ cup flour
1¼ cups milk
½ cup grated Cheddar cheese
salt and freshly ground black
  pepper
1 can (7 oz) tuna fish
1 can (12 oz) whole kernel corn
2 large tomatoes, finely sliced
1 package (2½ oz) salted potato
  chips

Melt the butter in a saucepan. Stir in the flour and cook for 1 minute. Gradually add the milk and bring to the boil, stirring constantly. Simmer for 2 minutes, stir in the cheese and season to taste. Flake the tuna and add to the sauce with the liquid from the can. Fold in the drained sweetcorn.

Use the tomato slices to line a greased ovenproof dish. Spoon the tuna mixture into the centre of the dish and crumble the potato crisps (chips) on top. Place in a moderate oven (180°C/350°F, Gas Mark 4) for about 20 minutes, until the top is brown and crisp. Serve with thick slices of French bread.

Fish Pasties (Turnovers)

METRIC/IMPERIAL
175 g/6 oz quantity shortcrust
  pastry (page 246)
350 g/12 oz cod fillet, cooked and
  flaked
100 g/4 oz peas, cooked
1½ tablespoons chopped parsley
1 tablespoon vinegar
½ quantity white coating sauce
  (page 242)
salt and pepper

AMERICAN
1½ cup quantity pie pastry (page
  246)
¾ lb cod fillet, cooked and flaked
1 cup peas, cooked
1½ tablespoons chopped parsley
1 tablespoon vinegar
½ quantity white coating sauce
  (page 242)
salt and pepper

Roll out the dough thinly and cut into 15 cm/6 inch rounds. Mix the fish with the peas, parsley, vinegar and white sauce. Season to taste with salt and pepper. Pile into the middle of the dough rounds. Dampen the edges, fold in two and press the edges together using a fork.

Put on a lightly buttered baking sheet. Bake in a preheated moderate oven (180°C/350°F, Gas Mark 4) for 25 to 35 minutes.

Sardine Eggs

METRIC/IMPERIAL
4 eggs, hard-boiled and shelled
1 x 124 g/4⅜ oz can sardines in oil,
    drained
1 teaspoon chopped parsley
2 teaspoons quick cook oats
2 tablespoons single cream
pinch of cayenne pepper
salt and freshly ground black
    pepper
TO FINISH:
lettuce leaves
parsley sprigs

AMERICAN
4 hard-cooked eggs, shelled
1 can (4⅜ oz) sardines in oil,
    drained
1 teaspoon chopped parsley
2 teaspoons quick cook oats
2 tablespoons light cream
pinch of cayenne
salt and freshly ground black
    pepper
TO FINISH:
lettuce leaves
parsley sprigs

Cut each egg in half lengthwise. Using a teaspoon, carefully remove the yolks and place them in a basin. Add the sardines to the egg yolks with the parsley, oats, cream and cayenne pepper. Mash with a fork then beat thoroughly until smooth and well blended. Season to taste and divide the mixture equally among the egg halves.

Place the stuffed eggs on a bed of lettuce leaves and garnish with parsley sprigs. Serve with brown bread and butter.

Smoked Cod Jumble

METRIC/IMPERIAL
225 g/8 oz macaroni
75 g/3 oz butter
350 g/12 oz smoked cod or
    haddock fillet, skinned and cut
    into chunks
4 tomatoes, chopped
6 spring onions, trimmed and
    chopped
salt and freshly ground black
    pepper

AMERICAN
2 cups macaroni
6 tablespoons butter
¾ lb smoked cod or haddock fillet,
    skinned and cut into chunks
4 tomatoes, chopped
6 scallions, trimmed and chopped
salt and freshly ground black
    pepper

Cook the macaroni in plenty of boiling slightly salted water. Drain well. Melt the butter in a saucepan. Add the fish, cover and cook very gently for 10 minutes, or until the fish is tender. Remove the lid, add the cooked macaroni, chopped tomato and spring onion (scallion) and season carefully. Stir the mixture lightly to avoid breaking up the fish, and reheat well. Serve with hot buttered toast.

Fish Balls

METRIC/IMPERIAL
3 medium potatoes
salt and pepper
225 g/8 oz haddock fillet, cooked
 and flaked
1 egg, beaten
4 tablespoons milk
oil for deep frying

AMERICAN
3 medium-size potatoes
salt and pepper
½ lb haddock fillet, cooked and
 flaked
1 egg, beaten
¼ cup milk
oil for deep frying

Cook the potatoes in boiling salted water until tender. Mash well, then add
the fish and egg and mix well. Beat in the milk and salt and pepper to taste
until light and fluffy.

Drop from a teaspoon into hot oil and deep fry for 2 to 3 minutes or until
golden brown. Drain on paper towels and serve hot.

Family Fish Pie

METRIC/IMPERIAL
1 kg/2 lb coley or other white fish,
 skinned
600 ml/1 pint milk
50 g/2 oz butter
50 g/2 oz flour
2 hard-boiled eggs, shelled and
 roughly chopped
salt and freshly ground black
 pepper
225 g/8 oz frozen peas, defrosted
1 kg/2 lb freshly cooked potatoes,
 mashed

AMERICAN
2 lb firm white fish, skinned
2½ cups milk
¼ cup butter
½ cup flour
2 hard-cooked eggs, shelled and
 roughly chopped
salt and freshly ground black
 pepper
1½ cups frozen peas, defrosted
2 lb freshly cooked potatoes,
 mashed

Place the fish in a saucepan, cover with the milk and poach for 10 minutes.
Lift out the fish with a slotted draining spoon, remove the bones and flake
the fish. Reserve the milk for the sauce.

Heat the butter in a saucepan, stir in the flour and cook for 2 minutes.
Gradually add the milk and bring to the boil, stirring constantly. Remove
from the heat. Stir in the flaked fish and chopped eggs and season to
taste. Pour the mixture into a buttered baking dish. Cover with the
defrosted peas and spread the mashed potatoes over the top. Bake in a
fairly hot oven (200°C/400°F, Gas Mark 6) for 30 minutes, or until
golden-brown on top.
Serves 6 to 8

Pilchard and Potato Cakes

METRIC/IMPERIAL
225 g/8 oz freshly cooked potatoes,
   mashed
1 x 225 g/8 oz can pilchards in
   tomato sauce, boned and flaked
1 teaspoon salt
freshly ground black pepper
½ teaspoon finely grated onion
½ teaspoon lemon juice
FOR COATING:
1 egg, beaten
75 g/3 oz dried breadcrumbs
vegetable oil for frying

AMERICAN
½ lb freshly cooked potatoes,
   mashed
1 x ½ lb can pilchards in tomato
   sauce, boned and flaked
1 teaspoon salt
freshly ground black pepper
½ teaspoon finely grated onion
½ teaspoon lemon juice
FOR COATING:
1 egg, beaten
¾ cup dried bread crumbs
vegetable oil for frying

Dry mash the potatoes (without adding any milk or butter) and place in a
bowl with the fish, seasoning, grated onion and lemon juice. Combine
gently with a fork until the mixture holds together. Shape into 8 round flat
cakes on a floured board. Dip the cakes into the beaten egg, making sure
that they are evenly covered, then coat with breadcrumbs.

Heat the oil gently in a deep-fat fryer or saucepan until it is hot enough to
turn a stale bread cube golden in 20 to 30 seconds (180°C/350°F). Lower
the cakes, 4 at a time, into the hot oil and fry for 1 to 2 minutes until crisp
and golden-brown on all sides. Drain on absorbent kitchen paper.

The fish cakes may also be shallow fried for 2 to 3 minutes on each side
or until golden-brown.
Makes 8 cakes

Cod in Cider

METRIC/IMPERIAL
500 g/1 lb cod fillets, cut into 5 cm/
   2 inch pieces
300 ml/½ pint dry cider
225 g/8 oz potatoes, grated
2 firm tomatoes, skinned and sliced
salt and pepper
1 small onion, chopped

AMERICAN
1 lb cod fillets, cut into 2 inch pieces
1¼ cups apple cider (or hard cider)
½ lb potatoes, grated
2 firm tomatoes, peeled and sliced
salt and pepper
1 small onion, chopped

Put the fish in a 1.5 litre/2½ pint (1½ quart) casserole dish. Heat the cider,
potatoes and tomatoes in a saucepan for 5 minutes. Season to taste with
salt and pepper and pour over the fish. Sprinkle the onion over the top.

Cover and cook in a preheated moderate oven (180°C/350°F, Gas Mark
4) for 30 to 45 minutes.

Cornish Casserole

METRIC/IMPERIAL
6 large fresh pilchards, cleaned
750 g/1 ½ lb potatoes, sliced
salt and pepper
300 ml/½ pint single cream
300 ml/½ pint double cream

AMERICAN
6 large fresh smelts, cleaned
1 ½ lb potatoes, sliced
salt and pepper
1 ¼ cups light cream
1 ¼ cups heavy cream

Put the fish into a 2 litre/3½ pint (2 quart) casserole dish and arrange the sliced potatoes over the top. Season to taste with salt and pepper. Mix the two creams together and pour over the top.

Cover and cook in a preheated moderate oven (160°C/325°F, Gas Mark 3) for 1 hour.

Smoked Haddock and Egg Lasagne

METRIC/IMPERIAL
1 tablespoon vegetable oil
175 g/6 oz lasagne verde
450 ml/¾ pint White Sauce (see page 242)
100 g/4 oz Cheddar cheese, grated
175 g/6 oz cooked smoked haddock fillet, skinned, boned and flaked
4 tablespoons double or single cream
salt and freshly ground black pepper
3 eggs
25 g/1 oz butter

AMERICAN
1 tablespoon vegetable oil
6 oz lasagne verde noodles
2 cups White Sauce (see page 242)
1 cup grated Cheddar cheese
6 oz cooked smoked haddock fillet, skinned, boned and flaked
4 tablespoons heavy or light cream
salt and freshly ground black pepper
3 eggs
2 tablespoons butter

Bring a large pan of lightly salted water to the boil and add the oil. Lower the lasagne, one sheet at a time, into the pan and cook for 5 minutes. Drain well and lay the sheets of lasagne on a large piece of greased greaseproof (waxed) paper or foil.

Heat the white sauce in a pan with half the grated cheese, the flaked smoked haddock, cream, and seasoning. Layer the lasagne and fish sauce in a greased ovenproof dish, starting and finishing with a layer of sauce. Bake in a fairly hot oven (190°C/375°F, Gas Mark 5) for 30 minutes.

Meanwhile, beat the eggs with the seasoning to taste. Melt the butter in a frying pan (skillet) and add the beaten eggs. Cook, stirring, over a gentle heat until the eggs begin to scramble. Remove from the heat and immediately spoon over the lasagne. Sprinkle with the remaining cheese and return to the oven for a further 10 minutes.

Stuffed Soused Herrings

METRIC/IMPERIAL
5 herrings
salt and freshly ground black
   pepper
1 small onion, peeled and cut into
   rings
1 small blade of mace
3 cloves
8 peppercorns
150 ml/¼ pint water
150 ml/¼ pint vinegar
FOR THE STUFFING:
50 g/2 oz quick cook oats
2 teaspoons chopped capers
grated zest of 1 small lemon
salt and freshly ground black
   pepper
25 g/1 oz butter, melted
1 egg, beaten

AMERICAN
5 herrings
salt and freshly ground black
   pepper
1 small onion, peeled and cut into
   rings
1 small blade of mace
3 cloves
8 peppercorns
⅔ cup water
⅔ cup vinegar
FOR THE STUFFING:
2 oz quick cook oats
2 teaspoons chopped capers
grated zest of 1 small lemon
salt and freshly ground black
   pepper
2 tablespoons butter, melted
1 egg, beaten

Clean and bone the herrings and lay them flat, skin side down. Sprinkle with salt and pepper.

To make the stuffing, place the oats, chopped capers, lemon zest and seasoning to taste in a bowl. Add the melted butter and beaten egg and mix thoroughly. The mixture should be stiff but not unmanageable. Add a little milk if necessary. Put equal quantities of the oat stuffing near the tail end of each herring, then roll up from the tail end.

Arrange the stuffed herrings, joins downwards, in a single layer in an ovenproof dish with the onion rings, mace, cloves and peppercorns. Mix together the water and vinegar and pour over the herrings. Bake in a fairly hot oven (190°C/375°F, Gas Mark 5) for 30 to 35 minutes. Serve hot or cold accompanied by a green salad.

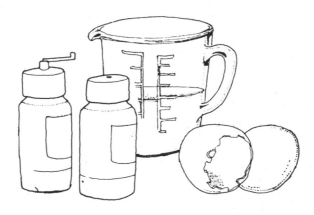

Fish in Pastry Envelopes

METRIC/IMPERIAL
225 g/8 oz flour
100 g/4 oz quick cook oats
pinch of salt
175 g/6 oz margarine
4–5 tablespoons cold water
1 egg, beaten
quick cook oats for sprinkling
FOR THE FILLING:
25 g/1 oz butter
1 tablespoon flour
150 ml/¼ pint milk
1 tablespoon chopped parsley
350 g/12 oz white fish fillets
salt and freshly ground black
  pepper

AMERICAN
2 cups flour
¼ lb quick cook oats
pinch of salt
¾ cup margarine
4–5 tablespoons cold water
1 egg, beaten
quick cook oats for sprinkling
FOR THE FILLING:
2 tablespoons butter
1 tablespoon flour
⅔ cup milk
1 tablespoon chopped parsley
¾ lb white fish fillets
salt and freshly ground black
  pepper

First make the filling. Melt the butter in a small saucepan. Stir in the flour and cook for 1 minute. Gradually stir in the milk and bring to the boil, stirring constantly. Add the parsley and cook for 2 minutes, stirring all the time.

Cut the fish into bite-sized pieces and place in a bowl with the parsley sauce and seasoning to taste. Mix thoroughly and allow to become cold.

Meanwhile, make the pastry. Mix together the flour, oats and salt in a bowl. Rub in the margarine and bind with cold water to give a stiff consistency. Roll out the pastry on a floured surface to a rectangle about 25 x 38 cm/10 x 15 inches and divide into six 12.5 cm/5 inch squares. Place equal quantities of the fish mixture in the centre of each pastry square. Brush the edges of the pastry with water and join the edges together to form envelopes. Brush each envelope with beaten egg and sprinkle with extra oats. Place on a lightly greased baking sheet and bake in a fairly hot oven (200°C/400°F, Gas Mark 6) for 10 minutes, then reduce the heat to cool (150°C/300°F, Gas Mark 2) and cook a further 20 to 25 minutes.
Makes 6

Turkey Plait

METRIC/IMPERIAL
25 g/1 oz butter
1 onion, peeled and sliced
75 g/3 oz button mushrooms, wiped and sliced
225 g/8 oz cooked turkey, boned and diced
175 g/6 oz Gouda cheese, grated
1 small red pepper, cored, seeded and sliced
½ level teaspoon dried mixed herbs
salt and freshly ground black pepper
1 egg, beaten
225 g/8 oz frozen puff pastry, defrosted

AMERICAN
2 tablespoons butter
1 onion, peeled and sliced
1 cup sliced button mushrooms
½ lb cooked turkey, boned and diced
1½ cups grated Gouda cheese
1 small red pepper, seeded and sliced
½ level teaspoon dried mixed herbs
salt and freshly ground black pepper
1 egg, beaten
½ lb frozen puff pastry, defrosted

Melt the butter in a saucepan and cook the sliced onion and mushrooms over moderate heat for 5 minutes, stirring occasionally. Stir in the diced turkey, grated cheese, sliced red pepper and mixed herbs. Season to taste and stir in most of the beaten egg, reserving a little for glazing.

Roll out the pastry to an oblong 34 x 30 cm/14 x 12 inches. Spoon the filling down the middle of the pastry, leaving a wide margin all round. Using a sharp knife cut parallel slits about 1 cm/½ inch wide, down each side of the oblong. Fold up the top and bottom of the oblong on to the filling. Plait the strips over the filling. Transfer on to a damp baking sheet.

Brush the turkey plait with the remainder of the beaten egg. Cook for 20 minutes in a hot oven (220°C/425°F, Gas Mark 7) and then reduce heat to fairly hot (190°C/375°F, Gas Mark 5) for a further 10 minutes.

Serve hot or cold with a green salad.

33

Chicken Pie

METRIC/IMPERIAL
1 boiling fowl, jointed
2 medium carrots
2 medium onions
2 medium celery stalks
1.2 litres/2 pints water
salt and pepper
40 g/1½ oz butter
40 g/1½ oz flour
300 ml/½ pint milk
4 tablespoons double cream
225 g/8 oz quantity milk puff pastry
  (page 248)
beaten egg to glaze

AMERICAN
1 stewing chicken, cut up
2 medium-size carrots
2 medium-size onions
2 medium-size celery stalks
5 cups water
salt and pepper
3 tablespoons butter
5 tablespoons flour
1¼ cups milk
¼ cup heavy cream
2 cup quantity milk puff pastry
  (page 248)
beaten egg to glaze

Put the chicken into a saucepan. Add the carrots, onions, and celery broken into small pieces. Pour in the water and add 2 teaspoons salt. Bring to the boil, skimming off any scum. Lower the heat, cover the pan and simmer for 2¼ to 2¾ hours or until the chicken is tender.

Lift the chicken out of the saucepan. Discard the skin and bones and cut the meat into bite-sized pieces. Strain the chicken stock and reserve 150 ml/¼ pint (⅔ cup).

Melt the butter in a clean saucepan. Add the flour and cook for 2 minutes without browning. Gradually stir in the reserved chicken stock and milk, with salt and pepper to taste. Cook, stirring, until the sauce comes to the boil and thickens. Remove from the heat and stir in the chicken and cream. Check the seasoning. Pour into a 900 ml/1½ pint (1 quart) pie dish.

Roll out the dough to 5 mm/¼ inch thick and cut out a lid 4 cm/1½ inches wider than the top of the dish. Moisten the edges of the dish with water and line with a strip of dough. Moisten the strip and cover with the lid of dough. Press the edges well together to seal. Flute with a fork and brush all over with beaten egg.

Place the dish on a baking sheet and bake in a preheated hot oven (220°C/425°F, Gas Mark 7) for 25 to 30 minutes or until the pastry is golden.

VARIATION:
Leftover cold roast chicken can be used instead of a boiling fowl as filling for this pie.

Chicken Casserole

METRIC/IMPERIAL
75 g/3 oz butter
4 chicken joints
100 g/4 oz streaky bacon, derinded
   and chopped
2 large onions, chopped
50 g/2 oz flour
600 ml/1 pint milk
1 bay leaf
1 teaspoon dried mixed herbs
1 chicken stock cube
salt and pepper
100 g/4 oz mushrooms, sliced

AMERICAN
6 tablespoons butter
4 chicken pieces
¼ lb slab bacon, chopped
2 large onions, chopped
½ cup flour
2½ cups milk
1 bay leaf
1 teaspoon dried Italian seasoning
1 chicken bouillon cube
salt and pepper
1 cup sliced mushrooms

Melt 50 g/2 oz (¼ cup) of the butter in a frying pan. Add the chicken and fry until golden brown on all sides. Remove to a large casserole.

Melt the remaining butter in the pan. Add the bacon and onions and fry for 5 minutes. Stir in the flour and cook, without browning, for 2 minutes. Gradually stir in the milk. Add the bay leaf, herbs and crumbled stock (bouillon) cube. Cook, stirring, until the sauce comes to the boil and thickens. Season to taste with salt and pepper and pour over the chicken.

Cover with foil or the lid and cook in a preheated moderate oven (160°C/325°F, Gas Mark 3) for 1 hour.

Add the mushrooms, cover again and cook for a further 30 minutes. Discard the bay leaf before serving.

Chicken Curry

METRIC/IMPERIAL
25 g/1 oz flour
salt and pepper
4 chicken joints
40 g/1 ½ oz butter
1 tablespoon olive or corn oil
2 large onions, chopped
1 large cooking apple, peeled,
  cored and chopped
1 tablespoon curry powder
½ teaspoon ground ginger
½ teaspoon ground cinnamon
1 tablespoon chutney
150 ml/¼ pint milk
150 ml/¼ pint water
150 ml/¼ pint natural yogurt
ACCOMPANIMENTS:
freshly boiled rice
50 g/2 oz salted peanuts, chopped
2 large tomatoes, sliced
chutney

AMERICAN
¼ cup flour
salt and pepper
4 chicken pieces
3 tablespoons butter
1 tablespoon olive or corn oil
2 large onions, chopped
1 large tart apple, peeled, cored
  and chopped
1 tablespoon curry powder
½ teaspoon ground ginger
½ teaspoon ground cinnamon
1 tablespoon chutney
⅔ cup milk
⅔ cup water
⅔ cup plain yogurt
ACCOMPANIMENTS:
freshly boiled rice
½ cup chopped salted peanuts
2 large tomatoes, sliced
chutney

Season the flour with salt and pepper and use to coat the chicken pieces.
Heat the butter and oil in a saucepan, add the chicken and fry until crisp
and golden on all sides. Remove to a plate.

Add the onions and apple to the pan and fry gently until pale gold. Stir in
the curry powder, ginger, cinnamon, chutney, milk, water and salt to taste.
Bring to the boil. Replace the chicken, cover and simmer for 45 minutes to
1 hour or until the chicken is tender.

Stir in the yogurt and heat through for a further 5 minutes. Serve with the
accompaniments.

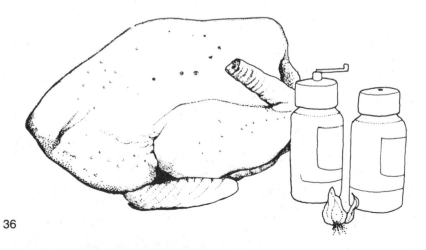

Coq au Vin

METRIC/IMPERIAL
25 g/1 oz flour
salt and pepper
2 large chicken joints
50 g/2 oz butter
1 tablespoon olive or corn oil
1 large onion, chopped
100 g/4 oz lean bacon, chopped
8 small onions or 10 shallots
1 small bay leaf
300 ml/½ pint dry red wine
4 tablespoons water
100 g/4 oz mushrooms

AMERICAN
¼ cup flour
salt and pepper
2 large chicken pieces
¼ cup butter
1 tablespoon olive or corn oil
1 large onion, chopped
¼ lb Canadian bacon, chopped
8 small onions or 10 shallots
1 small bay leaf
1¼ cups dry red wine
¼ cup water
¼ lb mushrooms

Season the flour with salt and pepper and use to coat the chicken. Heat the butter and oil in a large saucepan and add the chicken. Fry until crisp and golden on all sides. Remove to a plate.

Add the chopped onion and bacon to the pan and fry gently until pale gold. Replace the chicken, and add the small onions or shallots, bay leaf, wine and water. Bring to the boil, then lower the heat, cover and simmer for 1 hour. Add the mushrooms and simmer for a further 15 minutes.

Chicken Liver Risotto

METRIC/IMPERIAL
65 g/2½ oz butter
1 tablespoon vegetable oil
225 g/8 oz long-grain rice
175 g/6 oz chicken livers
175 g/6 oz button mushrooms,
* wiped and thinly sliced*
2 tablespoons tomato purée
450 ml/¾ pint chicken stock
sprigs of parsley to garnish

AMERICAN
¼ cup plus 1 tablespooon butter
1 tablespoon vegetable oil
1 scant cup long-grain rice
6 oz chicken livers
1½ cups wiped and thinly sliced
* button mushrooms*
2 tablespoons tomato paste
2 cups chicken stock
sprigs of parsley for garnish

Heat 50 g/2 oz (4 tablespoons) of the butter and the oil in a non-stick saucepan or one with a heavy base. Add the rice and cook, stirring occasionally, until just transparent.

Meanwhile, toss the chicken livers and sliced mushrooms in the remaining butter until the livers are just firm. Using kitchen scissors, snip up the livers into small pieces. Add the livers and mushrooms to the rice.

Dissolve the tomato purée in the hot stock, pour over the rice and bring to the boil. Stir gently, reduce the heat, cover and simmer for about 20 minutes, or until the rice is tender and all the liquid has been absorbed. Fluff up and serve hot, garnished with sprigs of parsley. Serve grated Parmesan cheese separately.

Spiced Chicken Pot Roast

METRIC/IMPERIAL

1½–1¾ kg/3–3½ lb oven-ready
  chicken with giblets
1 teaspoon ground coriander
1 teaspoon ground cumin seed
50 g/2 oz butter
225 g/8 oz cooked long-grain rice
1 small green pepper, cored,
  seeded and cut into strips
1 x approx. 100 g/4 oz can red
  pimientos, drained and chopped
2 large tomatoes, peeled and
  chopped
salt and freshly ground black
  pepper
1 large onion, peeled and chopped
1 tablespoon powdered turmeric

AMERICAN

3–3½ lb roasting chicken with
  giblets
1 teaspoon ground coriander
1 teaspoon ground cumin seed
¼ cup butter
1½ cups cooked long-grain rice
1 small green pepper, seeded and
  cut into strips
1 x approx 4 oz can red pimientos,
  drained and chopped
2 large tomatoes, peeled and
  chopped
salt and freshly ground black
  pepper
1 large onion, peeled and chopped
1 tablespoon powdered turmeric

Wash the chicken well, wash and drain the giblets, and cook the giblets in lightly salted water for about 20 minutes to make stock.

Meanwhile, prick the chicken all over with a fork. Combine the ground coriander and cumin seed and rub into the chicken.

Melt half the butter in a saucepan. Mix in the cooked rice, strips of green pepper, chopped pimiento and chopped tomato and season well. Use the mixture to stuff the chicken.

Heat the remaining butter in a frying pan (skillet). Add the chopped onion and turmeric and cook, stirring constantly, until golden-brown. Add the stuffed chicken, turning frequently, until coated with the mixture. Transfer the chicken with the onion and spices, to a casserole which fits it with little space to spare. Make up the strained giblet stock to 300 ml/ ½ pint (1¼ cups) with boiling water and pour into the frying pan (skillet). Stir well and pour over the chicken. Cover tightly and put the casserole into a moderate oven (180°C/350°F, Gas Mark 4) for 1½ hours. Serve with a salad and potatoes in their jackets.

Beef with Cheese Cobbler

METRIC/IMPERIAL
25 g/1 oz dripping
500 g/1 lb minced beef
2 tablespoons flour
500 g/1 lb onions, peeled and
  quartered
8 small pickled onions
2 tablespoons tomato purée
½ teaspoon sugar
½ teaspoon dried thyme
1 bay leaf, crushed
salt and freshly ground black
  pepper
300 ml/½ pint water
FOR THE CHEESE COBBLER:
225 g/8 oz self-raising flour
½ teaspoon dry mustard
salt and freshly ground black
  pepper
40 g/1½ oz butter
75 g/3 oz Cheddar cheese, finely
  grated
few drops Tabasco sauce
150 ml/¼ pint water
1 tablespoon milk

AMERICAN
2 tablespoons dripping
1 lb ground beef
2 tablespoons flour
1 lb onions, peeled and quartered
8 small pickled onions
2 tablespoons tomato paste
½ teaspoon sugar
½ teaspoon dried thyme
1 bay leaf, crushed
salt and freshly ground black
  pepper
1¼ cups water
FOR THE CHEESE COBBLER:
2 cups self-rising flour
½ teaspoon dry mustard
salt and freshly ground black
  pepper
3 tablespoons butter
¾ cup finely grated Cheddar
  cheese
few drops Tabasco sauce
⅔ cup water
1 tablespoon milk

Melt the dripping in a frying pan (skillet) and lightly fry the minced (ground) beef until brown, stirring occasionally. Transfer the meat to a casserole, sprinkle with the flour and stir well. Add the quartered onions, pickled onions, tomato purée (paste), sugar, herbs and salt and pepper to taste. Add the water or just sufficient water to cover the surface. Put the lid on the casserole and cook in a moderate oven (180°C/350°F, Gas Mark 4) for 1 hour.

To make the cheese cobbler, sift the flour then add the dry mustard and salt and pepper to taste. Rub in the butter until the mixture resembles fine breadcrumbs, mix in the grated cheese and Tabasco, and blend to a soft dough with the water. Roll out on a floured surface until 1 cm/½ inch thick. Cut into rounds with a 7 cm/2½ inch fancy cutter, and arrange on top of the meat mixture, overlapping in a decorative pattern. Brush the tops of the cobblers with the milk and return the uncovered casserole to the oven. Bake for a further 30 to 40 minutes or until golden.

Beef Brazilian-Style

METRIC/IMPERIAL
3 tablespoons oil
1 kg/2 lb stewing steak, cut into
　strips
3 onions, thinly sliced
1 garlic clove, crushed
25 g/1 oz flour
150 ml/¼ pint beef stock
1½–2 teaspoons instant coffee
　powder
150 ml/¼ pint boiling water
1 x 400 g/14 oz can tomatoes
pinch of grated nutmeg
2 teaspoons soft brown sugar
salt and pepper

AMERICAN
3 tablespoons oil
2 lb beef for stew, cut into strips
3 onions, thinly sliced
1 garlic clove, crushed
¼ cup flour
¾ cup beef broth
1½–2 teaspoons instant coffee
　powder
¾ cup boiling water
1 x 16 oz can tomatoes
pinch of grated nutmeg
2 teaspoons brown sugar
salt and pepper

Heat the oil in a flameproof casserole. Add the beef strips and fry quickly until browned. Lower the heat and add the onions and garlic. Cook until softened.

Sprinkle in the flour and continue to cook, stirring, for 1 to 2 minutes. Gradually add the stock (broth). Dissolve the coffee in the water and add with the tomatoes and their juice, the nutmeg, brown sugar, and salt and pepper to taste.

Bring to simmering point, then cover and transfer to a preheated moderate oven (160°C/325°F, Gas Mark 3). Cook for 2 hours.

Serve with buttered noodles and a green salad.

Beef Curry

METRIC/IMPERIAL
350 g/12 oz cooked beef, chopped
1 quantity curry sauce (page 239)
ACCOMPANIMENTS:
freshly boiled rice
25 g/1 oz desiccated coconut
150 ml/¼ pint natural yogurt
4 tomatoes, skinned and chopped
2 bananas, sliced and dipped in
　lemon juice
chutney

AMERICAN
2 cups chopped cooked beef
1 quantity curry sauce (page 239)
ACCOMPANIMENTS:
freshly boiled rice
3 tablespoons shredded coconut
¾ cup plain yogurt
4 tomatoes, peeled and chopped
2 bananas, sliced and dipped in
　lemon juice
chutney

Add the beef to the sauce and simmer gently for 15 minutes, stirring often.

Arrange a border of rice on a warm plate. Fill the centre with the hot beef curry and serve with the other accompaniments.

Fruited Beef Olives

METRIC/IMPERIAL
350 g/12 oz topside of beef
40 g/1½ oz beef dripping
1 medium onion, peeled and
   roughly chopped
25 g/1 oz flour
450 ml/¾ pint beef stock
2 teaspoons salt
freshly ground black pepper
FOR THE STUFFING:
5 tablespoons fresh white
   breadcrumbs
1 tablespoon shredded beef suet
4 dried apricots, soaked and
   chopped
1 rasher lean bacon, diced
1 teaspoon dried or 1 tablespoon
   fresh chopped mixed herbs
salt and freshly ground black
   pepper
1 egg, lightly beaten
8 stuffed green olives to garnish

AMERICAN
¾ lb top round of beef
3 tablespoons beef dripping
1 medium-size onion, peeled and
   roughly chopped
¼ cup flour
2 cups beef stock
2 teaspoons salt
freshly ground black pepper
FOR THE STUFFING:
5 tablespoons soft white bread
   crumbs
1 tablespoon shortening
4 dried apricots, soaked and
   chopped
1 slice lean bacon, diced
1 teaspoon dried or 1 tablespoon
   fresh chopped mixed herbs
salt and freshly ground black
   pepper
1 egg, lightly beaten
8 stuffed green olives for garnish

Cut the meat into slices across the grain, about 7.5 x 10 cm/3 x 4 inches. Flatten the slices by laying them between sheets of greaseproof (waxed) paper and batting out with a rolling pin.

Prepare the stuffing by mixing all the ingredients together well. Spread over the slices of meat. Roll up the meat tightly and secure the rolls with wooden cocktail sticks (toothpicks) or cotton thread.

Melt the dripping in a small casserole and brown the beef olives quickly on all sides. Remove them and fry the chopped onion until limp. Sprinkle in the flour and cook gently for another 2 minutes, stirring constantly, until the flour is golden-brown. Gradually stir in the stock and seasoning to taste. Bring to the boil, add the beef olives, cover with the lid and simmer gently for 2 hours.

Transfer the beef olives to a heated serving dish. Remove the cocktail sticks or cotton thread. Garnish each roll with an olive. Pour over a little of the sauce and serve the remainder separately. If liked, garnish each roll with a parsley sprig instead of an olive.

Hot Pot with Herb Dumplings

METRIC/IMPERIAL
flour for coating
salt and pepper
750 g/1½ lb braising steak, cubed
3 tablespoons oil
2 medium onions, sliced
4 leeks, trimmed and sliced
6 medium carrots, sliced
450 ml/¾ pint beef stock
1 x 400 g/14 oz can tomatoes
100 g/4 oz mushrooms, sliced
DUMPLINGS:
100 g/4 oz self-raising flour
50 g/2 oz shredded suet
2 teaspoons chopped fresh thyme
  or 1 teaspoon dried thyme
2 teaspoons chopped fresh sage or
  1 teaspoon dried sage

AMERICAN
flour for coating
salt and pepper
1½ lb beef for stew, cubed
3 tablespoons oil
2 medium-size onions, sliced
4 leeks, trimmed and sliced
6 medium-size carrots, sliced
2 cups beef broth
1 x 16 oz can tomatoes
1 cup sliced mushrooms
DUMPLINGS:
1 cup self-rising flour
¼ cup shredded beef suet
2 teaspoons chopped fresh thyme
  or 1 teaspoon dried thyme
2 teaspoons chopped fresh sage or
  1 teaspoon dried sage

Season flour with salt and pepper and use to coat the beef cubes. Heat the oil in a flameproof casserole, add the beef and brown quickly on all sides. Remove from the casserole.

Add the onions, leeks and carrots to the casserole and fry until softened. Add the stock (broth) and tomatoes with their juice. Bring to the boil, then return the meat to the casserole. Season to taste with salt and pepper. Cover and transfer to a preheated moderate oven (160°C/325°F, Gas Mark 3). Cook for 2 hours.

To make the dumplings, mix the flour and suet together. Add the herbs and season to taste with salt and pepper. Stir in enough water to make an elastic dough. Divide into eight portions.

Arrange the dumplings around the top edge of the casserole. Re-cover and cook for a further 15 to 20 minutes.

Souffléed Pasta Bolognese

METRIC/IMPERIAL
3 tablespoons vegetable oil
175 g/6 oz pasta shapes
1 large onion, peeled and finely
chopped
225 g/8 oz minced beef
1 clove of garlic, crushed
1 tablespoon tomato purée
1 x 396 g/14 oz can tomatoes
salt and freshly ground black
pepper
3 eggs, separated
25 g/1 oz grated Parmesan cheese

AMERICAN
3 tablespoons vegetable oil
6 oz pasta shapes
1 large onion, peeled and finely
chopped
½ lb ground beef
1 clove of garlic, crushed
1 tablespoon tomato paste
1 can (16 oz) tomatoes
salt and freshly ground black
pepper
3 eggs, separated
¼ cup grated Parmesan cheese

Bring a large pan of lightly salted water to the boil and add 1 tablespoon of the oil. Add the pasta shapes and cook until just tender – about 6 minutes. Drain well.

Fry the chopped onion gently in the remaining oil for 5 minutes. Add the minced (ground) beef and continue frying gently until lightly browned. Stir in the crushed garlic, tomato purée, canned tomatoes and their liquid and seasoning to taste. Simmer for 20 minutes. Allow to cool and then beat the egg yolks into the Bolognese sauce. Fold in the cooked pasta. Stiffly beat the egg whites and fold in. Put into a greased ovenproof dish and sprinkle the surface with grated Parmesan cheese. Bake in a fairly hot oven (190°C/375°F, Gas Mark 5) for 40 to 45 minutes until risen and golden-brown. Serve immediately with extra grated Parmesan cheese.
Serves 4 to 6

Cottage Pie

METRIC/IMPERIAL
350 g/12 oz cold cooked beef,
finely minced
1 quantity brown sauce (page 240)
500 g/1 lb mashed potatoes
50 g/2 oz Lancashire cheese,
crumbled

AMERICAN
¾ lb cold cooked beef, ground
(about 1½ cups)
1 quantity brown sauce (page 240)
2 cups mashed potatoes
½ cup crumbled Monterey Jack
cheese

Mix together the beef and brown sauce and spread out in a 900 ml/1½ pint (1 quart) pie or baking dish. Cover with the mashed potatoes and sprinkle with the cheese.

Bake in a preheated hot oven (220°C/425°F, Gas Mark 7) for 15 to 20 minutes or until piping hot and the top is browned.

Rice Rissoles

METRIC/IMPERIAL
350 g/12 oz lean minced beef
225 g/8 oz cooked long-grain rice
1 large onion, peeled and finely
*   chopped*
50 g/2 oz Cheddar cheese, grated
1 tablespoon chopped pickled
*   cucumber*
salt and freshly ground black
*   pepper*
3 eggs
2 tablespoons cold water
flour for coating
vegetable oil for frying

AMERICAN
¾ lb lean ground beef
1½ cups cooked long-grain rice
1 large onion, peeled and finely
*   chopped*
½ cup grated Cheddar cheese
1 tablespoon chopped dill pickles
salt and freshly ground black
*   pepper*
3 eggs
2 tablespoons cold water
flour for coating
vegetable oil for fyring

Stir together in a large bowl the minced (ground) beef, rice, chopped onion, grated cheese, chopped pickles and seasoning. Break in 2 eggs, mix thoroughly, and form with floured hands into 12 balls. Beat the remaining egg with the water and use to coat the balls. Roll them in flour and refrigerate on a plate, slipped inside a polythene bag, for at least 1 hour to become firm.

Fry in deep hot fat (190°C/375°F) (as for Macaroni Cheese Balls, see page 143) until a rich golden-brown.

Hamburgers

METRIC/IMPERIAL
500 g/1 lb minced beef
50 g/2 oz fresh white breadcrumbs
1 small onion, finely grated
4 tablespoons milk
½ teaspoon made mustard
1 teaspoon Worcestershire sauce
salt and pepper
40 g/1½ oz butter

AMERICAN
1 lb ground beef
1 cup soft white bread crumbs
1 small onion, finely grated
¼ cup milk
½ teaspoon prepared mustard
1 teaspoon Worcestershire sauce
salt and pepper
3 tablespoons butter

Mix together the beef, breadcrumbs, onion, milk, mustard, Worcestershire sauce, and salt and pepper to taste. Divide into eight equal portions and shape into 1 cm/½ inch thick patties.

Melt the butter in a frying pan. Add the hamburgers, a few at a time. Fry quickly for 1 minute on each side. Reduce the heat and continue cooking for 6 to 8 minutes, turning twice. Serve hot in soft baps (hamburger buns).

Minced Beef and Bacon Roll

METRIC/IMPERIAL
500 g/1 lb minced beef
225 g/8 oz minced bacon
 (trimmings may be used)
225 g/8 oz fresh white
 breadcrumbs
1 medium onion, peeled and finely
 chopped
1 teaspoon chopped parsley
pinch of dried thyme
pinch of dried marjoram
salt and freshly ground black
 pepper
2 eggs, lightly beaten

AMERICAN
1 lb ground beef
½ lb ground bacon (trimmings may
 be used)
4 cups soft white bread crumbs
1 medium-size onion, peeled and
 finely chopped
1 teaspoon chopped parsley
pinch of dried thyme
pinch of dried marjoram
salt and freshly ground black
 pepper
2 eggs, lightly beaten

Put the minced (ground) beef and bacon into a bowl and break up with a fork. Add the breadcrumbs, chopped onion, herbs and seasoning and blend well together. Bind the mixture with the beaten eggs and shape into a roll.

Wrap the roll in greased aluminium foil, sealing carefully by folding and crimping the edges of the foil.

Place in a steamer over gently bubbling water and cook for 2 hours, taking care that the pan does not boil dry. Replenish the pan with more boiling water if necessary. Remove the roll from the foil and serve hot immediately. If serving cold, allow the roll to cool in the foil.
NOTE: The prepared mixture may be divided and shaped to make 2 smaller rolls, one for serving hot and one cold.

Family Favourite

METRIC/IMPERIAL
750 g/1 ½ lb minced beef
1 medium onion, finely chopped
1 tablespoon flour
1 x 275 g/10 oz can condensed
 oxtail soup
1 soupcan water
350 g/12 oz carrots, quartered
 lengthways
salt and pepper

AMERICAN
1½ lb ground beef
1 medium-size onion, finely
 chopped
1 tablespoon flour
1 x 10 oz can condensed oxtail
 soup
1 soupcan water
¾ lb carrots, quartered lengthwise
salt and pepper

Place the beef and onion in a large saucepan and fry until browned. Stir in the flour and then the soup and water. Bring to the boil.

Add the carrots, and season to taste with salt and pepper. Simmer gently for 45 minutes to 1 hour or until the beef is quite tender.

45

Minced Beef and Kidney Pie

METRIC/IMPERIAL
225 g/8 oz flour
pinch of salt
100 g/4 oz lard, cut into pieces
2–3 tablespoons cold water
FOR THE FILLING:
25 g/1 oz dripping
1 small onion, peeled and chopped
½ kg/1 lb minced beef
100 g/4 oz ox kidney, trimmed and
   finely chopped
300 ml/½ pint water
1 teaspoon gravy powder
salt and freshly ground black
   pepper
1 tablespoon cornflour
a little milk to glaze
parsley sprigs to garnish

AMERICAN
2 cups flour
pinch of salt
½ cup shortening, cut into pieces
2–3 tablespoons cold water
FOR THE FILLING:
2 tablespoons dripping
1 small onion, peeled and chopped
1 lb ground beef
¼ lb ox kidney, trimmed and finely
   chopped
1¼ cups water
1 teaspoon gravy powder
salt and freshly ground black
   pepper
1 tablespoon cornstarch
a little milk to glaze
parsley sprigs for garnish

Sift the flour and salt into a bowl. Rub in the lard (shortening) until the mixture resembles fine breadcrumbs. Stir in just sufficient water to hold the mixture together, then form into a smooth ball. Wrap in foil or greaseproof (waxed) paper and chill in the refrigerator for 30 minutes.

Meanwhile, melt the dripping in a saucepan. Add the chopped onion and fry, stirring constantly, for 3 to 4 minutes. Add the minced (ground) beef and kidney and continue to fry, stirring until all the meat is brown and no lumps remain. Add the water, gravy powder and seasoning. Bring to the boil and stir well. Cover and simmer for 1 hour. Alternatively, cook in a pressure cooker for 20 minutes.

Blend the cornflour (cornstarch) with a little cold water. Add to the meat mixture and stir constantly until thickened. Simmer for a further 3 minutes. Cool.

Divide the pastry dough into two and roll out one half on a floured surface to form a circle to fit the base of a 20 cm/8 inch pie dish. Spoon in the meat mixture. Roll out the remaining pastry for the lid. Lay this over the filling, dampen the edges and press well together to seal. Flute the edge with finger and thumb or with a fork. Decorate the top using any pastry trimmings.

Brush the pie with milk and make a slit in the centre for the steam to escape.

Place the pie dish on a baking sheet and bake in a fairly hot oven (200°C/400°F, Gas Mark 6) for 20 minutes, or until golden-brown on top. Serve garnished with sprigs of parsley.

Corned Beef Cheeseburgers

METRIC/IMPERIAL
350 g/12 oz lean cut corned beef
1 medium onion, peeled
1 egg
1 tablespoon Worcestershire sauce
50 g/2 oz quick cook oats
1 tablespoon chopped parsley
salt and freshly ground black
  pepper
vegetable oil for frying
1 tomato, sliced
4 slices processed cheese

AMERICAN
¾ lb lean cut corned beef
1 medium-size onion, peeled
1 egg
1 tablespoon Worcestershire sauce
2 oz quick cook oats
1 tablespoon chopped parsley
salt and freshly ground black
  pepper
vegetable oil for frying
1 tomato, sliced
4 slices processed cheese

Place the corned beef in a medium-sized bowl and mash it with a fork until completely broken down. Grate the onion straight into the corned beef. Beat the egg and add to the meat mixture with the Worcestershire sauce, oats, parsley and seasoning to taste. Mix together thoroughly and allow the mixture to stand for 5 minutes. Divide into 4 equal parts and shape each into a round approx. 2.5 cm/1 inch thick.

Heat a little oil in a frying pan (skillet) and cook the burgers for 2 to 3 minutes on each side, until golden-brown. Remove from the pan and drain well on absorbent kitchen paper.

Meanwhile, heat the grill. Place the burgers in the grill pan, top each with a slice of tomato then with a slice of cheese. Place under the grill until the cheese melts. Serve with baps (see page 212) and sweet pickles.

Beef Cobbler

METRIC/IMPERIAL
2 large carrots, diced
1 large onion, chopped
600 ml/1 pint water
350 g/12 oz minced beef
1 quantity meat gravy (page 244)
225 g/8 oz quantity suet pastry
  (page 248)

AMERICAN
2 large carrots, diced
1 large onion, chopped
2½ cups water
¾ lb ground beef
1 quantity meat gravy (page 244)
2 cup quantity suet pastry (page
  248)

Put the carrots and onion in a large saucepan and add the water. Bring to the boil and simmer gently until softened. Add the beef and cover the pan. Simmer for 45 minutes.

Add the meat gravy and stir well. Pour into a deep pie or baking dish.

Roll out the suet pastry dough on a floured surface to 1 cm/½ inch thick. Using a pastry cutter, cut out enough rounds to cover the dish, without overlapping. Arrange over the beef filling.

Bake in a preheated moderately hot oven (190°C/375°F, Gas Mark 5) for 15 to 20 minutes or until the pastry is golden-brown.

Beef Casserole

METRIC/IMPERIAL
2 tablespoons flour
salt and pepper
750 g/1 ½ lb stewing steak, cut into
 2.5 cm/1 inch cubes
40 g/1 ½ oz butter
2 medium onions, chopped
3 medium carrots, sliced
½ small turnip, diced
450 ml/¾ pint water

AMERICAN
2 tablespoons flour
salt and pepper
1 ½ lb beef for stew, cut into 1 inch
 cubes
3 tablespoons butter
2 medium-size onions, chopped
3 medium-size carrots, sliced
½ small turnip, diced
2 cups water

Season the flour with salt and pepper to use to coat the beef cubes. Melt the butter in a frying pan, add the beef cubes and brown on all sides. Transfer to a casserole.

Add the vegetables and fry for 7 minutes. Add to the casserole.

Pour in the water and cover the casserole. Cook in a preheated moderate oven (160°C/325°F, Gas Mark 3) for 3 hours or until tender.

Beefy Cottage Pie

METRIC/IMPERIAL
2 tablespoons vegetable oil
2 medium onions, peeled and
 sliced
500 g/1 lb lean minced beef
1 tablespoon tomato purée
1 teaspoon sugar
1 teaspoon Worcestershire sauce
salt and freshly ground black
 pepper
150 ml/¼ pint hot water
1 teaspoon Bovril or Marmite
500 g/1 lb cooked potatoes,
 mashed and seasoned
3 tablespoons hot milk

AMERICAN
2 tablespoons vegetable oil
2 medium-size onions, peeled and
 sliced
1 lb lean ground beef
1 tablespoon tomato paste
1 teaspoon sugar
1 teaspoon Worcestershire sauce
salt and freshly ground black
 pepper
⅔ cup hot water
1 teaspoon Bovril or Marmite
1 lb cooked potatoes, mashed and
 seasoned
3 tablespoons hot milk

Heat the oil in a heavy saucepan or flameproof casserole. Add the sliced onions and fry until soft. Add the minced (ground) beef and fry gently for 5 minutes, breaking it up with a wooden spoon as it cooks. When all the meat has turned colour, add all the remaining ingredients except the mashed potato and milk. Cover and simmer for 30 minutes or until the meat is tender and most of the liquid absorbed. Taste and adjust the seasoning if necessary. Turn into a pie dish.

Beat the hot milk into the mashed potato, reserving 1 tablespoon, and spread the creamed potato over the meat. Brush with the remaining milk and bake in a hot oven (220°C/425°F, Gas Mark 7) for 10 minutes.

Chilli Con Carne

METRIC/IMPERIAL
225 g/8 oz dried haricot beans,
  soaked overnight
50 g/2 oz butter
2 teaspoons olive or corn oil
2 medium onions, finely chopped
2 garlic cloves, crushed
500 g/1 lb minced beef
225 g/8 oz tomatoes, skinned and
  chopped
1 medium green pepper, cored,
  seeded and diced
1 teaspoon chilli powder
¼ teaspoon salt
1 teaspoon caraway seeds
150 ml/¼ pint water
1 teaspoon flour
4 tablespoons single cream

AMERICAN
1 cup dried navy beans, soaked
  overnight
¼ cup butter
2 teaspoons olive or corn oil
2 medium-size onions, finely
  chopped
2 garlic cloves, crushed
1 lb ground beef
½ lb tomatoes, peeled and
  chopped
1 medium-size green pepper,
  cored, seeded and diced
1 teaspoon chili powder
¼ teaspoon salt
1 teaspoon caraway seeds
¾ cup water
1 teaspoon flour
¼ cup light cream

Drain the beans and place in a saucepan. Cover with fresh cold water, bring to the boil and simmer for about 45 minutes or until almost tender. Drain well.

Melt the butter with the oil in another saucepan. Add the onions and garlic and fry until golden. Add the meat and fry until brown, breaking it up with a fork and turning it all the time. Stir in the tomatoes, green pepper, beans, chilli powder, salt, caraway seeds and half the water. Cover and cook over low heat for 45 minutes to 1 hour or until the beans are soft.

Mix the flour with the rest of the water and add to the pan. Stir until the mixture thickens. Remove from the heat and stir in the cream. Serve hot.

School-Day Casserole

METRIC/IMPERIAL
2 medium onions, chopped
3 medium carrots, diced
600 ml/1 pint water
500 g/1 lb minced beef
1 x 200 g/7 oz can peas, drained
1 quantity meat gravy (page 244)

AMERICAN
2 medium-size onions, chopped
3 medium-size carrots, diced
2½ cups water
1 lb ground beef
1 x 7 oz can peas, drained
1 quantity meat gravy (page 244)

Put the onions and carrots in a saucepan, add the water and bring to the boil. Simmer until softened. Add the beef, cover and simmer for 45 minutes.

Stir in the peas and meat gravy and simmer, stirring, until thickened.

Stewed Beef with Dumplings

METRIC/IMPERIAL
2 tablespoons flour
salt and pepper
750 g/1½ lb stewing beef, cut into
    2.5 cm/1 inch cubes
175 g/6 oz ox kidney, cut into
    2.5 cm/1 inch cubes
40 g/1½ oz butter
2 medium onions, chopped
3 medium carrots, sliced
½ small turnip, diced
450 ml/¾ pint water
100 g/4 oz quantity suet pastry
    (page 248)

AMERICAN
2 tablespoons flour
salt and pepper
1½ lb beef for stew, cut into 1 inch
    cubes
6 oz beef kidney, cut into 1 inch
    cubes
3 tablespoons butter
2 medium-size onions, chopped
3 medium-size carrots, sliced
½ small turnip, diced
2 cups water
1 cup quantity suet pastry (page
    248)

Season the flour with salt and pepper and use to coat the beef and kidney pieces. Melt the butter in a saucepan, add the meat and brown all over. Remove to a plate.

Add the onions, carrots and turnip to the pan. Fry for 7 minutes or until well browned.

Return the meat to the pan, add the water and bring to the boil. Cover and simmer very gently for 1¾ to 2 hours or until the meat is tender.

Meanwhile, roll the suet dough into eight small balls. Twenty minutes before the stew has finished cooking, add these dumplings to the pan and continue cooking, covered.

VARIATION:
Stewed beef with tomatoes – make as above, omitting the suet dumplings, and adding 225 g/8 oz skinned and chopped tomatoes with the water.

Meat and Vegetable Pasties (Turnovers)

METRIC/IMPERIAL
175 g/6 oz stewing steak, diced
100 g/4 oz ox liver or kidney, diced
1 medium onion, chopped
1 large potato, diced
1 tablespoon water
½ teaspoon salt
pepper
225 g/8 oz quantity shortcrust
* pastry (page 246)*
milk for brushing

AMERICAN
1 cup diced beef for stew
1 cup diced beef liver or kidney
1 medium-size onion, chopped
1 large potato, diced
1 tablespoon water
½ teaspoon salt
pepper
2 cup quantity pie pastry (page
* 246)*
milk for brushing

Mix together the beef, liver or kidney, onion, potato, water, salt and pepper to taste.

Divide the pastry dough into four equal pieces and roll out each into a 15 to 18 cm/6 to 7 inch round. Moisten the edges with water. Put equal amounts of the filling onto each round and fold the rounds in half over the filling to form semi-circles. Press the edges well together to seal and mark with a fork. Transfer to a lightly buttered baking sheet and brush with milk.

Bake in a preheated hot oven (220°C/425°F, Gas Mark 7) for 20 minutes. Reduce the heat to moderate (160°C/325°F, Gas Mark 3) and bake for a further 45 minutes. Serve hot or cold.

Steak and Kidney Pudding

METRIC/IMPERIAL
225 g/8 oz quantity suet pastry
* (page 248)*
1 tablespoon flour
salt and pepper
500 g/1 lb stewing steak, cubed
175 g/6 oz ox kidney, cubed
1 large onion, chopped
3 tablespoons cold water

AMERICAN
2 cup quantity suet pastry
* (page 248)*
1 tablespoon flour
salt and pepper
1 lb beef for stew, cubed
6 oz beef kidney, diced
1 large onion, chopped
3 tablespoons cold water

Roll out two-thirds of the dough and use to line a well-greased 900 ml/ 1½ pint pudding basin (1 quart steaming mold). Season the flour with salt and pepper and use to coat the steak and kidney pieces. Place in the lined basin (mold) alternately with layers of onion. Pour in the water.

Roll out the rest of the dough to make a lid for the basin (mold). Place on top and press the edges well together. Cover with a double layer of well-buttered greaseproof (parchment) paper, or a single layer of foil.

Steam steadily for 3½ hours, topping up with boiling water when needed. Serve straight from the basin (mold).

Stewed Beef

METRIC/IMPERIAL
2 tablespoons flour
salt and pepper
750 g/1 ½ lb stewing beef, cut into
   2.5 cm/1 inch cubes
40 g/1 ½ oz butter
2 medium onions, chopped
3 medium carrots, sliced
2 sticks celery, chopped
450 ml/¾ pint water

AMERICAN
2 tablespoons flour
salt and pepper
1 ½ lb beef for stew, cut into 1 inch
   cubes
3 tablespoons butter
2 medium-size onions, chopped
3 medium-size carrots, sliced
2 sticks celery, chopped
2 cups water

Season the flour with salt and pepper and use to coat the beef cubes. Melt the butter in a saucepan, add the beef cubes and brown on all sides. Remove to a plate.

Add the vegetables to the pan. Fry for 7 minutes or until well browned.

Return the meat to the pan, add the water and bring to the boil. Cover and simmer very gently for 1¾ to 2 hours or until the meat is tender.

Steak and Kidney Plate Pie

METRIC/IMPERIAL
2 tablespoons flour
salt and pepper
500 g/1 lb stewing beef, cubed
175 g/6 oz ox kidney, diced
40 g/1 ½ oz butter
1 tablespoon oil
1 large onion, chopped
300 ml/½ pint beef stock or water
225 g/8 oz quantity milk puff pastry
   (page 248)
milk for brushing

AMERICAN
2 tablespoons flour
salt and pepper
1 lb beef for stew, cubed
6 oz beef kidney, diced
3 tablespoons butter
1 tablespoon oil
1 large onion, chopped
1 ¼ cups beef broth or water
2 cup quantity milk puff pastry
   (page 248)
milk for brushing

Season the flour with salt and pepper and use to coat the steak and kidney pieces. Melt the butter with the oil in a saucepan, add the steak and kidney and fry briskly until browned all over. Remove to a plate.

Add the onion to the pan and fry gently until pale gold. Replace the meat, pour in the stock (broth) or water and bring to the boil. Cover the pan and simmer gently for 1 ½ to 2 hours or until the meat is tender. Remove from the heat and leave until cold.

Roll out half the dough and use to line a lightly buttered 20 to 23 cm/8 to 9 inch pie plate (pan). Put the cold meat filling in the centre. Roll out the remaining dough and cover the pie. Press the edges well together.

Place the pie on a baking sheet, brush with milk and bake in a preheated hot oven (220°C/425°F, Gas Mark 7) for 25 to 30 minutes or until golden brown. Serve hot.

Meat Loaf

METRIC/IMPERIAL
500 g/1 lb minced beef
2 tablespoons minced parsley
1 tablespoon minced onion
2 tablespoons fresh breadcrumbs
15 g/½ oz butter, melted
1 egg, beaten
salt and pepper

AMERICAN
1 lb ground beef
2 tablespoons minced parsley
1 tablespoon minced onion
2 tablespoons soft bread crumbs
1 tablespoon butter, melted
1 egg, beaten
salt and pepper

Mix all the ingredients together with salt and pepper to taste. Pack into a well-greased 500 g/1 lb (7 x 3 inch) loaf pan, and cover with lightly buttered greaseproof (parchment) paper.

Bake in a preheated cool oven (150°C/300°F, Gas Mark 3) for 1 hour. Uncover and baste at least twice, then drain off excess juice. Turn the loaf onto a warmed serving dish and serve.

Spicy Beef with Beans

METRIC/IMPERIAL
1 large onion, chopped
500 g/1 lb minced beef
1 x 400 g/14 oz can tomatoes
2 teaspoons paprika
2 tablespoons Worcestershire
  sauce
150 ml/¼ pint + 3 tablespoons
  water
salt and pepper
1 x 425 g/15 oz can red kidney
  beans
2 tablespoons cornflour
butter
3 thick slices of bread

AMERICAN
1 large onion, chopped
1 lb ground beef
1 x 16 oz can tomatoes
2 teaspoons paprika
2 tablespoons Worcestershire
  sauce
⅔ cup + 3 tablespoons water
salt and pepper
1 x 16 oz can red kidney beans
2 tablespoons cornstarch
butter
3 thick slices of bread

Place the onion and beef in a large saucepan and fry for 5 minutes or until the onion is soft and the beef browned and crumbly. Add the undrained tomatoes, paprika, Worcestershire sauce, 150 ml/¼ pint (⅔ cup) of the water and salt and pepper to taste. Drain the red kidney beans, reserving the liquid, and add the liquid to the saucepan. Bring to the boil, then cover and simmer for 45 minutes.

Dissolve the cornflour (cornstarch) in the remaining water. Stir into the pan with the beans and simmer for a further 5 minutes, stirring well.

Butter the bread on both sides and cut into 2.5 cm/1 inch squares.

Pour the beef mixture into a flameproof serving dish and place the bread squares on top. Place under a preheated grill (broiler) and cook for 5 to 7 minutes or until golden brown.

Lamb Hot Pot

METRIC/IMPERIAL
500 g/1 lb potatoes, thinly sliced
750 g/1 ½ lb best end of neck of
   lamb, cut into cutlets and excess
   fat removed
2 lambs' kidneys, cored and sliced
225 g/8 oz onions, thinly sliced
salt and pepper
150 ml/¼ pint stock or water
25 g/1 oz butter, melted

AMERICAN
1 lb potatoes, thinly sliced
1 ½ lb lamb rib chops, trimmed of
   excess fat
2 lamb kidneys, cored and sliced
1 large onion, thinly sliced
salt and pepper
¾ cup broth or water
2 tablespoons butter, melted

Cover the bottom of a 1.5 litre/2½ pint (1½ quart) casserole or baking dish with about half the potato slices. Arrange the lamb on top, cover with the kidneys and onions and sprinkle with salt and pepper. Arrange the rest of the potatoes in overlapping rings on top. Pour on the stock (broth) or water and brush the potatoes with the butter.

    Cover the dish with a lid or foil and cook in a preheated moderate oven (180°C/350°F, Gas Mark 4) for 1½ hours.

    Remove the lid or foil and continue to cook for a further 30 minutes or until the potatoes on top are brown.

Lamb and Mushroom Hot Pot

METRIC/IMPERIAL
500 g/1 lb potatoes, thinly sliced
750 g/1 ½ lb best end of neck of
   lamb, cut into cutlets and excess
   fat removed
2 lambs' kidneys, cored and sliced
225 g/8 oz onions, thinly sliced
100 g/4 oz mushrooms
salt and pepper
150 ml/¼ pint stock or water
25 g/1 oz butter, melted

AMERICAN
1 lb potatoes, thinly sliced
1 ½ lb lamb rib chops, trimmed of
   excess fat
2 lamb kidneys, cored and sliced
1 large onion, thinly sliced
¼ lb mushrooms
salt and pepper
¾ cup broth or water
2 tablespoons butter, melted

Cover the bottom of a 1.2 to 1.5 litre/2 to 3 pint (1½ quart) casserole with some of the potatoes. Place the lamb on top and cover with the kidneys, onions and mushrooms. Sprinkle with salt and pepper to taste, then arrange the rest of the potatoes in overlapping rings on top. Pour on the stock (broth) or water.

    Brush the top layer of potatoes with the melted butter and cover the casserole with the lid or foil. Cook in a preheated moderate oven (180°C/350°F, Gas Mark 4) for 1½ hours.

    Remove the lid or foil and continue to cook for a further 30 minutes or until the potatoes are brown.

Lamb Curry

METRIC/IMPERIAL
25 g/1 oz butter
1 kg/2 lb middle neck of lamb, cut
    into bite-size pieces and excess
    fat removed
2 medium onions, thinly sliced
1 tablespoon curry powder
1 tablespoon flour
2 large tomatoes, skinned and
    chopped
1 bay leaf
4 cloves
1 teaspoon ground cinnamon
25 g/1 oz sultanas or raisins
1 large cooking apple, peeled,
    cored and grated
1 tablespoon sweet pickle
1 teaspoon salt
300 ml/½ pint stock or water
ACCOMPANIMENTS:
freshly boiled rice
150 ml/¼ pint natural yogurt
chopped salted peanuts
thinly sliced cucumber
chutney

AMERICAN
2 tablespoons butter
2 lb lamb for stew, cut into bite-size
    pieces
2 medium-size onions, thinly sliced
1 tablespoon curry powder
1 tablespoon flour
2 large tomatoes, peeled and
    chopped
1 bay leaf
4 cloves
1 teaspoon ground cinnamon
3 tablespoons golden raisins
1 large tart apple, peeled, cored
    and grated
1 tablespoon sweet pickle relish
1 teaspoon salt
1¼ cups broth or water
ACCOMPANIMENTS:
freshly boiled rice
¾ cup plain yogurt
chopped salted peanuts
thinly sliced cucumber
chutney

Melt the butter in a large saucepan. Add the lamb and onions and fry until the lamb is browned on all sides. Stir in the curry powder, flour, tomatoes, bay leaf, cloves, cinnamon, sultanas or raisins, apple, sweet pickle (relish) and salt. Gradually stir in the stock (broth) or water.

Bring slowly to the boil, then lower the heat, cover the pan and simmer gently for 1¼ to 1¾ hours or until the meat is tender.

Serve with the accompaniments.

Lamb Stew

METRIC/IMPERIAL
2 tablespoons flour
salt and pepper
1.5 kg/2½ lb scrag end of neck of
    lamb, cut into bite-size pieces
    and excess fat removed
25 g/1 oz butter
1 large onion, chopped
2 tablespoons well-washed pearl
    barley
450 ml/¾ pint stock or water

AMERICAN
2 tablespoons flour
salt and pepper
2½ lb lamb for stew, cut into
    bite-size pieces
2 tablespoons butter
1 large onion, chopped
2 tablespoons well-washed pearl
    barley
2 cups broth or water

Season the flour with salt and pepper and use to coat the pieces of lamb. Melt the butter in a large saucepan, add the lamb pieces and brown on all sides. Remove from the pan.

Add the onion to the pan and fry until golden brown. Replace the meat and add the barley, stock (broth) or water, and salt and pepper to taste.

Bring slowly to the boil, then lower the heat and cover the pan. Simmer gently for 1½ to 2 hours or until the meat is tender.

Barbecued Lamb Spare Ribs

METRIC/IMPERIAL
1 large breast of lamb, cut into ribs
600 ml/1 pint water
1 tablespoon malt vinegar
FOR THE SAUCE:
1 tablespoon soy sauce
1 tablespoon clear honey
1 tablespoon plum or other red jam
1 teaspoon malt vinegar
½ teaspoon Worcestershire sauce
½ teaspoon dry mustard
½ teaspoon tomato ketchup
½ teaspoon lemon juice
salt and black pepper

AMERICAN
1 large breast of lamb, cut into ribs
2½ cups water
1 tablespoon malt vinegar
FOR THE SAUCE:
1 tablespoon soy sauce
1 tablespoon honey
1 tablespoon plum or other red jam
1 teaspoon malt vinegar
½ teaspoon Worcestershire sauce
½ teaspoon dry mustard
½ teaspoon ketchup
½ teaspoon lemon juice
salt and black pepper

Remove any excess skin and fat from the ribs. Put the water and vinegar into a saucepan and bring to the boil. Place the ribs in the boiling water and simmer, covered, for 15 minutes. Remove the ribs and drain well. Place them in a roasting tin.

Mix together all the ingredients for the sauce in a small saucepan and simmer for 4 minutes. Taste and adjust the seasoning if necessary.

Pour the sauce over the meat and cook, covered, in a moderate oven (180°C/350°F, Gas Mark 4) for 30 minutes. Increase the temperature to (200°C/400°F, Gas Mark 6) and cook for a further 20 minutes.

Lamb Stew with Lentils

METRIC/IMPERIAL
2 tablespoons oil
1 kg/2 lb boned shoulder of lamb,
    cut into 4 cm/1½ inch pieces and
    excess fat removed
2 medium carrots, sliced
2 medium onions, chopped
1–2 garlic cloves, crushed
2 bay leaves
1 bouquet garni
good pinch of grated nutmeg
salt and pepper
450 ml/¾ pint beef stock
175 g/6 oz lentils, soaked in cold
    water for 2 hours
chopped parsley to garnish

AMERICAN
2 tablespoons oil
2 lb lamb for stew, cut into 1½ inch
    pieces
2 medium-size carrots, sliced
2 medium-size onions, chopped
1–2 garlic cloves, crushed
2 bay leaves
1 bouquet garni
large pinch of grated nutmeg
salt and pepper
2 cups beef broth
1 cup lentils, soaked in cold water
    for 2 hours
chopped parsley for garnish

Heat the oil in a flameproof casserole. Add the lamb and brown on all sides. Remove from the pot. Add the carrots and onions to the casserole and fry until softened.

Return the lamb to the casserole, and add the garlic, bay leaves, bouquet garni, nutmeg and salt and pepper to taste. Pour in the stock (broth) and bring to the boil. Cover and transfer to a preheated moderate oven (180°C/350°F, Gas Mark 4). Cook for 30 minutes.

Drain the lentils and add to the casserole. Re-cover and cook for a further 45 minutes.

Remove the bay leaves and bouquet garni, and serve garnished with chopped parsley.

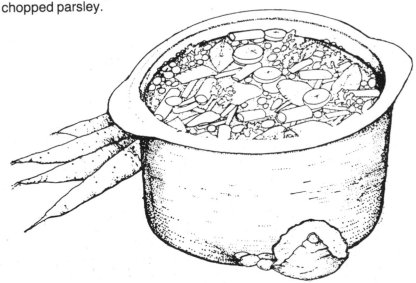

Stuffed Breast of Lamb

METRIC/IMPERIAL
1 kg/2 lb breast of lamb, boned and
  trimmed
salt and freshly ground black
  pepper
4 large potatoes, scrubbed
parsley sprigs to garnish
FOR THE STUFFING:
100 g/4 oz fresh white
  breadcrumbs
1 small onion, peeled and finely
  chopped
1 medium carrot, peeled and grated
1 medium turnip, peeled and grated
1 tablespoon chopped parsley
½ teaspoon dried sage
salt and freshly ground black
  pepper
1 egg, lightly beaten

AMERICAN
2 lb breast of lamb, boned and
  trimmed
salt and freshly ground black
  pepper
4 large potatoes, scrubbed
parsley sprigs for garnish
FOR THE STUFFING:
2 cups soft white bread crumbs
1 small onion, peeled and finely
  chopped
1 medium-size carrot, peeled and
  grated
1 medium-size turnip, peeled and
  grated
1 tablespoon chopped parsley
½ teaspoon dried sage
salt and freshly ground black
  pepper
1 egg, lightly beaten

Sew the breast of lamb together to make one piece, if necessary, and
sprinkle with a little seasoning. Prick the potatoes well.

To make the stuffing, mix together the breadcrumbs, chopped onion,
grated carrot, grated turnip, chopped parsley and sage. Season with salt
and pepper. Bind together with the lightly beaten egg. Spread the stuffing
over the inside of the breast of lamb. Roll up tightly and secure with string.
Place in a roasting tin. Put the potatoes round the joint. Bake in a
moderate oven (180°C/350°F, Gas Mark 4) for 1 hour. Turn the potatoes
over to coat evenly with the pan juices. Bake for another 45 minutes.
Serve garnished with parsley sprigs.

Lamb and Leek Pudding

METRIC/IMPERIAL
225 g/8 oz self-raising flour
1 teaspoon salt
100 g/4 oz shredded beef suet
150 ml/¼ pint water
FOR THE FILLING:
3 thin leeks, washed and sliced in
  rings
500 g/1 lb boned shoulder of lamb
  or best end of neck, trimmed of
  fat and cubed
2 tablespoons seasoned flour for
  coating
1 beef stock cube, crumbled
salt and freshly ground black
  pepper
1 teaspoon dried thyme

AMERICAN
2 cups self-rising flour
1 teaspoon salt
½ cup shortening
⅔ cup water
FOR THE FILLING:
3 thin leeks, washed and sliced in
  rings
1 lb boneless lamb for stew or rib
  lamb, trimmed of fat and cubed
2 tablespoons seasoned flour for
  coating
1 beef bouillon cube, crumbled
salt and freshly ground black
  pepper
1 teaspoon dried thyme

To make the pastry (dough), sift the flour and salt into a bowl. Stir in the shredded suet (shortening). Mix in just sufficient of the water to make a smooth dough that leaves the sides of the bowl clean. Turn out on to a lightly floured board and knead for 1 minute.

Form into two balls, one twice as large as the other. Roll the larger ball into a round big enough to line a 1 litre/1¾ pint pudding basin (1 quart steaming mold). Grease the pudding basin. Ease the pastry into position, making cuts down the sides of the pastry with clean kitchen scissors, if necessary, and sealing these together after brushing the cut edges with water.

Wash the sliced leeks thoroughly in a colander and drain well. Coat the cubed lamb with seasoned flour. Put both into the basin in alternate layers. Mix the crumbled stock (bouillon) cube, seasoning to taste and the dried thyme, with sufficient cold water to come halfway up the contents. Form the reserved pastry into a lid and place on top, sealing the edges of the pastry with cold water.

Cover the pudding with greased foil, making a pleat in the centre to allow for expansion. Tie a piece of string tightly round the bowl under the lip and across the top to form a handle. Place in a steamer or large saucepan of simmering water, making sure the water does not come more than halfway up the sides of the basin. Cover and steam for 3 hours, topping up the water level when necessary.

Remove the basin by the string handle, using the handle of a wooden spoon slipped under the string. Take off the foil and serve in wedges, taking care to spoon out a reasonable proportion of the filling with each serving. Diced carrots and peas make a good accompaniment.

Pork Loaf

METRIC/IMPERIAL
150 ml/¼ pint milk
1 teaspoon Worcestershire sauce
2 eggs
100 g/4 oz fresh white
   breadcrumbs
25 g/1 oz butter
1 onion, finely chopped
350 g/12 oz cold cooked pork,
   finely minced
½ teaspoon dried mixed herbs
salt and pepper
mushroom or onion sauce
   (page 242), to serve

AMERICAN
⅔ cup milk
1 teaspoon Worcestershire sauce
2 eggs
2 cups soft white bread crumbs
2 tablespoons butter
1 onion, finely chopped
2 cups finely ground cooked pork
½ teaspoon dried Italian seasoning
salt and pepper
mushroom or onion sauce
   (page 242), to serve

Beat the milk with the Worcestershire sauce and eggs, then mix with the breadcrumbs. Leave to soak.

Meanwhile, melt the butter in a frying pan, add the onion and fry until golden. Add to the breadcrumbs with the pork and herbs. Season to taste with salt and pepper and mix well together. Place in a well-buttered 1 kg/ 2 lb loaf tin (9 x 5 inch loaf pan).

Bake in a preheated moderate oven (180°C/350°F, Gas Mark 4) for 45 minutes to 1 hour or until firm. Serve hot with mushroom or onion sauce.

Pork Patties

METRIC/IMPERIAL
225 g/8 oz cooked pork, minced
100 g/4 oz lean bacon, derinded
   and finely minced
100 g/4 oz fresh white
   breadcrumbs
½ teaspoon dried sage
1 egg
150 ml/¼ pint milk
salt and pepper
300 ml/½ pint mustard coating
   sauce (page 242)

AMERICAN
1 cup ground cooked pork
½ cup ground Canadian bacon
2 cups soft white bread crumbs
½ teaspoon dried sage
1 egg
⅔ cup milk
salt and pepper
1½ cups mustard coating sauce
   (page 242)

Mix the pork with the bacon, breadcrumbs and herbs. Beat the egg and milk well together, then add to the pork mixture and combine thoroughly. Season to taste with salt and pepper.

Turn the mixture out onto a lightly floured board. Divide into eight equal pieces and shape each into a 2.5 cm/1 inch thick patty. Arrange in a baking dish, in one layer, and coat with the mustard sauce.

Bake in a preheated oven (190°C/375°F, Gas Mark 5) for 20 minutes.

Sausage Rolls

METRIC/IMPERIAL
225 g/8 oz quantity rough puff
  pastry (page 247)
1 teaspoon dried sage
1 small onion, finely chopped
350 g/12 oz pork sausagemeat
1 egg, beaten
beaten egg for brushing

AMERICAN
2 cup quantity rough puff pastry
  (page 247)
1 teaspoon dried sage
1 small onion, finely chopped
¾ lb pork sausage meat
1 egg, beaten
beaten egg for brushing

Roll out the dough into an oblong 1 cm/½ inch thick, and 25 x 20 cm/
10 x 8 inches. Cut into long strips 5 cm/2 inches wide.

Mix the sage, onion and sausagemeat together and bind with the beaten
egg. Mould the mixture into long thin sausage shapes, and place on the
strips of dough. Trim the edges and fold over. Brush with beaten egg and
press to seal. Cut each 'sausage' into five pieces, each about 5 cm/
2 inches long. Place on a baking sheet.

Bake in a preheated moderate oven (180°C/350°F, Gas Mark 4) for
15 minutes or until the pastry is well risen and golden brown.
Makes about 20

Pork and Apple Casserole

METRIC/IMPERIAL
25 g/1 oz dripping or lard
4 thick slices belly of pork
1 clove of garlic, crushed
4 juniper berries
2 medium onions, peeled and
  chopped
2 medium cooking apples, peeled,
  cored and chopped
salt and freshly ground black
  pepper
150 ml/¼ pint apple juice
1 kg/2 lb potatoes, peeled and
  thickly sliced
15 g/½ oz butter

AMERICAN
2 tablespoons dripping or
  shortening
4 thick fresh pork sides
1 clove of garlic, crushed
4 juniper berries
2 medium-size onions, peeled and
  chopped
2 medium-size tart apples, peeled,
  cored and chopped
salt and freshly ground black
  pepper
⅔ cup apple juice
2 lb potatoes, peeled and thickly
  sliced
1 tablespoon butter

Melt the dripping or lard (shortening) in a frying pan. Add the pork slices
and fry until golden-brown on both sides.

Arrange the meat in a shallow casserole. Add the crushed garlic and
juniper berries and cover with a layer of chopped onion and apple. Season
to taste. Pour on the apple juice and cover with overlapping potato slices.
Dot with butter, cover and bake in a cool oven (160°C/325°F, Gas Mark 3)
for 1½ hours. Uncover and cook for a further 30 minutes to brown the top.

Pork Pie

METRIC/IMPERIAL
350 g/12 oz quantity hot water crust pastry (page 247)
500 g/1 lb lean boneless pork, diced
1 small onion, grated
1 teaspoon dried sage
large pinch of grated nutmeg
150 ml/¼ pint water
pepper
beaten egg for brushing
1½ teaspoons gelatine

AMERICAN
3 cup quantity hot water crust pastry (page 247)
1 lb lean boneless pork, diced
1 small onion, grated
1 teaspoon dried sage
large pinch of grated nutmeg
⅔ cup water
pepper
beaten egg for brushing
1½ teaspoons unflavored gelatin

Roll out two-thirds of the dough and mould over the outside of a well-floured 15 cm/6 inch round deep cake pan, covering the base and sides completely. Turn over onto a lightly buttered baking sheet, and carefully remove the cake pan.

Mix the diced pork with the onion, sage, nutmeg, 4 tablespoons of the water and pepper to taste. Pack into the pastry case and moisten the edges with water.

Roll out the rest of the dough to make a lid for the pastry case. Cover the pie and press the edges well together to seal. Tie a strip of double thickness foil around the outside of the pie to keep its shape. Make a hole in the lid to allow steam to escape. Brush all over with beaten egg. Decorate with leaves made from the leftover dough and brush with more egg.

Bake in a preheated moderately hot oven (200°C/400°F, Gas Mark 6) for 15 minutes, then reduce the heat to moderate (180°C/350°F, Gas Mark 4) and bake for a further 1¾ hours.

Remove from the oven. Heat the rest of the water, then add the gelatine and stir briskly until dissolved. Pour into the hot pie, through the hole in the lid using a small plastic funnel. Leave until completely cold before cutting.

Quick Cassoulet

METRIC/IMPERIAL
2 tablespoons vegetable oil
1 large onion, peeled and sliced
500 g/1 lb chipolata sausages
100 g/4 oz streaky bacon, chopped
1 x 436/15 oz can red kidney
   beans, drained
150 ml/¼ pint beef stock
salt and freshly ground black
   pepper
8 thin slices French bread
50 g/2 oz Cheddar cheese, grated

AMERICAN
2 tablespoons vegetable oil
1 large onion, peeled and sliced
1 lb chipolata sausages
¼ lb streaky bacon, chopped
1 can (16 oz) red kidney beans,
   drained
⅔ cup beef stock
salt and freshly ground black
   pepper
8 thin slices French bread
½ cup grated Cheddar cheese

Heat the oil in a frying pan (skillet). Add the onion and fry gently for
5 minutes. Add the chipolata sausages and the chopped bacon and fry
gently for a further 5 minutes, turning the sausages occasionally.

Put the sausages, onion and bacon into a casserole. Add the drained
red kidney beans, stock and seasoning to taste. Cover and cook in a
moderate oven (180°C/350°F, Gas Mark 4) for 40 minutes. Remove the lid
and cover the sausage and bean mixture with slices of French bread.
Sprinkle with the grated cheese and return the cassoulet to the oven for a
further 10 to 15 minutes, until the cheese bubbles.

Quick Bean Casserole

METRIC/IMPERIAL
50 g/2 oz butter
1 small onion, finely chopped
25 g/1 oz green pepper, cored,
   seeded and chopped
75 g/3 oz flour
450 ml/¾ pint milk
1 teaspoon salt
1 x 425 g/15 oz can butter beans
150–175 g/5–6 oz cooked ham,
   diced
3 hard-boiled eggs, quartered
50 g/2 oz Cheddar cheese, grated

AMERICAN
¼ cup butter
1 small onion, finely chopped
¼ cup chopped green pepper
¾ cup flour
2 cups milk
1 teaspoon salt
1 x 16 oz can lima beans, drained
1 cup diced cooked ham
3 hard-cooked eggs, quartered
½ cup grated Cheddar cheese

Melt the butter in a frying pan, add the onion and green pepper and fry until
soft. Slowly mix in the flour, milk and salt, stirring all the time. Cook for
about 5 minutes or until thick and smooth. Add the rest of the ingredients
and mix well.

Pour into a 1.5 litre/2½ pint (1½ quart) casserole dish. Bake in a
preheated moderate oven (180°C/350°F, Gas Mark 4) for 15 to 20 minutes
or until bubbly.

Pork and Bean Pot

METRIC/IMPERIAL
1 kg/2 lb belly of pork
1 kg/2 lb dried white beans,
(cannellini or haricot) soaked
overnight
2 tablespoons olive or corn oil
1 or 2 cloves of garlic, crushed
1 x 156 g/5½ oz can tomato purée
1 tablespoon soft brown sugar
2 small bay leaves
salt and freshly ground black
pepper
50 g/2 oz fresh brown breadcrumbs
15 g/½ oz butter

AMERICAN
2 lb fresh pork sides
2 lb dried white beans (cannellini or
navy) soaked overnight
2 tablespoons olive or corn oil
1 or 2 cloves of garlic, crushed
1 can (5½ oz) tomato paste
1 tablespoon firmly packed light
brown sugar
2 small bay leaves
salt and freshly ground black
pepper
1 cup soft brown bread crumbs
1 tablespoon butter

Remove any bones from the pork and cut the meat into 2.5 cm/1 inch squares. Drain the beans and rinse under cold running water. Place in a large saucepan. Add the bones from the pork and a little salt. Cover with cold water. Bring to the boil and remove any scum with a slotted draining spoon. Boil for 10 minutes, then cover and simmer for 1 hour, or until tender. Discard the bones.

Heat the oil in a sauté or large frying pan (skillet). Add the cubes of pork and cook turning frequently until golden-brown. Add the crushed garlic, tomato purée, sugar, bay leaves and 300 ml/½ pint (1¼ cups) of liquid from the beans. Season well and simmer gently for 10 minutes.

Put a deep layer of drained beans in a large earthenware casserole. Cover with the meat mixture and then the remaining beans. Add sufficient bean stock just to cover. Top with the brown breadcrumbs. Dot with a little butter and bake uncovered in a warm oven (160°C/325°F, Gas Mark 3) for 1½ to 2 hours.

Just before serving stir the crumb topping into the pork and beans. Serve with a tossed green salad, fresh crusty bread and an inexpensive red wine.
Serves 12

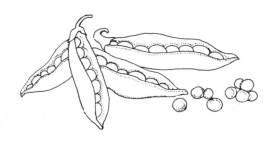

Ham and Beef Fricassée

METRIC/IMPERIAL
1 gammon bone with a little meat
1 bouquet garni
1 small onion, peeled
1 slice of white bread, crust
   removed
1 tablespoon corn oil
500 g/1 lb lean minced beef
2 tablespoons seedless raisins
1 tablespoon flour
salt and black pepper

AMERICAN
1 ham bone with a little meat
1 bouquet garni
1 small onion, peeled
1 slice of white bread, crust
   removed
1 tablespoon corn oil
1 lb lean ground beef
2 tablespoons seedless raisins
1 tablespoon flour
salt and black pepper

On a clean chopping board remove all the lean meat from the ham bone. Put the bone on to boil with enough water just to cover it. Add the bouquet garni and simmer for 30 minutes.

Mince the ham with the onion, then put the bread through the mincer. Heat the corn oil in a flameproof casserole and fry the minced (ground) beef gently until brown, turning constantly. Add the ham mixture and the raisins, sprinkle with the flour, and season to taste. Cook, still stirring, for a further 2 minutes. Measure 150 ml/¼ pint (⅔ cup) of the ham stock and add to the casserole. Cover and simmer for 30 minutes. Add more stock if the mixture becomes dry. Taste and adjust the seasoning if necessary.

Bacon and Beef Casserole

METRIC/IMPERIAL
25 g/1 oz butter
50 g/2 oz bacon, chopped
2 large onions, sliced
750 g/1 ½ lb stewing steak, cut into
   2.5 cm/1 inch cubes
500 g/1 lb potatoes, cubed
25 g/1 oz flour
1 fresh thyme sprig
1 bay leaf
600 ml/1 pint beef stock
salt and pepper

AMERICAN
2 tablespoons butter
½ cup chopped bacon
2 large onions, sliced
1 ½ lb chuck steak, cut into 1 inch
   cubes
1 lb potatoes, cubed
¼ cup flour
1 fresh thyme sprig
1 bay leaf
2½ cups beef broth
salt and pepper

Heat the butter in a frying pan, add the bacon and brown all over. Add the onions and fry until soft. Add the beef and fry quickly until browned. Put the beef mixture and potatoes in a 1.8 litre/3 pint (2 quart) casserole dish.

Stir the flour and herbs into the fat in the frying pan, then gradually stir in the beef stock (broth). Season to taste with salt and pepper. Bring to the boil, stirring. Pour over the vegetables and meat in the casserole dish.

Cover and cook in a preheated moderate oven (160°C/325°F, Gas Mark 3) for 1½ to 2 hours. Discard the bay leaf before serving.

Cowboy's Delight

METRIC/IMPERIAL
25 g/1 oz butter
150 g/5 oz cooked ham, chopped
1 x 447 g/15¾ oz can baked beans
1 x 425 g/15 oz can red kidney
    beans, drained
1 x 425 g/15 oz can butter beans,
    drained
1 tablespoon made mustard
120 ml/4 fl oz tomato sauce
1 tablespoon brown sugar
3 tablespoons vinegar
salt and pepper
1 medium onion, sliced

AMERICAN
2 tablespoons butter
1 cup chopped cooked ham
1 x 15¾ oz can baked beans
1 x 16 oz can red kidney beans,
    drained
1 x 16 oz can lima beans, drained
1 tablespoon prepared mustard
½ cup tomato sauce
1 tablespoon brown sugar
3 tablespoons vinegar
salt and pepper
1 medium-size onion, sliced

Melt the butter in a frying pan, add the ham and brown all over. Mix together the baked beans, kidney beans, butter (lima) beans, mustard, tomato sauce, sugar and vinegar. Add the ham and any butter left in the pan and season to taste with salt and pepper.

 Pour the mixture into a 1.8 litre/3 pint (2 quart) casserole, and arrange the onion slices on top. Bake in a preheated moderate oven (180°C/350°F, Gas Mark 4) for 45 minutes to 1 hour.

Sweet and Sour Pork and Pasta

METRIC/IMPERIAL
500 g/1 lb pork shoulder steaks
salt and black pepper
4 tablespoons vinegar
2 tablespoons brown sugar
2 tablespoons soy sauce
50 g/2 oz butter
1 x 396 g/14 oz can tomatoes
1 tablespoon tomato purée
juice and grated zest of 1 large
    orange
350 g/12 oz pasta shells

AMERICAN
1 lb pork shoulder steaks
salt and black pepper
4 tablespoons vinegar
2 tablespoons brown sugar
2 tablespoons soy sauce
¼ cup butter
1 can (16 oz) tomatoes
1 tablespoon tomato paste
juice and grated zest of 1 large
    orange
¾ lb pasta shells

Cut the pork into thin strips. Put into a shallow dish with seasoning, vinegar, brown sugar and soy sauce. Cover and chill in the refrigerator overnight. Remove the meat from the marinade and drain well. Heat the butter in a pan and fry the pork strips gently until browned on all sides. Add the marinade, canned tomatoes and their liquid, tomato purée and orange juice and zest. Cover and simmer for 30 to 35 minutes.

 Meanwhile, cook the pasta in rapidly boiling salted water, for about 6 to 8 minutes. Drain. Pile up on to a warm dish and spoon over the sauce.

Bacon Collar with Apricots

METRIC/IMPERIAL
1–1½ kg/2–3 lb joint collar bacon
1 bouquet garni
100 g/4 oz dried apricots
500 g/1 lb parsnips, peeled and
  quartered
25 g/1 oz sultanas
salt and freshly ground black
  pepper
1 teaspoon cornflour (optional)
1 tablespoon water (optional)

AMERICAN
2–3 lb joint collar bacon
1 bouquet garni
⅔ cup dried apricots
1 lb parsnips, peeled and quartered
3 tablespoons golden raisins
salt and freshly ground black
  pepper
1 teaspoon cornstarch (optional)
1 tablespoon water (optional)

Soak the joint overnight in cold water. Drain and place in a casserole with the bouquet garni and almost cover with fresh water. Put the lid on the casserole and cook in a moderate oven (180°C/350°F, Gas Mark 4) for 1 hour.

Add the apricots, parsnips, sultanas (golden raisins), a little pepper, and salt if needed. Cook covered, for a further 1 hour. Discard the bouquet garni.

Take out the bacon, remove the rind, slice the meat and place on a heated serving dish garnished with the apricots and parsnips. Serve the sauce separately.

If a slightly thicker sauce is required, moisten the cornflour (cornstarch) with the water and stir into the casserole 15 minutes before the joint is done.

Serve with boiled or mashed potatoes, and do not add salt to the water when cooking them in case the bacon sauce is slightly salty.

Boiled Gammon (Ham) with Pease Pudding

METRIC/IMPERIAL

500 g/1 lb yellow split peas, washed, covered with hot water and soaked overnight
1 corner gammon joint (about 1½ kg/3 lb), soaked in cold water overnight
1 bouquet garni
salt and freshly ground black pepper
50 g/2 oz butter

VEGETABLES FOR THE SOUP:
4 medium carrots, peeled and chopped
4 medium onions, peeled and chopped
4 leeks, white and pale green part washed, trimmed and chopped
6 large celery stalks, scrubbed and chopped

VEGETABLES FOR THE FIRST MEAL:
4 medium carrots, peeled and quartered
4 medium onions, peeled and quartered
4 leeks, white and pale green part washed and halved
1 small swede, peeled and cut into large chunks

AMERICAN

2 cups yellow split peas, washed, covered with hot water and soaked overnight
1 corner ham joint (about 3 lb), soaked in cold water overnight
1 bouquet garni
salt and freshly ground black pepper
¼ cup butter

VEGETABLES FOR THE SOUP:
4 medium-size carrots, peeled and chopped
4 medium-size onions, peeled and chopped
4 leeks, white and pale green part washed, trimmed and chopped
6 large sticks of celery, scrubbed and chopped

VEGETABLES FOR THE FIRST MEAL:
4 medium-size carrots, peeled and quartered
4 medium-size onions, peeled and quartered
4 leeks, white and pale green part washed and halved
1 small rutabaga, peeled and cut into large chunks

Drain the split peas, rinse under cold running water and tie all but a handful in a scalded muslin cloth. Drain the gammon (ham) and place in a large saucepan with the bouquet garni, loose and tied peas, seasoning and soup vegetables. Cover with about 2 litres/3½ pints (9 cups) cold water and bring to the boil, skimming with a slotted draining spoon. Lower the heat and simmer gently for about 1½ hours (allowing 25 to 30 minutes per ½ kg/1 lb) or until the gammon (ham) is tender. Taste the soup and adjust the seasoning if necessary.

Remove the gammon from the pan, strip off the rind and keep the joint hot. Turn the peas from the muslin into a serving dish. Add the butter and beat with a fork until smooth. Taste and adjust the seasoning, if necessary, and keep hot. Meanwhile add the vegetables for the first meal to the saucepan. Bring back to the boil and simmer for 15 minutes or until tender.

Remove the vegetables for the first meal carefully with a slotted draining spoon. Serve with the gammon, pease pudding, English mustard and, if desired, plain boiled potatoes or wholemeal bread. Any remaining pease pudding may be blended into the soup to be served the following day or fried gently in a little butter and served with bacon.

NOTE: In the interest of economy, this dish may be prepared with a gammon (ham) shank or forehock.

Fidget Pie

METRIC/IMPERIAL

FOR THE PASTRY:
225 g/8 oz flour
pinch of salt
100 g/4 oz lard, cut into small
*   pieces*
2-3 tablespoons cold water
FOR THE FILLING:
1 large potato, peeled and chopped
1 large onion, peeled and chopped
225 g/8 oz smoked streaky or collar
*   bacon, diced*
1 large cooking apple, peeled,
*   cored and chopped*
salt and freshly ground black
*   pepper*
150 ml/¼ pint water
a little milk to glaze

AMERICAN

FOR THE PASTRY:
2 cups flour
pinch of salt
½ cup shortening, cut into small
*   pieces*
2-3 tablespoons cold water
FOR THE FILLING:
1 large potato, peeled and chopped
1 large onion, peeled and chopped
½ lb smoked streaky or collar
*   bacon, diced*
1 large cooking apple, peeled,
*   cored and chopped*
salt and freshly ground black
*   pepper*
⅔ cup water
a little milk to glaze

Sift the flour and salt into a bowl, add the lard (shortening) and rub in with the fingertips until the mixture resembles fine breadcrumbs. Add enough cold water to mix to a stiff dough with a palette knife. Knead lightly on a floured surface for 1 minute until smooth. Wrap in foil or greaseproof (waxed) paper and chill in the refrigerator for 30 minutes.

Grease a 1 litre/1¾ pint (4¾ cup) pie dish and into it put layers of the chopped potato, chopped onion and lastly the diced bacon and chopped apple mixed. Season each layer well. Add the water.

Roll out the pastry fairly thickly, to fit the top of the pie dish, cutting a strip to go round the lip of the dish from the trimmings. Dampen the strip with cold water and put the pastry lid on top of this, pressing down well to seal. Cut two small steam vents in the lid. Decorate the top of the pie with the rest of the pastry trimmings. Brush with milk.

Bake in a fairly hot oven (200°C/400°F, Gas Mark 6) for about 30 minutes or until the pastry is golden-brown. Reduce the temperature to 160°C/325°F, Gas Mark 3 and cook for a further 1 hour, covering the pastry with foil, if necessary, to prevent it from becoming too brown. Serve hot.

Veal and Vegetable Casserole

METRIC/IMPERIAL
1 kg/2 lb pie veal, cubed
salt and freshly ground black
    pepper
2 tablespoons vegetable oil
1 clove of garlic, crushed
6 spring onions, trimmed and
    chopped
2 small turnips, peeled and diced
225 g/8 oz baby carrots, scrubbed
½ teaspoon dried thyme
½ teaspoon dried marjoram
4 medium potatoes, peeled and
    thinly sliced
300 ml/½ pint water
1 chicken stock cube, crumbled
150 ml/¼ pint dry cider
TO GARNISH:
100 g/¼ lb cottage cheese
1 teaspoon snipped chives
1 tablespoon chopped parsley
salt and freshly ground black
    pepper

AMERICAN
2 lb boneless veal for stew, cubed
salt and freshly ground black
    pepper
2 tablespoons vegetable oil
1 clove garlic, crushed
6 scallions, trimmed and chopped
2 small turnips, peeled and diced
½ lb baby carrots, scrubbed
½ teaspoon dried thyme
½ teaspoon dried marjoram
4 medium-size potatoes, peeled
    and thinly sliced
1¼ cups water
1 chicken bouillon cube, crumbled
⅔ cup apple cider
FOR GARNISH:
½ cup cottage cheese
1 teaspoon chopped chives
1 tablespoon chopped parsley
salt and freshly ground black
    pepper

Sprinkle the meat with salt and pepper. Heat the oil in a large frying pan, add the meat, crushed garlic and chopped spring onions (scallions) and cook for 5 minutes, turning several times to brown the meat on all sides. Remove with a slotted draining spoon to a casserole.

Cook the diced turnips and carrots in the oil left in the pan for 5 minutes. Add the vegetables to the meat in the casserole, sprinkle in the herbs and cover with a layer of potato slices.

Mix together the water, chicken stock cube and the cider in a saucepan, bring to the boil and pour into the casserole. Cover and cook in a cool oven (150°C/300°F, Gas Mark 2) for 2 hours. Taste and adjust seasoning if necessary.

Mix the cottage cheese with the snipped chives and chopped parsley and a little seasoning, if liked, and spread over the potatoes. Raise the heat to fairly hot (200°C/400°F, Gas Mark 6) for a further 10 minutes to form a cheesy crust. Serve at once.

Sausages with Horseradish Mayonnaise

METRIC/IMPERIAL
500 g/1 lb pork sausages
4 tablespoons French dressing
FOR THE HORSERADISH MAYONNAISE:
2 egg yolks
1 tablespoon wine vinegar
2 teaspoons French mustard
300 ml/½ pint olive oil
salt and freshly ground black
* pepper*
4 tablespoons whipped cream
1 tablespoon creamed horseradish
2 stalks of celery, scrubbed and
* chopped*
2 eating apples, grated
2 tablespoons chopped gherkin

AMERICAN
1 lb pork sausages
¼ cup French dressing
FOR THE HORSERADISH MAYONNAISE:
2 eggs yolks
1 tablespoon wine vinegar
2 teaspoons Dijon-style mustard
1¼ cups olive oil
salt and freshly ground black
* pepper*
¼ cup whipped cream
1 tablespoon creamy horseradish
* sauce*
2 celery sticks, scrubbed and
* chopped*
2 eating apples, grated
2 tablespoons chopped gherkin

Grill the pork sausages for about 10 minutes, until golden-brown all over and cooked through. While they are still warm put them in a shallow dish and spoon over the French dressing. Cover the dish and chill in the refrigerator for 2 hours.

To make the horseradish mayonnaise, beat the egg yolks with the wine vinegar and then add the mustard. Gradually add the oil, in a fine trickle, whisking continuously until it is all absorbed. Season to taste and stir in the whipped cream and creamed horseradish. Fold in the chopped celery, grated apple and chopped gherkin.

Arrange the marinated sausages on a serving platter and spoon over the horseradish mayonnaise. Serve with rye bread.

Sausage Kedgeree

METRIC/IMPERIAL
500 g/1 lb chipolata sausages
2 eggs
175 g/6 oz long-grain rice
50 g/2 oz butter
salt and black pepper
4 tablespoons chopped parsley
lemon twists to garnish

AMERICAN
1 lb chipolata sausages
2 eggs
1 cup long-grain rice
¼ cup butter
salt and black pepper
4 tablespoons chopped parsley
lemon twists for garnish

Grill the chipolata sausages until golden-brown on all sides and cooked through. Cut into bite-sized pieces. Put the eggs into cold water, bring to the boil and simmer for 10 minutes. Remove the eggs, lightly crack the shells and plunge them into a bowl of cold water. Cook the long-grain rice in rapidly boiling salted water for about 10 minutes until just tender. Drain thoroughly and toss with a fork to separate the grains. Shell the hard-boiled (hard-cooked) eggs and chop roughly. Melt the butter in a pan, add the sausage pieces and the cooked rice and season to taste. Add the chopped hard-boiled (hard-cooked) egg and stir with a fork over a gentle heat for a few minutes, until the kedgeree is heated through. Add half the chopped parsley and pile up on a hot serving dish. Sprinkle with the remaining parsley. Serve hot, garnished with lemon twists.

Sausage Hot-Pot

METRIC/IMPERIAL
750 g/1 ½ lb ox kidney, skinned,
   cored and chopped
225 g/8 oz pork sausages, each cut
   into thirds
15 g/½ oz flour
50 g/2 oz butter
2 carrots, sliced
1 onion, sliced
300 ml/½ pint beef stock
100 g/4 oz button mushrooms
salt and pepper
chopped parsley to garnish

AMERICAN
1 ½ lb beef kidney, skinned, cored
   and chopped
½ lb pork link sausages, each cut
   into thirds
2 tablespoons flour
¼ cup butter
2 carrots, sliced
1 onion, sliced
1 ¼ cups beef broth
¼ lb button mushrooms
salt and pepper
chopped parsley for garnish

Coat the kidney and sausages in the flour. Heat the butter in a frying pan, add the kidney and sausages and fry for 3 minutes. Remove from the pan and add the carrots and onion. Fry until lightly browned. Slowly stir in the stock (broth) and bring to the boil.

Pour into a 1.8 litre/3 pint (2 quart) casserole dish and add the kidney, sausages, mushrooms and salt and pepper to taste. Cook in a preheated moderate oven (160°C/325°F, Gas Mark 3) for 2 hours. Sprinkle with chopped parsley before serving.

Baked Stuffed Hearts

METRIC/IMPERIAL
4 calves' hearts
½ quantity pork sage stuffing
(page 253)
50 g/2 oz butter
3 tablespoons stock or water

AMERICAN
4 veal hearts
½ quantity pork sage stuffing
(page 253)
¼ cup butter
3 tablespoons broth or water

Wash the hearts well, drain and remove any veins and fat. Cut through the centre divisions to make a cavity in each heart. Fill each heart loosely with equal amounts of stuffing and place in a casserole.

Dot with the butter and pour on the stock (broth) or water. Cover tightly and cook in a preheated moderate oven (160°C/325°F, Gas Mark 3) for 1½ hours. Baste occasionally with the liquid in the casserole.

Uncover and cook for a further 30 minutes or until the hearts are tender.

Casseroled Stuffed Hearts

METRIC/IMPERIAL
4 lambs' or calves' hearts
3 tablespoons oil
2 tablespoons flour
600 ml/1 pint beef stock
salt and pepper
2 onions, sliced
4 carrots, sliced
1 bouquet garni
STUFFING:
1 onion, finely chopped
1 celery stalk, finely chopped
2 walnuts, finely chopped
40 g/1½ oz fresh breadcrumbs
grated rind of 1 orange
15 g/½ oz butter, melted
½ egg, beaten
salt and pepper

AMERICAN
4 veal or lamb hearts
3 tablespoons oil
2 tablespoons flour
2½ cups beef broth
salt and pepper
2 onions, sliced
4 carrots, sliced
1 bouquet garni
STUFFING:
1 onion, finely chopped
1 celery stalk, finely chopped
2 walnuts, finely chopped
¾ cup soft bread crumbs
grated rind of 1 orange
1 tablespoon butter, melted
½ egg, beaten
salt and pepper

Wash the hearts well, drain and remove any veins and fat. Cut through the centre divisions to make a cavity in each heart. Mix all the stuffing ingredients, season, and fill the hearts. Sew up the openings.

Heat the oil in a frying pan, add the hearts and brown all over. Place in a casserole. Sprinkle the flour onto the fat in the pan and cook, stirring constantly, for 1 minute. Gradually stir in the stock (broth) and bring to the boil, stirring. Season to taste with salt and pepper and pour over the hearts. Add the onions, carrots and bouquet garni.

Cover the casserole and place in a preheated moderate oven (160°C/325°F, Gas Mark 3). Cook for 3 hours.

Baked Stuffed Hearts in Cider

METRIC/IMPERIAL
4 lambs' hearts
15 g/½ oz butter or margarine
1 small onion, peeled and finely
* chopped*
50 g/2 oz fresh white breadcrumbs
1 teaspoon dried mixed herbs
2 tablespoons seedless raisins
salt and freshly ground black
* pepper*
1 egg, beaten
450 ml/¾ pint beef stock
150 ml/¼ pint dry cider
4 stalks celery, scrubbed and
* chopped*
100 g/4 oz carrots, peeled and
* chopped*

AMERICAN
4 lambs' hearts
1 tablespoon butter or margarine
1 small onion, peeled and finely
* chopped*
1 cup soft white bread crumbs
1 teaspoon dried mixed herbs
2 tablespoons seedless raisins
salt and freshly ground black
* pepper*
1 egg, beaten
2 cups beef stock
⅔ cup apple cider
4 celery sticks, scrubbed and
* chopped*
¼ lb carrots, peeled and chopped

Trim the hearts and remove all blood vessels and membranes from the outside.

Melt the butter or margarine in a saucepan. Add the onion and cook gently until soft but not brown. Stir in the breadcrumbs, herbs, raisins and season to taste. Moisten with the beaten egg and use to stuff the hearts. Sew up the openings with a needle and white cotton thread.

Put the hearts into an ovenproof dish and pour over the stock and cider. Cover and cook in a warm oven (160°C/325°F, Gas Mark 3) for 1 hour. Add the chopped celery and carrots, cover and return to the oven for a further 1 hour, or until the hearts are tender. Serve with mashed potatoes.

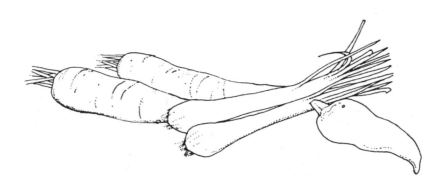

Braised Liver

METRIC/IMPERIAL
25 g/1 oz flour
salt and pepper
500 g/1 lb ox liver, cut into 2.5 cm/
  1 inch cubes
50 g/2 oz butter
1 medium onion, chopped
2 medium carrots, grated
1 large potato, grated
2 celery stalks, chopped
2 tablespoons chopped parsley
300 ml/½ pint water
1 medium lemon, sliced

AMERICAN
¼ cup flour
salt and pepper
1 lb beef liver, cut into 1 inch cubes
¼ cup butter
1 medium-size onion, chopped
2 medium-size carrots, grated
1 large potato, grated
2 celery stalks, chopped
2 tablespoons chopped parsley
1¼ cups water
1 medium-size lemon, sliced

Season the flour with salt and pepper and use to coat the liver cubes. Melt the butter in a saucepan, add the liver cubes and fry until golden brown, turning all the time. Remove to a plate.

Add the onion to the pan and fry gently until pale gold. Stir in any leftover flour along with the carrots, potato, celery, parsley, ½ teaspoon salt and the water. Bring to the boil.

Replace the liver in the pan and cover with the sliced lemon. Lower the heat and cover the pan. Simmer for 30 to 40 minutes or until tender.

Fried Liver

METRIC/IMPERIAL
500 g/1 lb lamb's or pig's liver,
  thinly sliced
cold milk
25 g/1 oz flour
salt and pepper
1 large egg, beaten
6–8 tablespoons toasted
  breadcrumbs
75 g/3 oz butter
TO GARNISH:
lemon slices
watercress

AMERICAN
1 lb lamb or pork liver, thinly sliced
cold milk
¼ cup flour
salt and pepper
1 large egg, beaten
6–8 tablespoons toasted bread
  crumbs
6 tablespoons butter
FOR GARNISH:
lemon slices
watercress

Put the liver in a shallow dish and cover with milk. Soak for 30 minutes.

Drain the liver and pat dry with paper towels. Season the flour with salt and pepper and use to coat the liver slices. Coat twice with the egg and crumbs, then leave for 15 minutes.

Melt the butter in a frying pan and add the liver, one or two slices at a time. Fry for 2 to 3 minutes on each side or until crisp and golden. Drain on paper towels and serve hot, garnished with sliced lemon and watercress.

Liver Italian-Style

METRIC/IMPERIAL
25 g/1 oz flour
salt and pepper
500 g/1 lb lamb's liver, cut into strips
40 g/1½ oz butter
4 onions, sliced into rings
4 tomatoes, skinned and sliced
300 ml/½ pint chicken stock
2 tablespoons tomato purée
dash of Tabasco sauce
½ teaspoon dried thyme
½ teaspoon dried oregano
150 ml/¼ pint double cream
chopped red pepper to garnish

AMERICAN
¼ cup flour
salt and pepper
1 lb lamb liver, cut into strips
3 tablespoons butter
4 onions, sliced into rings
4 tomatoes, peeled and sliced
1¼ cups chicken broth
2 tablespoons tomato paste
dash of hot pepper sauce
½ teaspoon dried thyme
½ teaspoon dried oregano
¾ cup heavy cream
chopped red pepper for garnish

Season the flour with salt and pepper and use to coat the liver strips. Melt the butter in a flameproof casserole, add the onions and fry gently until soft. Remove and put to one side.

Add the liver to the casserole and fry until lightly browned all over. Replace the onions and add the tomatoes, stock (broth), tomato purée (paste), Tabasco sauce and herbs. Bring to the boil, then cover and transfer to a preheated moderate oven (180°C/350°F, Gas Mark 4). Cook for 30 minutes.

Stir in the cream and heat through without boiling. Garnish with red pepper and serve with spaghetti.

Moorland Hot-Pot

METRIC/IMPERIAL
500 g/1 lb lamb's liver, sliced
25 g/1 oz flour
50 g/2 oz butter
100 g/4 oz lean bacon, derinded
  and chopped
2 large onions, sliced
300 ml/½ pint beef stock
salt and pepper
500 g/1 lb potatoes, sliced

AMERICAN
1 lb lamb liver, sliced
¼ cup flour
¼ cup butter
¼ lb Canadian bacon, chopped
2 large onions, sliced
1¼ cups beef broth
salt and pepper
1 lb potatoes, sliced

Coat the liver slices with the flour. Heat the butter in a frying pan, add the liver, bacon and onions and fry until golden brown. Slowly stir in the beef stock (broth) and season to taste with salt and pepper.

Pour into a 1.5 litre/2½ pint (1½ quart) casserole dish and arrange the potatoes around the top edge. Cover and bake in a preheated moderate oven (180°C/350°F, Gas Mark 4) for 1 hour. Uncover and bake for a further 30 minutes or until the potatoes are browned.

Layered Liver and Bacon

METRIC/IMPERIAL
150 g/½ oz lard
500 g/1 lb pig's liver, thinly sliced
4 rashers streaky bacon, rind
    removed
2 medium onions, peeled and
    chopped
2 medium cooking apples, peeled,
    cored and chopped
1 teaspoon dried thyme
1 tablespoon chopped parsley
salt and freshly ground black
    pepper
8 tablespoons fresh white
    breadcrumbs
300 ml/½ pint hot water

AMERICAN
1 tablespoon shortening
1 lb pig's liver, thinly sliced
4 slices streaky bacon, rind
    removed
2 medium-size onions, peeled and
    chopped
2 medium-size cooking apples,
    peeled, cored and chopped
1 teaspoon dried thyme
1 tablespoon chopped parsley
salt and freshly ground black
    pepper
8 tablespoons soft white bread
    crumbs
1¼ cups hot water

Grease the inside of a casserole with the lard (shortening). Place half the sliced liver in a layer at the bottom and cover with 2 rashers of bacon. Mix together the chopped onion, apple, herbs and seasoning and place half the mixture over the bacon slices. Sprinkle half the breadcrumbs over it. Continue to fill the casserole with another layer each of liver, bacon and onion and apple mixture, finishing with the breadcrumbs. Pour in the hot water or just sufficient to cover the surface. Put the lid on the casserole and cook in a moderate oven (180°C/350°F, Gas Mark 4) for 1½ hours. Remove the lid, add a little more hot water if the contents appear too dry, and cook for another 30 minutes to allow the surface to brown.

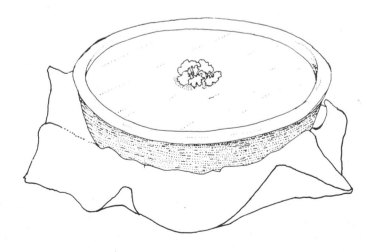

Glazed Lambs' Tongues

METRIC/IMPERIAL	AMERICAN
4 lambs' tongues	4 lambs' tongues
4 cloves	4 cloves
1 small onion, peeled	1 small onion, peeled
1 teaspoon salt	1 teaspoon salt
1 bay leaf	1 bay leaf
1 x 2.5 cm/1 inch piece of cinnamon stick	1 x 1 inch piece of cinnamon stick
3 tablespoons malt vinegar	3 tablespoons malt vinegar
4 small tomatoes	4 small tomatoes
1 tablespoon lemon juice	1 tablespoons lemon juice
1 teaspoon gelatine	1 teaspoon gelatin

Wash the tongues well in cold running water and place in a saucepan. Stick the cloves in the onion and add to the tongues together with the salt, bay leaf and cinnamon stick. Cover with cold water and bring to the boil. Put on the lid and simmer for 45 minutes. Add the vinegar and continue to simmer for a further 30 minutes. Take out the tongues, allow to cool, skin and remove any small bones from the cut ends.

Stand the tongues on their sides with their bases towards the centre, on a serving plate, and place the tomatoes between the tongues.

Strain 7 tablespoons of the cooking liquid into a small saucepan and add the lemon juice. Mix the gelatine with 2 tablespoons of the remaining cold stock and leave until it has softened and become spongy. Stir the softened gelatine into the liquid in the saucepan and heat until it has completely dissolved. Allow to cool and become syrupy.

Slowly spoon the setting glaze over the tongues and repeat several times to achieve a really good coating.

Serve with green salad and either rice or potato salad.

Lambs' Tongues with Herb Dumplings

METRIC/IMPERIAL
4 small lamb's tongues
1 tablespoon salt
2 large onions, peeled and sliced
1 bouquet garni
25 g/1 oz butter
1 tablespoon flour
2 tablespoons capers
2 tablespoons lemon juice
FOR THE DUMPLINGS:
225 g/8 oz self-raising flour
100 g/4 oz shredded beef suet
½ teaspoon dried thyme
salt and freshly ground black
　pepper

AMERICAN
4 small lambs' tongues
1 tablespoon salt
2 large onions, peeled and sliced
1 bouquet garni
2 tablespoons butter
1 tablespoon flour
2 tablespoons capers
2 tablespoons lemon juice
FOR THE DUMPLINGS:
2 cups of self-rising flour
½ cup beef suet
½ teaspoon dried thyme
salt and freshly ground black
　pepper

Wash the tongues thoroughly. Put into a large saucepan, cover with water and add the salt. Bring to the boil, and drain. Cover the tongues with fresh water, add the sliced onion and bouquet garni, and bring to the boil. Reduce the heat, cover and simmer for 1¼ hours, or until the tongues are tender. Remove the tongues and leave to cool, then skin and take out any little bones. Cool the stock and skim off the fat from the surface. Remove the bouquet garni.

Melt the butter in a small saucepan and gradually stir in the flour. Cook for 2 minutes, stirring all the time. Add the stock (if necessary, make up to 450 ml/¾ pint (2 cups) with boiling water), the capers and lemon juice. Continue stirring until the sauce has thickened.

Prepare the dumpling mixture by mixing together the flour, suet, thyme, seasoning and enough water to form a fairly stiff dough. Form the dough into about 12 round dumplings.

Dice the tongues, put into a casserole and cover with the sauce. Place the dumplings on top so that the surface is completely covered. Bake in a fairly hot oven (190°C/375°F, Gas Mark 5) for 30 minutes.

VARIATION:
An ox tongue can be used in this recipe instead of the lambs' tongues. If you use an ox tongue, you should extend the cooking time by 1 hour.

Kidneys in Rich Mustard Sauce

METRIC/IMPERIAL
8 lambs' kidneys
25 g/1 oz butter
1 small onion, peeled and sliced
225 g/8 oz mushrooms, sliced
salt and freshly ground black
    pepper
1 tablespoon mild French mustard
4 tablespoons milk
4 tablespoons single cream
½ teaspoon grated nutmeg
½ teaspoon freshly ground black
    pepper
225 g/8 oz freshly cooked long-
    grain rice

AMERICAN
8 lamb kidneys
2 tablespoons butter
1 small onion, peeled and sliced
2 cups sliced mushrooms
salt and freshly ground black
    pepper
1 tablespoon mild Dijon-style
    mustard
¼ cup milk
¼ cup light cream
½ teaspoon grated nutmeg
½ teaspoon freshly ground black
    pepper
1½ cups freshly cooked long-grain
    rice

Trim and slice the kidneys. Sauté the sliced kidneys in the butter in a large frying pan (skillet), remove them and keep warm.

Cook the sliced onion and mushrooms in the same pan, adding a little more butter if it has all been absorbed before the onion is soft. Season to taste, stir in the mustard, milk and cream mixed together. Add the kidneys and reheat slowly to boiling point, remove from the heat.

Fold the nutmeg and pepper into the hot cooked rice. Spoon heaps of rice on to 4 warm plates, make a dent in the centre of each heap with the back of a spoon. Fill with the kidney mixture.

Tripe and Onions

METRIC/IMPERIAL
1 kg/2 lb dressed tripe, washed and
    cut into 5 cm/2 inch squares
1 large onion, thinly sliced
450 ml/¾ pint + 2 tablespoons milk
1 teaspoon salt
1 teaspoon cornflour
15 g/½ oz butter
pepper

AMERICAN
2 lb prepared tripe, washed and cut
    into 2 inch squares
1 large onion, thinly sliced
2 cups + 2 tablespoons milk
1 teaspoon salt
1 teaspoon cornstarch
1 tablespoon butter
pepper

Place the tripe and onion in a saucepan with 450 ml/¾ pint (2 cups) of the milk and the salt. Bring to the boil, then lower the heat and cover the pan. Simmer very gently for 35 to 45 minutes or until the tripe is tender.

Mix the cornflour (cornstarch) with the remaining milk to make a smooth paste. Add to the saucepan and cook, stirring, until thickened. Add the butter and season to taste with pepper. Serve hot.

Kidney in Oriental Sauce

METRIC/IMPERIAL
500 g/1 lb ox kidney
1 tablespoon vegetable oil
300 ml/½ pint dry ginger ale
2 teaspoons malt vinegar
salt and freshly ground black
* pepper*
25 g/1 oz butter
100 g/4 oz mushrooms, wiped and
* sliced*
25 g/1 oz flaked almonds
25 g/1 oz sultanas
1 tablespoon gravy powder
3 tablespoons cold water

AMERICAN
1 lb ox kidney
1 tablespoon vegetable oil
1¼ cups dry ginger ale
2 teaspoons malt vinegar
salt and freshly ground black
* pepper*
2 tablespoons butter
1 cup sliced mushrooms
¼ cup slivered almonds
3 tablespoons golden raisins
1 tablespoons gravy powder
3 tablespoons cold water

Cut the ox kidney in slices about 2 cm/¾ inch thick. Remove the core and chop the slices. Heat the vegetable oil in a saucepan and fry the pieces of kidney, turning several times, until lightly coloured all over, about 3 minutes. Add the ginger ale, vinegar and seasoning and bring to the boil. Simmer, covered, for 30 minutes. Meanwhile melt the butter in a frying pan (skillet) and cook the sliced mushrooms for 3 minutes, turning frequently. Add the fried mushrooms, flaked almonds and sultanas (raisins) to the kidney mixture, stir well and simmer for a further 10 minutes. Dissolve the gravy powder in the cold water and stir into the saucepan. Bring to the boil, stirring constantly. Simmer for a further 5 minutes. Taste and adjust the seasoning if necessary. Serve with boiled rice.

Stewed Oxtail

METRIC/IMPERIAL	AMERICAN
25 g/1 oz butter	2 tablespoons butter
1 large onion, sliced	1 large onion, sliced
1 medium oxtail, jointed	1 medium-size oxtail, cut up
1 medium carrot, sliced	1 medium-size carrot, sliced
½ small turnip, diced	½ small turnip, diced
6 peppercorns	6 peppercorns
3 whole cloves	3 whole cloves
3 parsley sprigs	3 parsley sprigs
450 ml/¾ pint boiling water	2 cups boiling water
salt and pepper	salt and pepper
2 teaspoons flour	2 teaspoons flour
3 tablespoons cold water	3 tablespoons cold water
2 teaspoons vinegar	2 teaspoons vinegar
chopped parsley to garnish	chopped parsley for garnish

Melt the butter in a large saucepan. Add the onion and fry until pale gold. Add the oxtail, carrot and turnip and fry briskly for 5 minutes, turning all the time.

Tie the peppercorns, cloves and parsley sprigs in a small muslin (cheesecloth) bag. Add to the pan with the boiling water and salt to taste. Bring to the boil, cover and simmer for 3 hours or until the oxtail is tender.

Remove the seasoning bag and leave the stew overnight in a cold place.

The next day, remove the hard layer of fat that will have formed on the surface of the stew and discard. Bring the stew to the boil. Mix the flour to a smooth paste with the cold water and vinegar. Add to the pan and cook, stirring, until thickened. Simmer for 5 minutes.

Taste and adjust the seasoning, then serve, sprinkled with chopped parsley.

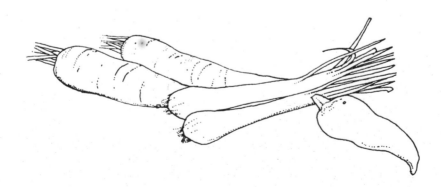

Partridges in Piquant Sauce

METRIC/IMPERIAL
4 small partridges, plucked and
    drawn
50 g/2 oz lard
3 medium onions, peeled and
    sliced
2 stalks of celery, scrubbed and
    chopped
1 cooking apple, peeled, cored and
    roughly chopped
2 tablespoons flour
300 ml/½ pint chicken stock
2 tablespoons Worcestershire
    sauce
50 g/2 oz seedless raisins
salt and freshly ground black
    pepper
150 ml/¼ pint plain yogurt
pastry fleurons to finish

AMERICAN
4 small partridges, plucked and
    drawn
¼ cup shortening
3 medium-size onions, peeled and
    sliced
2 celery sticks, scrubbed and
    chopped
1 tart apple, peeled, cored and
    roughly chopped
2 tablespoons flour
1¼ cups chicken stock or broth
2 tablespoons Worcestershire
    sauce
⅓ cup seedless raisins
salt and freshly ground black
    pepper
⅔ cup plain yogurt
pastry fleurons to finish

Wash the partridges and dry well with absorbent kitchen paper. Melt the lard (shortening) in a heavy pan and lightly brown the partridges on all sides. Remove them from the pan and place in a casserole. Cook the onion gently in the remaining fat in the pan for 5 minutes or until limp, then add the chopped celery and the apple. Stir in the flour and cook for another 2 minutes. Gradually add the stock and the Worcestershire sauce, bring to the boil and add the raisins. Add seasoning to taste.

Pour the sauce over the partridges, cover lightly with foil and cook in a moderate oven (180°C/350°F, Gas Mark 4) for 1½ hours, or until the partridges are tender. Remove them and place on a warm serving dish together with the onions, apples and raisins strained from the sauce. Taste the sauce, and adjust the seasoning if necessary. Stir in the yogurt and reheat without boiling. Pour a little of the sauce over the partridges, surround them with the fleurons and serve the rest of the sauce separately in a sauceboat.

To make the fleurons: Defrost and roll out a small piece of frozen puff pastry thinly and cut out circles with a small biscuit cutter. Using the same cutter, make crescent shapes and ovals from the circles. Bake on a dampened baking sheet in a hot oven (220°C/425°F, Gas Mark 7) for 10 to 12 minutes or until golden-brown, raising the oven temperature immediately after removing the partridges.

Pigeon Casserole with Grapes

METRIC/IMPERIAL
25 g/1 oz butter
1 tablespoon vegetable oil
2 pigeons, split
1 medium onion, peeled and
    chopped
100 g/4 oz button mushrooms,
    wiped and sliced
1 tablespoons flour
150 ml/¼ pint dry cider
150 ml/¼ pint strong chicken stock
salt and freshly ground black
    pepper
100 g/4 oz seedless grapes
2 teaspoons cornflour
1 tablespoon water

AMERICAN
2 tablespoons butter
1 tablespoon vegetable oil
2 pigeons, split
1 medium-size onion, peeled and
    chopped
1 cup sliced button mushrooms
1 tablespoon flour
⅔ cup apple cider
⅔ cup strong chicken stock or
    broth
salt and freshly ground black
    pepper
1 cup seedless grapes
2 teaspoons cornstarch
1 tablespoon water

Melt the butter and oil together in a large heavy saucepan or flameproof casserole. Brown the pigeons quickly in the fat on both sides. Remove from the pan. Add the chopped onion to the fat and cook gently, covered, for a few minutes until soft. Add the sliced mushrooms, and fry for 2 minutes. Stir in the flour, cook for 1 minute, then add the cider, stock, seasoning to taste, and bring to the boil.

Return the pigeon halves to the pan, skin side down, and sprinkle the grapes round them. Cover and simmer for 1½ to 2 hours. Remove the pigeon halves and place, skin side up, on a warm serving dish.

Moisten the cornflour (cornstarch) with the water, stir into the sauce and bring back to the boil. Cook gently for 3 minutes then pour over the pigeons.

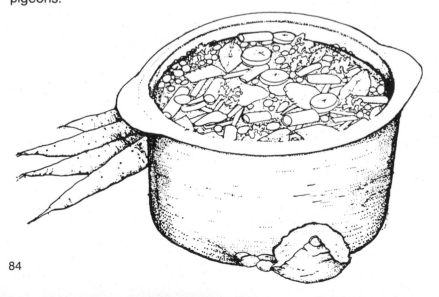

Pigeons Braised with Cabbage

METRIC/IMPERIAL
2 tablespoons chicken fat, or butter
2 large pigeons, split
2 thick rashers streaky bacon, rinds
    removed and chopped
2 large carrots, peeled and
    chopped
1 large onion, peeled and chopped
salt and freshly ground black
    pepper
1 medium cabbage (750 g–1 kg/
    1½–2 lb), trimmed and quartered
½ teaspoon ground bay leaves
1 chicken stock cube, crumbled
TO FINISH:
½ teaspoon grated lemon zest
1 tablespoon cornflour
2 tablespoons lemon juice

AMERICAN
2 tablespoons chicken fat, or butter
2 large pigeons, split
2 thick slices streaky bacon, rinds
    removed and chopped
2 large carrots, peeled and
    chopped
1 large onion, peeled and chopped
salt and freshly ground black
    pepper
1 medium cabbage (1½–2 lb),
    trimmed and quartered
½ teaspoon ground bay leaves
1 chicken bouillon cube, crumbled
TO FINISH:
½ teaspoon grated lemon zest
1 tablespoon cornstarch
2 tablespoons lemon juice

Heat the chicken fat or butter in a large, deep, flameproof casserole and sauté the pigeon halves in it, until lightly coloured on both sides. Remove and keep warm.

Fry the chopped bacon in the casserole until the fat begins to run, then add the diced carrot and chopped onion. Fry until just coloured, then return the pigeon halves to the casserole, breast side down, and season well. Surround with the cabbage quarters, add the ground bay leaves and the stock cube dissolved in 450 ml/¾ pint (2 cups) boiling water. Bring to the boil. Cover closely, and simmer for 2 to 2½ hours or until the pigeons are tender. (Test with a fine skewer in the leg meat.)

Remove the vegetables and pigeon halves, breast side uppermost, on to a warm serving dish with a slotted draining spoon. Add the grated lemon zest to the sauce. Boil for 1 to 2 minutes to reduce slightly.

Mix the cornflour (cornstarch) with the lemon juice and stir into the sauce. Cook, stirring, over moderate heat for 3 minutes. Taste the sauce and adjust the seasoning if necessary. Spoon the sauce over the pigeon breasts. Serve with fluffy boiled rice or buttered noodles.

VARIATION:
Substitute grated orange zest and fresh orange juice for the lemon zest and juice.

Rabbit in Mustard Sauce

METRIC/IMPERIAL
4 rabbit joints
4 tablespoons French mustard
4 tablespoons seasoned flour for coating
50 g/2 oz butter
50 g/2 oz salt pork, rind removed and diced
1 medium onion, peeled and chopped
1 clove of garlic, crushed
300 ml/½ pint milk
salt and freshly ground black pepper
TO GARNISH:
parsley sprigs
8 large bread croûtons, fried in butter

AMERICAN
4 rabbit joints
4 tablespoons Dijon-style mustard
¼ cup seasoned flour for coating
¼ cup butter
2 oz salt pork, rind removed and diced
1 medium-size onion, peeled and chopped
1 clove of garlic, crushed
1¼ cups milk
salt and freshly ground black pepper
FOR GARNISH:
parsley sprigs
8 large bread croûtons, fried in butter

On the day before you wish to serve the meal soak the rabbit joints for 2 hours in lightly salted water. Remove them and dry them well with absorbent kitchen paper. Coat the joints on all sides with the mustard and leave, covered, in the refrigerator overnight.

Coat the joints with the seasoned flour. Melt the butter in a flameproof casserole. Brown the joints on all sides, then add the diced salt pork, chopped onion and crushed garlic. Cover and cook for another 20 minutes, stirring occasionally. Then add the milk and seasoning and stir. Transfer the casserole to a warm oven (160°C/325°F, Gas Mark 3) and cook for another 45 minutes.

Place the rabbit joints on a heated serving dish, cover with the sauce from the casserole and garnish with parsley sprigs and the fried bread croûtons.

BUDGET

Vegetables

MEALS

Sweet and Sour White Cabbage

METRIC/IMPERIAL
1 white cabbage, cored and
  shredded
50 g/2 oz butter
2 tablespoons water
2 tablespoons vinegar
2 teaspoons soft brown sugar
pinch of mixed spice
¼ teaspoon salt

AMERICAN
1 head of white cabbage, cored and
  shredded
¼ cup butter
2 tablespoons water
2 tablespoons vinegar
2 teaspoons brown sugar
pinch of apple pie spice
¼ teaspoon salt

Put the cabbage into a saucepan with all the remaining ingredients. Cover the pan and cook over a low heat for 15 to 20 minutes or until the cabbage is just tender but still crisp. Shake the pan often to prevent sticking.

Uncover the pan and cook quickly until all the liquid has evaporated.

Crisp Boiled Cabbage

METRIC/IMPERIAL
salt
750 g–1 kg (1½–2 lb) young
  cabbage, cored and shredded
50 g/2 oz butter

AMERICAN
salt
1½–2 lb young cabbage, cored and
  shredded
¼ cup butter

Place 5 to 7.5 cm/2 to 3 inches water in a saucepan, add salt and bring to the boil. Add the cabbage, cover the pan and simmer for 6 to 8 minutes.

Drain the cabbage and return to the pan. Add the butter. Cover and cook over a low heat for a further 5 minutes, shaking the pan often.

Spicy Red Cabbage

METRIC/IMPERIAL
1 kg/2 lb red cabbage, core
  removed and finely shredded
500 g/1 lb onions, peeled and finely
  chopped
500 g/1 lb cooking apples, peeled,
  cored and finely chopped
salt and freshly ground black
  pepper
good pinch of ground mixed spice
2 tablespoons soft brown sugar
2 tablespoons wine vinegar
25 g/1 oz butter

AMERICAN
2 lb red cabbage, core removed
  and finely shredded
1 lb onions, peeled and finely
  chopped
1 lb tart apples, peeled, cored and
  finely chopped
salt and freshly ground black
  pepper
good pinch of ground mixed spice
2 tablespoons firmly packed light
  brown sugar
2 tablespoons wine vinegar
2 tablespoons butter

Put a layer of shredded cabbage in the bottom of a casserole. Arrange a layer of chopped onions and apples over the top. Season and add a little mixed spice and a sprinkling of sugar. Fill up the dish with alternating layers of onion and apple mixture and cabbage, seasoning each layer and sprinkling with the spices and sugar. Pour in the wine vinegar and dot the surface with the butter. Cover and bake in a cool oven (150°C/300°F, Gas Mark 2) for 2 hours.

Baked Cabbage with Cream

METRIC/IMPERIAL
500 g/1 lb cabbage, cored and
  shredded
150 ml/¼ pint single cream
1 teaspoon caster sugar
½ teaspoon salt
½ teaspoon paprika
4 tablespoons toasted
  breadcrumbs
75 g/3 oz Cheddar cheese, grated

AMERICAN
1 lb cabbage, cored and shredded
¾ cup light cream
1 teaspoon sugar
½ teaspoon salt
½ teaspoon paprika
¼ cup toasted bread crumbs
¾ cup grated Cheddar cheese

Place the cabbage in a large buttered baking dish. Mix the cream with the sugar, salt and paprika, and pour over the cabbage. Sprinkle the breadcrumbs over the top.

Cover the dish and bake in a preheated moderate oven (160°C/325°F, Gas Mark 3) for 45 minutes.

Remove from the oven and top with the cheese. Brown under a hot grill (broiler).

Braised Red Cabbage

METRIC/IMPERIAL
100 g/4 oz streaky bacon, derinded
  and chopped
1 red cabbage, cored and shredded
1 onion, sliced
2 cooking apples, peeled, cored
  and chopped
50 g/2 oz sultanas
3 tablespoons wine vinegar
2 tablespoons soft brown sugar
pinch of grated nutmeg
300 ml/½ pint chicken stock
grated rind of ½ lemon
salt and pepper
25 g/1 oz butter

AMERICAN
¼ lb slab bacon, chopped
1 red cabbage, cored and shredded
1 onion, sliced
2 tart apples, peeled, cored and
  chopped
⅓ cup golden raisins
3 tablespoons wine vinegar
2 tablespoons brown sugar
pinch of grated nutmeg
1¼ cups chicken broth
grated rind of ½ lemon
salt and pepper
2 tablespoons butter

Fry the bacon in a flameproof casserole until crisp. Lower the heat and add
the cabbage. Mix well together and braise gently for 5 minutes. Add the
onion, apples, sultanas (raisins), wine vinegar, sugar, nutmeg, stock
(broth) and lemon rind. Season to taste with salt and pepper. Mix
thoroughly and cover tightly.

Transfer to a preheated cool oven (150°C/300°F, Gas Mark 2) and cook
for 1½ to 2 hours. Dot with the butter before serving.

Brussels Sprouts and Chestnuts

METRIC/IMPERIAL
175 g/6 oz chestnuts
1½ teaspoons cooking oil
500 g/1 lb Brussels sprouts
salt
40 g/1½ oz butter

AMERICAN
6 oz chestnuts
1½ teaspoons cooking oil
1 lb Brussels sprouts
salt
3 tablespoons butter

Wash the chestnuts, cut a gash in the flat side of each and coat them with
cooking oil. Place them in a heat-proof dish and bake in a preheated oven
(180°C/350°F, Gas Mark 4) for about 10 minutes or until the skins come off
easily. Peel off the skins, using a sharp kitchen knife. Put the peeled
chestnuts into a heavy saucepan, cover with boiling salted water and cook
for 15 to 25 minutes or until they are tender when pierced with a cocktail
stick. Drain the chestnuts and set aside.

Remove the discoloured outer leaves from the sprouts and make a
cross-cut in each stem. Soak in cold salted water for 10 minutes. Drain
and cook in boiling salted water for 10 minutes.

Drain and return to the saucepan. Add the chestnuts and butter and
cook over a low heat for 5 to 7 minutes, shaking the pan often.

Crumbed Brussels Sprouts

METRIC/IMPERIAL
500 g/1 lb Brussels sprouts
salt
40 g/1½ oz butter
2 tablespoons fresh breadcrumbs
¼ teaspoon dry mustard

AMERICAN
1 lb Brussels sprouts
salt
3 tablespoons butter
2 tablespoons soft bread crumbs
¼ teaspoon dry mustard

Remove the discoloured outer leaves from the sprouts and make a cross-cut in each stem. Soak in cold salted water for 10 minutes. Drain and cook in boiling salted water for 10 minutes.

Meanwhile, melt the butter in another saucepan. Add the breadcrumbs and mustard. Fry gently until golden.

Drain the sprouts and place in a warmed serving dish. Coat with the fried breadcrumb mixture and serve hot.

Glazed Carrots and Parsnips

METRIC/IMPERIAL
50 g/2 oz butter
4 large carrots, peeled and cut into
  rings
2 large parsnips or turnips, peeled
  and cut into rings
½ teaspoon ground ginger
½ teaspoon grated nutmeg
salt and freshly ground black
  pepper
2 tablespoons lemon juice
2 tablespoons soft brown sugar

AMERICAN
¼ cup butter
4 large carrots, peeled and cut into
  rings
2 large parsnips or turnips, peeled
  and cut into rings
½ teaspoon ground ginger
½ teaspoon grated nutmeg
salt and freshly ground black
  pepper
2 tablespoons lemon juice
2 tablespoons firmly packed light
  brown sugar

Melt half the butter in a heavy saucepan and use to sauté the sliced carrots and parsnips gently, turning frequently, for 2 minutes. Add the ground ginger, grated nutmeg and seasoning to taste. Stir well, add the lemon juice and just sufficient water to cover the vegetables. Put on the lid and simmer, covered, for 12 to 15 minutes or until the vegetables are just tender and most of the liquid absorbed. Add the brown sugar and remaining butter and increase the heat slightly. Toss the vegetables frequently in the pan to glaze them evenly. Taste and adjust the seasoning if necessary. Serve as a snack with fried bacon or fried liver.

Spiced Carrots and Swede (Rutabaga)

METRIC/IMPERIAL
4 large carrots, peeled and sliced
500 g/1 lb swede, peeled and diced
25 g/1 oz butter, melted
2 tablespoons orange juice
1 teaspoon grated orange zest
good pinch of ground ginger
good pinch of grated nutmeg
salt and pepper

AMERICAN
4 large carrots, peeled and sliced
1 lb rutabaga, peeled and diced
2 tablespoons butter, melted
2 tablespoons orange juice
1 teaspoon grated orange zest
good pinch of ground ginger
good pinch of grated nutmeg
salt and pepper

Place the sliced carrots and diced swede (rutabaga) in an ovenproof dish.

Combine the melted butter, orange juice, grated orange zest, ground ginger and grated nutmeg and seasoning to taste. Pour over the vegetables.

Lightly cover with foil and bake in a fairly hot oven (190°C/375°F, Gas Mark 5) for 45 minutes.

NOTE: Potatoes can be peeled, sliced and baked in seasoned milk in a similar dish on the same shelf of the oven. Both dishes should then be read to serve at the same time.

Carrots in Parsley Sauce

METRIC/IMPERIAL
500 g/1 lb new carrots
salt
1 quantity parsley sauce (page
    242)

AMERICAN
1 lb new carrots
salt
1 quantity parsley sauce (page
    242)

Cook the carrots in boiling salted water until tender. Drain and transfer to a warm serving dish. Coat with the hot sauce and serve.

Vichy Carrots

METRIC/IMPERIAL
500 g/1 lb carrots, thinly sliced
50 g/2 oz butter
1 teaspoon caster sugar
1 teaspoon lemon juice
¼ teaspoon salt
1 tablespoon finely chopped
    parsley

AMERICAN
1 lb carrots, thinly sliced
¼ cup butter
1 teaspoon sugar
1 teaspoon lemon juice
¼ teaspoon salt
1 tablespoon finely chopped
    parsley

Put the carrots in a saucepan with water to cover, the butter, sugar, lemon juice and salt. Cover and simmer gently for 15 to 20 minutes or until tender and glazed. Transfer to a warm serving dish, and sprinkle with parsley.

Baked Buttered Carrots

METRIC/IMPERIAL
50 g/2 oz butter
1 medium onion, chopped
500 g/1 lb carrots, coarsely grated
½ teaspoon salt
5 tablespoons water

AMERICAN
¼ cup butter
1 medium-size onion, chopped
1 lb carrots, coarsely grated
½ teaspoon salt
5 tablespoons water

Melt the butter in a frying pan. Add the onion and fry gently until pale gold. Add the carrots and salt and mix well together. Transfer to a 600 ml/1 pint (2½ cup) baking dish. Add the water and cover the dish.

Bake in a preheated moderate oven (180°C/350°F, Gas Mark 4) for 35 to 45 minutes or until the carrots are tender.

Cauliflower Sauté

METRIC/IMPERIAL
1 medium cauliflower
salt
50 g/2 oz butter
2 teaspoons finely grated onion
½ teaspoon paprika

AMERICAN
1 medium-size cauliflower
salt
¼ cup butter
2 teaspoons finely grated onion
½ teaspoon paprika

Cook the cauliflower in boiling salted water for 12 to 15 minutes or until tender. Drain and divide into florets.

Melt the butter in a saucepan, add the onion and fry for 2 minutes. Add the cauliflower and fry gently, turning often, until golden. Place in a warm serving dish and sprinkle with the paprika.

Cauliflower with Cheese Sauce

METRIC/IMPERIAL
1 medium cauliflower
salt
1 quantity cheese coating sauce
   (page 242)
75 g/3 oz Lancashire or Cheddar
   cheese, grated

AMERICAN
1 medium-size cauliflower
salt
1 quantity cheese coating sauce
   (page 242)
¾ cup grated Cheddar cheese

Cook the cauliflower in boiling salted water for 12 to 15 minutes or until tender. Drain and divide into florets. Place in a warm flameproof serving dish. Coat with the hot cheese sauce and sprinkle with the cheese. Brown under a hot grill (broiler) and serve.

Cauliflower Cheese with Onion and Bacon

METRIC/IMPERIAL
1 large cauliflower, broken into
  florets
salt and pepper
225 g/8 oz streaky bacon, derinded
  and chopped
2 onions, chopped
40 g/1½ oz butter
25 g/1 oz flour
300 ml/½ pint milk
2 tablespoons cream
150 g/5 oz Cheddar cheese, grated
grated nutmeg
parsley sprig to garnish

AMERICAN
1 large cauliflower, broken into
  florets
salt and pepper
½ lb slab bacon, chopped
2 onions, chopped
3 tablespoons butter
¼ cup flour
1½ cups milk
2 tablespoons cream
1¼ cups grated Cheddar cheese
grated nutmeg
parsley sprig for garnish

Cook the cauliflower in boiling salted water for 10 minutes.

Meanwhile, fry the bacon in a saucepan until golden. Remove from the pan. Fry the onions in the bacon fat and butter until softened. Add the flour and cook, stirring, for 1 minute. Gradually stir in the milk and bring to the boil, stirring. Remove from the heat and add the cream, 100 g/4 oz (1 cup) of the cheese, the bacon, and salt, pepper and nutmeg to taste.

Drain the cauliflower and place in a heatproof serving dish. Pour over the sauce and sprinkle with the rest of the cheese. Bake in a preheated moderately hot oven (190°C/375°F, Gas Mark 5) for 30 to 40 minutes or until golden and bubbly. Garnish with the parsley and serve.

Corn on the Cob

METRIC/IMPERIAL
4 corn on the cob
50 to 75 g/2 to 3 oz butter

AMERICAN
4 ears of corn
4 to 6 tablespoons butter

Remove the husks and silk from the corn. Place in a large pan of boiling water and simmer for 4 to 5 minutes, turning once if the water does not cover the corn.

Drain and serve with the butter dotted along the top.

Braised Celery

METRIC/IMPERIAL
1 medium bunch of celery
juice of 1 lemon
½ teaspoon salt
5 tablespoons water
50 g/2 oz butter, melted
2 teaspoons cornflour
2 tablespoons milk

AMERICAN
1 medium-size head of celery
juice of 1 lemon
½ teaspoon salt
5 tablespoons water
¼ cup butter, melted
2 teaspoons cornstarch
2 tablespoons milk

Remove the leaves from the celery and cut the stalks into 7.5 to 10 cm/3 to 4 inch lengths. Put in a saucepan and sprinkle with the lemon juice and salt. Pour in the water and melted butter. Cover and simmer gently for 25 minutes or until tender.

Place the celery in a warm serving dish and keep hot. Reduce the liquid left in the saucepan to about 150 ml/¼ pint (⅔ cup) by boiling briskly. Mix the cornflour (cornstarch) to a smooth paste with the milk and add to the liquid left in the saucepan. Cook, stirring, until the sauce comes to the boil and thickens. Simmer for 1 minute, then pour over the celery.

Corn Fritters

METRIC/IMPERIAL
100 g/4 oz self-raising flour
pinch of grated nutmeg
½ teaspoon salt
½ teaspoon dry mustard
2 eggs, beaten
2 tablespoons milk
225 g/8 oz canned or frozen
   sweetcorn kernels, cooked and
   drained
oil for deep frying

AMERICAN
1 cup self-rising flour
pinch of grated nutmeg
½ teaspoon salt
½ teaspoon dry mustard
2 eggs, beaten
2 tablespoons milk
2 cups canned or frozen whole
   kernel corn, cooked and drained
oil for deep frying

Sift the flour, nutmeg, salt and mustard together. Whisk the eggs and milk well together, then gradually beat into the dry ingredients. When smooth and creamy, stir in the corn.

Heat oil in a deep frying pan. Drop about 16 spoonfuls of the mixture into the hot oil. Fry for about 5 minutes, or until puffed and golden.

Drain on paper towels and serve hot.

Corn with Almonds

METRIC/IMPERIAL
75 g/3 oz butter
50 g/2 oz blanched almonds,
   slivered
1 x 350 g/12 oz can sweetcorn
   kernels, drained

AMERICAN
6 tablespoons butter
½ cup slivered blanched almonds
1 x 12 oz can whole kernel corn,
   drained

Melt the butter in a saucepan. Add the almonds and fry gently until pale gold. Add the corn and heat through gently. Serve hot.

Chinese-Style Green Beans

METRIC/IMPERIAL
500 g/1 lb runner beans, thinly
   sliced diagonally
salt
40 g/1½ oz butter
4 lean bacon rashers, derinded and
   chopped.
1 small onion, grated
½ garlic clove, chopped
2 tablespoons soy sauce

AMERICAN
1 lb green beans, thinly sliced
   diagonally
salt
3 tablespoons butter
4 Canadian bacon slices, chopped
1 small onion, grated
½ garlic clove, chopped
2 tablespoons soy sauce

Cook the beans in boiling salted water for 15 to 20 minutes or until tender.
   Meanwhile, melt the butter in a frying pan. Add the bacon, onion and garlic and fry until pale gold. Drain the beans and add to the frying pan with the soy sauce. Heat through gently, shaking the pan all the time.

Creamed Green Beans

METRIC/IMPERIAL
500 g/1 lb French or runner beans,
   thinly sliced diagonally
salt
25 g/1 oz butter
50 g/2 oz mushrooms, sliced
150 ml/¼ pint double cream

AMERICAN
1 lb green beans, thinly sliced
   diagonally
salt
2 tablespoons butter
½ cup sliced mushrooms
⅔ cup heavy cream

Cook the beans in boiling salted water for 15 to 20 minutes or until tender.
   Melt the butter in a frying pan. Add the mushrooms and fry until golden. Drain the beans and return to the saucepan. Add the mushrooms and pan juices along with the cream. Mix well together and reheat gently.

White Beans with Tomatoes

METRIC/IMPERIAL
350 g/12 oz dried white haricot
   beans, soaked overnight and
   drained
1 teaspoon salt
225 g/8 oz tomatoes, skinned and
   chopped
100 g/4 oz lean bacon, derinded
   and chopped
1 medium onion, chopped
75 g/3 oz Lancashire cheese,
   crumbled

AMERICAN
2 cups dried navy beans, soaked
   overnight and drained
1 teaspoon salt
2 cups peeled and chopped
   tomatoes
½ cup chopped Canadian bacon
1 medium-size onion, chopped
¾ cup shredded cheese

Place the beans in a saucepan and cover with fresh cold water. Add the
salt. Bring to the boil, then lower the heat, cover and simmer until tender.
   Drain the beans and mix with the tomatoes, bacon and onion. Place in a
1.2 litre/2 pint (5 cup) baking dish and sprinkle with the cheese.
   Bake in a preheated moderately hot oven (190°C/375°F, Gas Mark 5) for
30 minutes.

Sautéed Marrow (Squash)

METRIC/IMPERIAL
40 g/1½ oz butter
1 tablespoon vegetable oil
1 medium marrow, peeled, seeds
   removed and diced
6 spring onions, trimmed and finely
   chopped
1 tablespoon fresh tarragon,
   chopped or 1 teaspoon dried
   tarragon
salt and freshly ground black
   pepper

AMERICAN
3 tablespoons butter
1 tablespoon vegetable oil
1 medium-size squash, peeled,
   seeds removed and diced
6 scallions, trimmed and finely
   chopped
1 tablespoon fresh tarragon,
   chopped or 1 teaspoon dried
   tarragon
salt and freshly ground black
   pepper

Melt the butter with the oil in a saucepan. Add the diced marrow (squash)
and finely chopped onions. Sauté for 3 minutes, turning frequently, until
the juices begin to run from the marrow (squash). Sprinkle in the tarragon
and season to taste. Reduce the heat, cover and cook for 5 minutes,
shaking the covered pan occasionally. Test one of the marrow (squash)
dice with a skewer and if tender serve immediately in a warm vegetable
dish. If not cooked, add 2 tablespoons water and replace the pan over
moderate heat until the marrow (squash) is tender.

Marrow (Squash) Provençale

METRIC/IMPERIAL
75 g/3 oz butter
1 medium marrow, peeled, seeded
   and cut into 2.5 cm/1 inch cubes
1 medium onion, grated
1 small green pepper, cored,
   seeded and chopped
100 g/4 oz tomatoes, skinned and
   chopped
100 g/4 oz Lancashire or Cheddar
   cheese, grated

AMERICAN
6 tablespoons butter
1 medium-size summer squash,
   peeled, seeded and cut into
   1 inch cubes
1 medium-size onion, grated
1 small green pepper, cored,
   seeded and chopped
1 cup peeled and chopped
   tomatoes
1 cup shredded cheese

Melt the butter in a large saucepan. Add the marrow (squash) and fry for 6 to 7 minutes or until golden. Remove to a plate.

Add the onion and green pepper to the saucepan and fry until pale gold. Add the tomatoes and marrow (squash) and mix well together.

Put half the mixture into a large baking dish. Cover with half of the cheese, then add the rest of the vegetable mixture and sprinkle over the remainder of the cheese. Bake in a preheated moderately hot oven (190°C/375°F, Gas Mark 5) for 30 minutes.

Courgette (Zucchini) Neapolitan

METRIC/IMPERIAL
500 g/1 lb fresh tomatoes, skinned,
   or 1 x 396 g/14 oz can tomatoes
1 small onion, peeled and chopped
salt and freshly ground black
   pepper
750 g/1½ lb courgettes
2 tablespoons flour
25 g/1 oz butter
225 g/8 oz Edam cheese, thinly
   sliced

AMERICAN
1 lb fresh tomatoes, skinned or
   1 can (16 oz) tomatoes
1 small onion, peeled and chopped
salt and freshly ground black
   pepper
1½ lb zucchini
2 tablespoons flour
2 tablespoons butter
½ lb Edam cheese, thinly sliced

Chop the tomatoes and heat in a saucepan with the chopped onion and seasoning to taste, for 10 minutes, to make a thick tomato sauce. Slice the courgettes (zucchini) into 1 cm/½ inch rings and then into quarters. Shake in a bag with the flour to coat evenly. Melt the butter in a large frying pan (skillet) and fry the courgettes (zucchini) until brown on both sides. Put alternate layers of courgette (zucchini), the tomato mixture and the cheese in a shallow baking dish, finishing with a layer of cheese. Bake in a fairly hot oven (190°C/375°F, Gas Mark 5) for 30 minutes. Serve topped with grilled bacon.

Mushrooms with Cream

METRIC/IMPERIAL	AMERICAN
50 g/2 oz butter	¼ cup butter
350 g/12 oz mushrooms, sliced	3 cups sliced mushrooms
150 ml/¼ pint double cream	¾ cup heavy cream
1 teaspoon snipped chives	1 teaspoon chopped chives
1 tablespoon chopped parsley	1 tablespoon chopped parsley
¼ teaspoon salt	¼ teaspoon salt

Melt the butter in a frying pan. Add the mushrooms and fry gently for 5 minutes. Stir in the remaining ingredients and heat through gently without boiling.

Mushroom Fritters

METRIC/IMPERIAL	AMERICAN
350 g/12 oz button mushrooms, stalks trimmed	¾ lb button mushrooms, stems trimmed
½ quantity savoury fritter batter (page 137)	½ quantity savory fritter batter (page 137)
oil for deep frying	oil for deep frying
1 tablespoon finely chopped parsley	1 tablespoon finely chopped parsley

Dry the mushrooms and coat with the batter. Deep-fry in hot oil until golden. Drain on paper towels and serve hot, sprinkled with the parsley.

Savoury Mushroom Toasts

METRIC/IMPERIAL	AMERICAN
40 g/1½ oz butter	3 tablespoons butter
100 g/4 oz button mushrooms, wiped and thinly sliced	1 cup wiped and thinly sliced button mushrooms
4 large slices white bread	4 large slices white bread
1 x 75 g/3 oz jar chicken and bacon spread	1 jar (3 oz) chicken and bacon spread
2 teaspoons chopped parsley to garnish	2 teaspoons chopped parsley for garnish

Melt 15 g/½ oz (1 tablespoon) of the butter in a small frying pan (skillet) and use to fry the sliced mushrooms until golden. Meanwhile, toast the bread lightly and spread one side of each slice with the remaining butter. Spread the buttered toast fairly thickly with the chicken and bacon spread and arrange the cooked mushrooms on top.

Place the toasts under a hot grill for 2 minutes. Serve hot, scattered with chopped parsley and cut into fingers.

Baked-Stuffed Onions

METRIC/IMPERIAL	AMERICAN
4 large onions	4 large onions
salt and pepper	salt and pepper
100 g/4 oz lean bacon, derinded and chopped	¼ lb Canadian bacon, chopped
50 g/2 oz fresh white breadcrumbs	1 cup soft bread crumbs
2–3 tablespoons single cream	2–3 tablespoons light cream
25 g/1 oz butter	2 tablespoons butter

Cook the onions in boiling salted water for 30 minutes. Drain, reserving 5 tablespoons of the cooking liquid. Slice off the top of each onion and carefully remove the centres, leaving 1 to 2 cm/½ to ¾ inch outer shells.

Finely chop the onion centres and mix with the bacon and breadcrumbs. Bind with the cream and season to taste with salt and pepper. Use the mixture to stuff the onion shells.

Place the onions in a shallow baking dish and pour in the reserved cooking liquid. Dot each onion with butter.

Bake in a preheated moderately hot oven (190°C/375°F, Gas Mark 5) for 45 minutes or until tender.

VARIATION:
Cheese and Parsley Stuffed Onions – make as above, making the stuffing with the chopped onion centres, 100 g/4 oz (1 cup) grated Wensleydale (Monterey Jack) cheese, 50 g/2 oz (1 cup) fresh breadcrumbs, 1 tablespoon chopped parsley, 2 to 3 tablespoons single (light) cream, and salt and pepper to taste.

Buttered Onions

METRIC/IMPERIAL	AMERICAN
8 small onions	8 small onions
salt	salt
50 g/2 oz butter, melted	¼ cup butter, melted
grated nutmeg	grated nutmeg

Cook the onions in boiling salted water for 25 to 40 minutes or until tender. Drain and transfer to a warm serving dish. Coat with the melted butter and sprinkle lightly with nutmeg.

VARIATION:
Onions in Cheese Sauce – Cook the onions as above, then coat with 1 quantity cheese coating sauce (page 242) and sprinkle with 1 tablespoon toasted breadcrumbs.

Fried Onions

METRIC/IMPERIAL
50 g/2 oz butter
3 medium onions, thinly sliced into
   rings

AMERICAN
¼ cup butter
3 medium-size onions, thinly sliced
   into rings

Melt the butter in a large frying pan. Add the onions and fry until golden brown, stirring to prevent them burning.

French-Fried Onion Rings

METRIC/IMPERIAL
self-raising flour
salt and pepper
4 medium onions, thinly sliced into
   rings
cold milk
oil for deep frying

AMERICAN
self-rising flour
salt and pepper
4 medium-size onions, thinly sliced
   into rings
cold milk
oil for deep frying

Season the flour with salt and pepper. Dip the onion rings into milk, then coat with the flour. Deep fry in hot oil until crisp and golden. Drain on paper towels and serve hot.

Glazed Onions

METRIC/IMPERIAL
12 small onions
salt
50 g/2 oz butter
1 tablespoon soft brown sugar

AMERICAN
12 small onions
salt
¼ cup butter
1 tablespoon brown sugar

Cook the onions in boiling salted water for 25 minutes. Drain well.
   Melt the butter in a frying pan, add the sugar and ½ teaspoon salt and heat for 1 minute. Add the onions and toss in this mixture until well coated. Cook over a very low heat for about 15 minutes or until glazed and golden.

Stuffed Peppers

METRIC/IMPERIAL	AMERICAN
4 medium green peppers	4 medium-size green peppers
salt and pepper	salt and pepper
50 g/2 oz butter	1/4 cup butter
1 medium onion, grated	1 medium-size onion, grated
225 g/8 oz minced beef	1/2 lb ground beef
225 g/8 oz cooked rice	1 1/3 cups cooked rice
1 teaspoon Worcestershire sauce	1 teaspoon Worcestershire sauce
5 tablespoons cold water	5 tablespoons water

Cut the tops off the peppers and remove the seeds and fibres from inside. Put the peppers in a saucepan and cover with boiling salted water. Simmer for 2 minutes. Remove from the pan and leave to drain, upside down, on paper towels.

Melt 25 g/1 oz (2 tablespoons) of the butter in a frying pan. Add the onion and fry until pale gold. Add the beef and fry for 7 minutes, turning often. Stir in the rice and Worcestershire sauce. Season to taste with salt and pepper.

Place the peppers in a shallow baking dish and fill with the rice and meat mixture. Pour the water into the dish and dot the peppers with the remaining butter. Bake in a preheated moderate oven (180°C/350°F, Gas Mark 4) for 15 minutes.

VARIATION:
Stuffed Peppers with Rice and Cheese – make as above, stuffing the peppers with a mixture of 225 g/8 oz (1 1/3 cups) cooked rice, 225 g/8 oz (2 cups) grated Cheddar cheese, 300 ml/1/2 pint single cream (1 1/4 cups light cream), 1/2 teaspoon made mustard, and salt and pepper to taste. After dotting the stuffed peppers with butter, bake covered with a lid or foil.

Baked Parsnips

METRIC/IMPERIAL	AMERICAN
4 medium parsnips, halved lengthways	4 medium-size parsnips, halved lengthwise
50 g/2 oz butter, melted	1/4 cup butter, melted
1/2 teaspoon salt	1/2 teaspoon salt
150 ml/1/4 pint water	2/3 cup water
chopped parsley to garnish	chopped parsley for garnish

Arrange the parsnips in a baking dish. Coat with the butter and sprinkle with the salt. Pour the water into the dish and cover with a lid or foil.

Bake in a preheated moderately hot oven (190°C/375°F, Gas Mark 5) for 45 minutes or until tender. Sprinkle with parsley and serve.

French-Style Peas

METRIC/IMPERIAL
350–500 g (12 oz–1 lb) shelled
    fresh or frozen peas
6 large lettuce leaves, shredded
2 teaspoons finely grated onion
50 g/2 oz butter
5 tablespoons water
½ teaspoon caster sugar
¼ teaspoon salt

AMERICAN
¾–1 lb shelled fresh or frozen peas
    (3 to 4 cups)
6 large lettuce leaves, shredded
2 teaspoons finely grated onion
¼ cup butter
5 tablespoons water
½ teaspoon sugar
¼ teaspoon salt

Place all the ingredients in a saucepan and slowly bring to the boil. Lower the heat and cover the pan. Simmer very gently for 15 to 20 minutes or until the peas are tender. Add extra water if the peas become too dry. Serve moist, but not soggy.

Pease Pudding

METRIC/IMPERIAL
500 g/1 lb dried split peas, soaked
    overnight and drained
salt and pepper
15 g/½ oz butter, melted
1 egg yolk

AMERICAN
1 lb (2½ cups) split peas, soaked
    overnight and drained
salt and pepper
1 tablespoon butter, melted
1 egg yolk

Put the peas into a saucepan and cover with fresh cold water. Add ½ teaspoon salt and bring slowly to the boil. Reduce the heat, cover and simmer gently for 1½ to 2 hours, adding more water if the peas begin to get dry. Stir occasionally.

Rub the peas through a sieve or purée in a blender or food processor. Add the butter and egg yolk. Mix well. Season to taste with salt and pepper.

Place in a buttered 600 ml/1 pint (2½ cup) baking dish. Bake in a preheated moderate oven (180°C/350°F, Gas Mark 4) for 30 minutes.

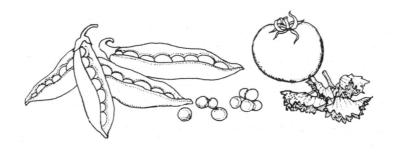

Swiss Peas with Rice

METRIC/IMPERIAL
350 g/12 oz shelled fresh or frozen
  peas
½ teaspoon salt
50 g/2 oz butter
1 small onion, chopped
175 g/6 oz cooked rice
50 g/2 oz stuffed olives, sliced
2 tablespoons finely chopped
  parsley

AMERICAN
3 cups shelled fresh or frozen peas
½ teaspoon salt
¼ cup butter
1 small onion, chopped
1 cup cooked rice
¼ cup sliced stuffed olives
2 tablespoons finely chopped
  parsley

Put the fresh peas into a saucepan, cover with boiling water and add the salt. Cover and simmer for 10 to 15 minutes or until tender. (Cook frozen peas according to packet instructions.) Drain.

Melt the butter in a saucepan, add the onion and fry until pale gold. Add the rice, peas, olives and parsley. Mix well together, and heat through gently for 5 to 7 minutes, stirring often.

Potato and Onion Cakes

METRIC/IMPERIAL
225 g/8 oz self-raising flour
pinch of salt
1 teaspoon dry mustard
100 g/4 oz butter
1 small onion, peeled and grated
1 large potato, peeled and grated
2 tablespoons chopped parsley
50 g/2 oz Cheddar cheese, grated
1 egg
2 tablespoons milk
vegetable oil or fat for greasing the
  griddle

AMERICAN
2 cups self-rising flour
pinch of salt
1 teaspoon dry mustard
½ cup butter
1 small onion, peeled and grated
1 large potato, peeled and grated
2 tablespoons chopped parsley
½ cup grated Cheddar cheese
1 egg
2 tablespoons milk
vegetable oil or fat for greasing the
  griddle

Sift the flour, salt and mustard into a bowl. Rub (cut) in the butter until the mixture resembles fine breadcrumbs. Add the grated onion, grated potato, chopped parsley and grated cheese and mix to a fairly stiff dough with the egg and the milk. Knead lightly on a floured surface and roll the scone dough to a circle about 22.5 cm/9 inches in diameter. Divide the scone round into 8 equal sections.

Grease and warm a griddle or heavy-based frying pan (skillet). The griddle is hot enough when a piece of the mixture placed on it turns golden-brown underneath in 30 seconds.

Cook the cakes for 2 to 3 minutes on each side. Serve hot.
Makes 8

Stuffed Baked Potatoes

METRIC/IMPERIAL
4 large potatoes
oil
25 g/1 oz butter
4 tablespoons milk
1 teaspoon made mustard
100 g/4 oz Cheddar or other full-
   flavoured cheese, grated
salt and pepper

AMERICAN
4 large potatoes
oil
2 tablespoons butter
¼ cup milk
1 teaspoon prepared mustard
1 cup grated Cheddar or other
   sharp cheese
salt and pepper

Make small slits in each potato with a sharp knife. Brush with oil and place on a baking sheet. Bake in a preheated moderately hot oven (190°C/375°F, Gas Mark 5) for 1½ to 2 hours or until the potatoes feel tender when squeezed slightly.

Remove from the oven and cut each potato in half lengthways. Scoop out the insides into a bowl and mash finely with the butter, milk and mustard. Add the cheese and mix well together. Season to taste.

Return the mixture to the potato cases. Increase the oven temperature to hot (220°C/425°F, Gas Mark 7). Reheat the potatoes for 10 to 15 minutes.

VARIATIONS:
Make as above, adding 2 tablespoons finely chopped parsley to the potato stuffing.
Make as above, using 175 g/6 oz (¾ cup) finely chopped fried bacon instead of the cheese.
Make as above, adding 50 g/2 oz (½ cup) finely chopped cooked ham to the potato stuffing.

Bake the potatoes as above, then cut a cross in the top of each. Hold a potato in a clean tea (dish) towel and squeeze gently to open the cross. Put a large pat of butter in the top of each potato and serve.

Roast Potatoes

METRIC/IMPERIAL
750 g/1½ lb potatoes, quartered if
   large
salt
50 g/2 oz butter
2 teaspoons olive or corn oil

AMERICAN
1½ lb potatoes, quartered if large
salt
¼ cup butter
2 teaspoons olive or corn oil

Cook the potatoes in boiling salted water for 5 to 7 minutes. Drain well.

Heat the butter and oil in a roasting pan. Add the potatoes and turn until well coated in butter and oil. Roast in a preheated moderately hot oven (200°C/400°F, Gas Mark 6) for 45 minutes or until crisp and golden, basting the potatoes at least twice with the fat in the pan.

Casseroled Potatoes

METRIC/IMPERIAL
750 g/1½ lb potatoes, thinly sliced
salt and pepper
50 g/2 oz butter
300 ml/½ pint milk

AMERICAN
1½ lb potatoes, thinly sliced
salt and pepper
¼ cup butter
1¼ cups milk

Dry the potatoes well with paper towels or a clean tea (dish) towel. Fill a 1.2 litre/2 pint (5 cup) buttered pie dish with layers of potatoes, seasoning each layer with salt and pepper.

Melt 40 g/1½ oz (3 tablespoons) of the butter and mix with the milk. Pour onto the potatoes. Dot the top with the rest of the butter cut into thin flakes.

Bake in a preheated moderately hot oven (190°C/375°F, Gas Mark 5) for 1 hour or until the potatoes are tender.

VARIATION:
Casseroled Potatoes with Cheese – sprinkle 75 g/3 oz (¾ cup) grated Cheddar cheese between the layers of potatoes before dotting with the flakes of butter. Bake as above.

Creamed Potatoes

METRIC/IMPERIAL
750 g/1½ lb potatoes
salt and pepper
40 g/1½ oz butter
3 tablespoons milk

AMERICAN
1½ lb potatoes
salt and pepper
3 tablespoons butter
3 tablespoons milk

Cook the potatoes in boiling salted water until tender. Drain well and return to the saucepan. Mash finely with a fork or potato masher (or use a potato ricer).

Add the butter, milk and salt and pepper to taste and beat over a low heat until light and creamy.

VARIATION:
Snow Potatoes – make as above, using 500 g/1 lb potatoes, 25 g/1 oz (2 tablespoons) butter, 150 ml/¼ pint (¾ cup) hot milk, and salt and pepper to taste. Beat until the potatoes are very light and fluffy.

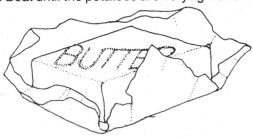

Minted New Potatoes

METRIC/IMPERIAL
750 g/1½ lb new potatoes, peeled
salt
40 g/1½ oz butter
3 fresh mint leaves

AMERICAN
1½ lb new potatoes, peeled
salt
3 tablespoons butter
3 fresh mint leaves

Cook the potatoes in boiling salted water until tender. Drain, then return the pan to low heat. Add the butter and mint, cover and heat gently for 2 to 3 minutes, shaking the pan often. Remove the mint leaves before serving.

Duchesse Potatoes

METRIC/IMPERIAL
500 g/1 lb potatoes
salt
25 g/1 oz butter
2 small egg yolks
2 teaspoons hot milk
a little egg white

AMERICAN
1 lb potatoes
salt
2 tablespoons butter
2 small egg yolks
2 teaspoons hot milk
a little egg white

Cook the potatoes in boiling salted water until tender. Drain well. Return to the saucepan and mash well with fork or masher (or use a potato ricer). Place the pan over low heat and add the butter, egg yolks and milk. Beat until smooth.

Spoon the potato mixture into a piping (pastry) bag fitted with a large star nozzle (tube). Pipe small mounds on to a buttered baking sheet and leave until cold.

Brush with egg white and bake in a preheated hot oven (220°C/425°F, Gas Mark 7) for 15 minutes or until golden.

Sauté Potatoes

METRIC/IMPERIAL
750 g/1½ lb potatoes
salt and pepper
50 g/2 oz butter
2 tablespoons olive or corn oil
chopped parsley to garnish

AMERICAN
1½ lb potatoes
salt and pepper
¼ cup butter
2 tablespoons olive or corn oil
chopped parsley for garnish

Cook the potatoes in boiling salted water for 5 to 7 minutes. Drain and cool. Cut into 5 mm/¼ inch thick slices.

Heat the butter and oil in a large, heavy frying pan. Add the potato slices and fry until golden brown on both sides, turning occasionally. Season to taste with salt and pepper and sprinkle with parsley before serving.

Stewed Potatoes

METRIC/IMPERIAL
750 g/1 ½ lb potatoes, cut into
   5mm/¼ inch thick slices
1 quantity white pouring sauce
   (page 242)
chopped chives or leeks to garnish

AMERICAN
1 ½ lb potatoes, cut into ¼ inch
   thick slices
1 quantity white pouring sauce
   (page 242)
chopped chives or leeks for garnish

Place the potatoes in a saucepan with the white sauce. Cover and simmer
gently until the potatoes are tender.
   Serve hot, garnished with chives or leeks.

VARIATION:
Stewed Potatoes with Cheese – make as above, then pour the potatoes
into a flameproof serving dish. Sprinkle over 50 g/2 oz (½ cup) crumbled
Lancashire (Brick) cheese and brown under a preheated grill (broiler).

Potatoes Anna

METRIC/IMPERIAL
750 g/1 ½ lb potatoes, very thinly
   sliced
75 g/3 oz butter, melted
salt and pepper

AMERICAN
1 ½ lb potatoes, very thinly sliced
6 tablespoons butter, melted
salt and pepper

Dry the potatoes well with paper towels or a clean tea (dish) towel. Brush a
1.2 litre/2 pint (5 cup) pie dish with a little butter and fill with layers of potato
slices in overlapping circles. Brush each layer thickly with butter and
sprinkle with salt and pepper. Brush the top layer with the remaining
butter.
   Cover the dish with foil and bake in a preheated moderately hot oven
(190°C/375°F, Gas Mark 5) for 1¼ hours.
   Turn out onto a warm ovenproof plate (the potatoes should stay in the
shape of the pie dish). Return to the oven and bake for a further 20 to
30 minutes or until the surface is golden brown.

Potatoes Lyonnaise

METRIC/IMPERIAL	AMERICAN
750 g/1½ lb potatoes	1½ lb potatoes
salt and pepper	salt and pepper
50 g/2 oz butter	¼ cup butter
225 g/8 oz onions, sliced	1 large onion, sliced
2 tablespoons olive or corn oil	2 tablespoons olive or corn oil
chopped parsley to garnish	chopped parsley for garnish

Cook the potatoes in boiling salted water for 5 to 7 minutes. Drain and cool. Cut into 5 mm/¼ inch thick slices.

Melt the butter in a frying pan, add the onions and fry until golden. Remove from the pan. Add the oil to the butter in the pan and heat. Add the potato slices and fry until golden brown on both sides, turning occasionally. Add the fried onions and salt and pepper to taste and mix well together. Sprinkle with parsley and serve hot.

Turnip and Potato Purée

METRIC/IMPERIAL	AMERICAN
40 g/1½ oz butter	3 tablespoons butter
350 g/12 oz young turnips, peeled and sliced	¾ lb young turnips, peeled and sliced
350 g/12 oz potatoes, peeled and sliced	¾ lb potatoes, peeled and sliced
1 small onion, peeled and sliced	1 small onion, peeled and sliced
salt and freshly ground black pepper	salt and freshly ground black pepper
300 ml/½ pint milk	1¼ cups milk
½ teaspoon grated nutmeg	½ teaspoon grated nutmeg
25 g/1 oz butter to finish	2 tablespoons butter to finish

Heat the butter in a saucepan until just melted, add the sliced turnip, potato and onion. Sauté the vegetables, stirring frequently, for 3 minutes. Season to taste, add the milk and sprinkle in the grated nutmeg. Bring to the boil, reduce the heat, cover and cook gently for 10 minutes or until the vegetables are tender. Liquidize in an electric blender or pass through a sieve. Return the purée to the saucepan and reheat.

Spoon on to individual plates, and mound up each serving. Make a dent in the top of each mound with the back of a spoon and put in a knob of butter.

Vegetable Curry of Your Choice

METRIC/IMPERIAL

1 tablespoon turmeric
1 tablespoon flour
1 kg/2 lb mixed fresh vegetables,
    prepared and cut into suitable
    pieces, e.g., cauliflower sprigs,
    sliced beans, carrots, celery,
    courgettes, green or red
    peppers, potatoes
4 tablespoons vegetable oil or 50 g/
    2 oz dripping, for frying
3 medium onions, peeled and
    chopped
2 medium cooking apples, peeled,
    cored and chopped
2 tablespoons curry powder
1 x 397 g/14 oz can tomatoes
1 teaspoon ground coriander
225 g/8 oz haricot or red kidney
    beans or chick peas or a
    combination of these, soaked
    overnight and cooked
salt
3 hard-boiled eggs, shelled and
    halved, to finish (optional)

AMERICAN

1 tablespoon turmeric
1 tablespoon flour
2 lb mixed fresh vegetables,
    prepared and cut into suitable
    pieces, e.g., cauliflower sprigs,
    sliced beans, carrots, celery,
    zucchini, green or red peppers,
    potatoes
¼ cup vegetable oil or dripping, for
    frying
3 medium-size onions, peeled and
    chopped
2 medium-size cooking apples,
    peeled, cored and chopped
2 tablespoons curry powder
1 can (16 oz) tomatoes
1 teaspoon ground coriander
1½ cups navy or red kidney beans
    or chick peas or a combination of
    these, soaked overnight and
    cooked
salt
3 hard-cooked eggs, shelled and
    halved, to finish (optional)

Mix the turmeric and flour together in a large bowl. Put in the prepared fresh vegetables and toss to coat lightly with the mixture.

Heat the oil or dripping in a large frying or sauté pan. Add the fresh vegetables and fry for 3 to 4 minutes. Remove from the pan with a slotted draining spoon and set aside.

Add the chopped onion and apple to the fat remaining in the pan and fry gently for 5 minutes. Stir in the curry powder and continue frying for a further 3 minutes. Pour in the tomatoes and their liquid, add the coriander, mixed vegetables and the cooked beans or chick peas. Add salt to taste and bring to the boil. Cover and simmer for 30 minutes or until the vegetables are tender. Stir occasionally to prevent the curry powder from sticking and, if the sauce becomes too thick, add a little water.

Just before serving add the hard-boiled (hard-cooked) eggs, if using, and heat through.

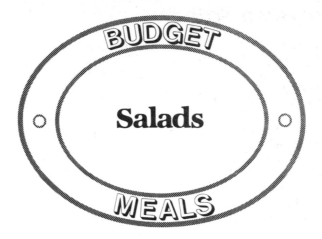

Chicory (Endive) and Grapefruit Salad

METRIC/IMPERIAL	AMERICAN
1 large ripe grapefruit	1 large ripe grapefruit
4 large heads chicory, trimmed and separated into leaves	4 large heads endive, trimmed and separated into leaves
FOR THE DRESSING:	FOR THE DRESSING:
150 ml/¼ pint soured cream	⅔ cup sour cream
½ teaspoon French mustard	½ teaspoon Dijon-style mustard
½ teaspoon salt	½ teaspoon salt
good pinch of freshly ground black pepper	good pinch of freshly ground black pepper
1 tablespoon white vinegar	1 tablespoon white vinegar
1 tablespoons vegetable oil	1 tablespoon vegetable oil
1 teaspoon clear honey	1 teaspoon honey

Grate a little zest from the skin of the grapefruit. (As it is strongly flavoured, add it gradually to the finished dressing, tasting to make sure the flavour does not become too strong.) Peel the grapefruit, remove all white pith, separate into segments, and cut each of these in half. Place in a bowl. Reserve about 16 well-shaped leaves of chicory (endive) to line a salad bowl and chop the rest roughly and add to the grapefruit. Place the reserved chicory (endive) leaves in a polythene bag to keep them fresh.

To make the dressing, put the soured cream in a small basin and beat in the mustard, salt, pepper, vinegar and oil. Stir in the honey. Add sufficient grated zest to give a hint of grapefruit to the flavour. Pour the dressing over the chopped grapefruit segments and chicory (endive) and toss lightly.

Arrange the chicory (endive) leaves to make a decorative border on a round platter and pile up the salad in the centre.

Green Bean Salad

METRIC/IMPERIAL
500 g/1 lb young green beans,
sliced
salt and pepper
4 tablespoons olive oil
¼ teaspoon dry mustard
¼ teaspoon icing sugar
2 tablespoons wine vinegar
2 tablespoons finely chopped
parsley
2 tablespoons snipped chives or
green part of a leek
4 tablespoons double cream

AMERICAN
1 lb young green beans, sliced
salt and pepper
¼ cup olive oil
¼ teaspoon dry mustard
¼ teaspoon confectioners' sugar
2 tablespoons wine vinegar
2 tablespoons finely chopped
parsley
2 tablespoons snipped chives or
green part of a leek
¼ cup heavy cream

Cook the beans in boiling salted water until tender.

Meanwhile, beat the olive oil with the mustard, sugar and ¼ teaspoon salt. Season to taste with pepper. Slowly beat in the vinegar and keep beating until the dressing becomes thick. Stir in 1 tablespoon each of the parsley and chives or leek.

Drain the beans and, while still hot, toss with the dressing. Cool, then chill for 2 hours.

Just before serving, stir in the cream, and sprinkle the rest of the parsley and chives or leek on the top. Serve with meat, poultry, duck, turkey, cheese, eggs and fish dishes.

Green Pepper and Onion Salad

METRIC/IMPERIAL
½ curly endive, separated into
leaves
2 medium green peppers, cored,
seeded and cut into thin strips
2 medium onions, thinly sliced
1 quantity cream cheese dressing
(page 242)
1 large hard-boiled egg, sliced
paprika

AMERICAN
½ head of chicory, separated into
leaves
2 medium-size green peppers,
cored, seeded and cut into thin
strips
2 medium-size onions, thinly sliced
1 quantity cream cheese dressing
(page 242)
1 large hard-cooked egg, sliced
paprika

Cover the bottom of a serving dish with the endive (chicory). Arrange the pepper strips and slices of onion on top. Spoon the dressing over the top, garnish with the slices of egg and sprinkle with paprika. Serve with veal, lamb, duck, poultry and egg dishes.

Potato Cream Salad

METRIC/IMPERIAL
500 g/1 lb potatoes, cooked and
*   cubed*
1 teaspoon finely grated onion, or
*   2 spring onions, finely chopped*
150 ml/¼ pint mayonnaise
5 tablespoons double cream
snipped chives or paprika to
*   garnish*

AMERICAN
1 lb potatoes, cooked and cubed
1 teaspoon finely grated onion, or
*   2 scallions, finely chopped*
¾ cup mayonnaise
5 tablespoons heavy cream
chopped chives or paprika for
*   garnish*

Put the potatoes into a large bowl and add the onion, mayonnaise and cream. Stir gently until the potato cubes are thickly coated. Put into a serving dish and sprinkle with chives or paprika.

Carrot, Apple and Nut Salad

METRIC/IMPERIAL
1 tablespoon lemon juice
1 red-skinned dessert apple, cored
*   and thinly sliced*
2 large carrots, peeled and grated
100 g/4 oz white cabbage, core
*   removed and finely shredded*
1 leek, white and pale green part
*   only, washed and finely sliced*
8 walnut halves
FOR THE DRESSING:
1 tablespoon lemon juice
½ teaspoon caster sugar
½ teaspoon salt
pinch of freshly ground black
*   pepper*
2 tablespoons vegetable oil
1 tablespoon smooth peanut butter

AMERICAN
1 tablespoon lemon juice
1 red-skinned dessert apple, cored
*   and thinly sliced*
2 large carrots, peeled and grated
1½ cups finely shredded white
*   cabbage*
1 leek, white and pale green part
*   only, washed and finely sliced*
8 walnut halves
FOR THE DRESSING:
1 tablespoon lemon juice
½ teaspoon sugar
½ teaspoon salt
pinch of freshly ground black
*   pepper*
2 tablespoons vegetable oil
1 tablespoon smooth peanut butter

Pour the lemon juice into a saucer. Dip the apple slices in the lemon juice and coat both sides to prevent discoloration. Arrange the grated carrot, shredded cabbage, sliced leek and apple slices in a salad bowl. Scatter the walnut halves over the top.
   To make the dressing, place the lemon juice, sugar, salt and pepper in a small basin and beat vigorously until blended. Gradually beat in the oil and peanut butter alternately, until the dressing is smooth and slightly thickened. To save time, place all the ingredients in a screw-topped jar and shake briskly until the dressing emulsifies. Pour the dressing over the salad and toss lightly before serving.

Courgette (Zucchini) and Anchovy Salad

METRIC/IMPERIAL
1 tablespoon vegetable oil
500 g/1 lb courgettes, trimmed and
  thinly sliced
6 spring onions, trimmed and
  chopped
150 ml/¼ pint chicken stock
1 x 50 g/2 oz can anchovy fillets
2 tablespoons white vinegar
1 teaspoon caster sugar
freshly ground black pepper
1 clove of garlic, crushed

AMERICAN
1 tablespoon vegetable oil
1 lb zucchini, trimmed and thinly
  sliced
6 scallions, trimmed and chopped
⅔ cup chicken stock
1 can (2 oz) anchovy fillets
2 tablespoons white vinegar
1 teaspoon sugar
freshly ground black pepper
1 clove of garlic, crushed

Heat the oil in a saucepan. Add the sliced courgettes (zucchini) and spring onions (scallions) and sauté over moderate heat until the vegetables are limp. Add the stock, cover and simmer for 5 minutes. Remove from the heat, stir well, cover again and allow to cool.

Remove the anchovies from the can, place on a board, and chop finely. Mix the vinegar, caster sugar, black pepper to taste and crushed garlic with the anchovy oil from the can. Stir in the chopped anchovies. Drain the cooked courgettes (zucchini), toss them lightly in the dressing and serve in a glass dish. (No salt should be added to the cooking water for the courgettes (zucchini) or the basic dressing, as the anchovies are sufficiently salty.)

Green Salad

METRIC/IMPERIAL
1 garlic clove, halved
1 Webb's Wonder, cos or round
  lettuce, torn into bite-sized
  pieces
bunch of watercress (optional)
French dressing (page 240)

AMERICAN
1 garlic clove, halved
1 head of iceberg, romaine or
  Boston lettuce, torn into bite-
  sized pieces
bunch of watercress (optional)
French dressing (page 240)

Rub the cut side of the garlic over the inside of a salad bowl. Discard the garlic. Put the lettuce leaves into the bowl. Add the watercress, if using.

Just before serving, pour over the dressing and toss until every piece of lettuce is coated with dressing.

Russian Salad

METRIC/IMPERIAL
1 lettuce heart, separated into
 leaves
225 g/8 oz carrots, cooked and
 cubed
225 g/8 oz potatoes, cooked and
 cubed
100 g/4 oz peas, cooked
100 g/4 oz green beans, cooked
mayonnaise
1 large hard-boiled egg, cut into
 wedges
4 gherkins, sliced

AMERICAN
1 lettuce heart, separated into
 leaves
½ lb carrots, cooked and cubed
 (about 1 cup)
½ lb potatoes, cooked and cubed
 (about 1 cup)
1 cup peas, cooked
¼ lb green beans, cooked (about
 1 cup)
mayonnaise
1 large hard-cooked egg, cut into
 wedges
4 gherkins, sliced

Place the lettuce in a salad bowl. Put the carrots, potatoes, peas and beans in a mixing bowl. Mix well together. Gently fold in enough mayonnaise to coat the vegetables fairly thickly. Pile on top of the lettuce and garnish with the egg wedges and gherkins.

Stuffed Pepper Salad

METRIC/IMPERIAL
2 medium red or green peppers
100 g/4 oz cream cheese
2 tablespoons double cream
½ teaspoon paprika
1 teaspoon finely grated onion
3 tablespoons finely chopped
 cooked ham or salted cashew
 nuts
salt and pepper
½ round lettuce, separated into
 leaves
1 large tomato, cut into wedges

AMERICAN
2 medium-size red or green
 peppers
½ cup cream cheese
2 tablespoons heavy cream
½ teaspoon paprika
1 teaspoon finely grated onion
3 tablespoons finely chopped
 cooked ham or salted cashew
 nuts
salt and pepper
½ head of Boston lettuce,
 separated into leaves
1 large tomato, cut into wedges

Cut the top off the stem end of each pepper and remove all the seeds from inside. Mix the cream cheese with the cream, paprika, onion and ham or nuts. Season to taste with salt and pepper. Stuff the peppers with the cheese mixture, wrap in foil and chill overnight.

Before serving, cover the bottom of a serving dish with the lettuce leaves. Cut each pepper into six slices and arrange on top of the lettuce leaves in a circle. Fill the centre of the circle with the tomato wedges.

Syrian Salad

METRIC/IMPERIAL
½ cos or Webb's Wonder lettuce,
   torn into bite-sized pieces
100 g/4 oz green beans, cooked
100 g/4 oz peas, cooked
100 g/4 oz carrot, cooked and diced
100 g/4 oz cucumber, coarsely
   grated
150 ml/¼ pint natural yogurt
4 tablespoons single cream
¼–½ teaspoon salt
chopped fresh mint to garnish

AMERICAN
½ head of romaine or iceberg
   lettuce, torn into bite-sized
   pieces
¼ lb green beans, cooked (about
   1 cup)
1 cup peas, cooked
½ cup diced carrot, cooked
½ cup coarsely grated cucumber
¾ cup plain yogurt
¼ cup light cream
¼–½ teaspoon salt
chopped fresh mint for garnish

Cover the bottom of four plates with the lettuce. Arrange the green beans, peas, carrot and cucumber in separate piles on top of the lettuce.

Mix the yogurt with the cream and salt and spoon over the vegetables. Garnish with the chopped mint and serve.

Tomato and Onion Salad

METRIC/IMPERIAL
500 g/1 lb tomatoes
French dressing (page 240)
1 teaspoon finely chopped onion
1 ½ tablespoons finely chopped
   parsley

AMERICAN
1 lb tomatoes
French dressing (page 240)
1 teaspoon finely chopped onion
1 ½ tablespoons finely chopped
   parsley

Put the tomatoes into a bowl, cover with boiling water and leave for 30 seconds, then drain. Skin the tomatoes. Return them to the bowl, cover with very cold water and leave for 5 minutes.

Drain well and cut into very thin slices. Arrange in a large shallow serving dish. Pour the French dressing over and sprinkle with the onion and parsley. Serve chilled.

VARIATION:
Tomato and Parsley Salad – skin and slice the tomatoes as above and arrange in a serving dish. Coat with cream cheese and nut dressing (page 243) and sprinkle over 4 tablespoons finely chopped parsley, in neat rows. Serve chilled.

Winter Coleslaw

METRIC/IMPERIAL	AMERICAN
1 small or ½ medium white cabbage, cored and shredded	1 small or ½ medium head of white cabbage, cored and shredded
2 eating apples, peeled, cored and coarsely grated	2 apples, peeled, cored and coarsely grated
1 tablespoon finely grated onion	1 tablespoon finely grated onion
50 g/2 oz Leicester cheese, grated	½ cup grated cheese
2½ tablespoons finely chopped parsley	2½ tablespoons finely chopped parsley
150 ml/¼ pint soured cream	¾ cup sour cream
2 tablespoons milk	2 tablespoons milk
2 teaspoons rosehip syrup	2 teaspoons rosehip syrup
½ teaspoon Worcestershire sauce	½ teaspoon Worcestershire sauce
1 tablespoon lemon juice	1 tablespoon lemon juice
½ teaspoon salt	½ teaspoon salt

Put the cabbage into a large bowl and add the apples, onion, cheese and parsley. Mix well together.

Combine the soured cream, milk, rosehip syrup, Worcestershire sauce, lemon juice and salt and pour over the cabbage and apple mixture. Toss well with a spoon and fork and serve.

Orange, Cottage Cheese and Ham Salad

METRIC/IMPERIAL	AMERICAN
2 oranges	2 oranges
225 g/8 oz cottage cheese	1 cup cottage cheese
225 g/8 oz cooked ham, chopped	1 cup chopped cooked ham
1 onion, peeled and grated	1 onion, peeled and grated
salt and freshly ground black pepper	salt and freshly ground black pepper
25 g/1 oz stem ginger, chopped	1 tablespoon chopped preserved ginger
sprigs of watercress to garnish	sprigs of watercress for garnish

Finely grate the zest from 1 orange. Remove all the peel and pith from both oranges. Cutting between each section membrane, remove the segments from the oranges, discarding the pips.

Mix the cottage cheese with the grated orange zest, chopped ham, grated onion, salt and pepper to taste, and the chopped ginger.

Spoon the salad into the centres of 4 small dishes or plates, and arrange the orange segments and sprigs of watercress around the edges. Serve with slices of pumpernickel.

Orange, Chicken and Bean Sprout Salad

METRIC/IMPERIAL
175 g/6 oz cooked, boned chicken
2 oranges
175 g/6 oz fresh bean sprouts
FOR THE DRESSING:
4 tablespoons orange juice
2 tablespoons lemon juice
150 ml/¼ pint olive or corn oil
salt and freshly ground black
   pepper
TO GARNISH:
2 tablespoons chopped parsley
25 g/1 oz cashew nuts, chopped

AMERICAN
6 oz cooked, boned chicken
2 oranges
3 cups fresh bean sprouts
FOR THE DRESSING:
¼ cup orange juice
2 tablespoons lemon juice
⅔ cup olive or corn oil
salt and freshly ground black
   pepper
FOR GARNISH:
2 tablespoons chopped parsley
¼ cup chopped cashew nuts

Remove any skin from the chicken meat and pull it into shreds. (This is more easily done while the chicken is still warm, and it is best to take any leftovers from the carcass of a chicken as soon after cooking as possible.)

Remove all the peel and white pith from the oranges. Cutting between each section membrane, remove the segments from the oranges, discarding the pips. Put the orange segments into a bowl with the bean sprouts and chicken. To make the dressing, put the orange and lemon juices into a screw-topped jar with the oil and seasoning to taste. Shake vigorously.

Pour the dressing over the chicken, orange segments and bean sprouts, and toss lightly together. Spoon the salad out on 4 small dishes or plates, and sprinkle with chopped parsley and cashew nuts.

Cucumber Salad

METRIC/IMPERIAL
½ cos or Webb's Wonder lettuce,
   torn into bite-sized pieces
1 small cucumber, peeled and
   diced
150 ml/¼ pint natural yogurt
2 tablespoons mayonnaise
1 tablespoon lemon juice
salt and pepper

AMERICAN
½ head of romaine or iceberg
   lettuce, torn into bite-sized
   pieces
1 small cucumber, peeled and
   diced
¾ cup plain yogurt
2 tablespoons mayonnaise
1 tablespoon lemon juice
salt and pepper

Mix the lettuce with the cucumber in a serving bowl.

Combine the yogurt with the mayonnaise and lemon juice. Season to taste with salt and pepper. Pour over the lettuce and cucumber and toss well. Serve with poultry, fish, turkey, cheese and egg dishes.

Orange, Grapefruit and Date Salad

METRIC/IMPERIAL
2 oranges
1 grapefruit
8 fresh dates, stoned and chopped
3 tablespoons clear honey
3 teaspoons French mustard
2 tablespoons lemon juice
salt and freshly ground black
   pepper

AMERICAN
2 oranges
1 grapefruit
8 fresh dates, pitted and chopped
3 tablespoons honey
3 teaspoons Dijon-style mustard
2 tablespoons lemon juice
salt and freshly ground black
   pepper

Remove all the peel and pith from the oranges and the grapefruit. Cut the fruits into thin slices, and cut each slice into 3 or 4 sections.

Mix together the orange and grapefruit pieces in a bowl with the chopped fresh dates. Combine the honey, mustard, lemon juice and seasoning to taste.

Spoon the mustard and honey dressing over the prepared fruit and toss lightly. Chill for at least 1 hour.

Spoon the salad out on 4 small dishes, and serve with sliced salami, or other Continental sausage.

Apple and Walnut Salad

METRIC/IMPERIAL
½ cos or small Webb's Wonder
   lettuce, torn into bite-sized
   pieces
3 large eating apples
6 celery stalks, chopped
75 g/3 oz walnuts, coarsely
   chopped
150 ml/¼ pint mayonnaise
5 tablespoons double cream
1 tablespoon vinegar
juice of 1 medium lemon

AMERICAN
½ head romaine or small iceberg
   lettuce, torn into bite-sized
   pieces
3 large apples
6 celery stalks, chopped
¾ cup coarsely chopped walnuts
¾ cup mayonnaise
5 tablespoons heavy cream
1 tablespoon vinegar
juice of 1 medium-size lemon

Cover the bottom of a serving dish with the lettuce. Peel, core and slice two of the apples, add the celery and chopped nuts and mix well together.

Mix the mayonnaise with the cream and vinegar, pour over the apple mixture and toss until all the ingredients are thickly coated. Arrange over the lettuce.

Cut the third apple, unpeeled, into thin slices, dip in lemon juice to stop from going brown and arrange on top of the salad. Serve with meat, poultry, duck or turkey dishes.

Chinese Leaf Salad

METRIC/IMPERIAL
½ head Chinese leaves, washed
250 g/8 oz cooked broad beans
2 tablespoons mustard sauce from
   a jar of piccalilli
4 tablespoons mayonnaise
FOR THE GARLIC CROÛTONS:
2 tablespoons vegetable oil
1 clove of garlic, very finely
   chopped
2 slices white bread, trimmed and
   cut into dice

AMERICAN
½ head Chinese leaves, washed
1½ cups cooked fava or lima beans
2 tablespoons mustard sauce from
   a jar of piccalilli
¼ cup mayonnaise
FOR THE GARLIC CROÛTONS:
2 tablespoons vegetable oil
1 clove of garlic, very finely
   chopped
2 slices white bread, trimmed and
   cut into dice

Reserve one large outer leaf from the Chinese leaves for serving and shred the remainder finely. Place the shredded vegetable in a bowl with the broad (fava or lima) beans.

Mix together the mustard sauce and the mayonnaise, pour over the leaves and beans and toss lightly. Allow to stand while preparing the garlic croûtons.

Heat the oil in a frying pan. Add the garlic and stir well. Drop in the bread cubes and fry them, stirring frequently, until crisp and golden-brown. Drain well.

Spoon the salad on to the reserved leaf on a serving dish and scatter over the garlic croûtons.

Creamed Cabbage and Caraway Salad

METRIC/IMPERIAL
1 small or ½ medium white
   cabbage (about 225 g/8 oz),
   cored and grated
1 teaspoon finely grated onion
1 teaspoon caraway seeds
300 ml/½ pint soured cream
4 tablespoons lemon juice
2 teaspoons soft brown sugar
salt and pepper

AMERICAN
1 small or ½ medium head of white
   cabbage (about ½ lb), cored and
   grated
1 teaspoon finely grated onion
1 teaspoon caraway seeds
1¼ cups sour cream
¼ cup lemon juice
2 teaspoons brown sugar
salt and pepper

Put the cabbage into a large mixing bowl with the onion and caraway seeds and mix well together. Mix the soured cream with the lemon juice, brown sugar and salt and pepper to taste. Pour over the cabbage mixture and toss well. Transfer to a serving dish. Serve with frankfurters or sausages.

Hot New Potato Salad

METRIC/IMPERIAL
500 g/1 lb new potatoes, scrubbed
1 chicken stock cube
150 ml/¼ pint boiling water
225 g/8 oz frozen peas
4 tablespoons mayonnaise
2 tablespoons mixed chopped
    parsley and dill
2 oz gherkins, finely sliced, to
    garnish

AMERICAN
1 lb new potatoes, scrubbed
1 chicken bouillon cube
⅔ cup boiling water
½ lb frozen peas
¼ cup mayonnaise
2 tablespoons chopped parsley and
    dill
2 oz gherkins, finely sliced, for
    garnish

Place the potatoes in a saucepan, cover with lightly salted water and bring to the boil. Cover and simmer until tender. Drain well and halve any larger potatoes while still warm. Transfer to a salad bowl.

Meanwhile, crumble the stock cube into the boiling water and stir until dissolved. Rinse out the saucepan in which the potatoes were cooked, pour in the stock, add the frozen peas and bring to the boil, stirring gently to separate the peas. Remove from the heat and transfer the peas from the stock to the potatoes with a slotted draining spoon.

Allow the stock to cool slightly then beat in the mayonnaise and stir in the chopped herbs. Pour this mixture over the potatoes and peas and fold over several times to coat the vegetables evenly with the dressing. Serve warm garnished with the sliced gherkin.

Mushroom Macédoine Salad

METRIC/IMPERIAL
225 g/8 oz button mushrooms
3 tablespoons vegetable oil
4 tablespoons salad cream
2 tablespoons single cream
350 g/12 oz frozen mixed
    vegetables, cooked
1 teaspoon finely chopped onion
salt and freshly ground black
    pepper
watercress sprigs to garnish

AMERICAN
2 cups button mushrooms
3 tablespoons vegetable oil
4 tablespoons salad cream
2 tablespoons light cream
¾ lb frozen mixed vegetables,
    cooked
1 teaspoon finely chopped onion
salt and freshly ground black
    pepper
watercress sprigs for garnish

Wipe the mushrooms, but do not peel. Trim off the stalks level with the caps. Slice the mushrooms. Heat the oil in a frying pan (skillet) and use to sauté the mushroom stalks and sliced caps for 2 minutes, until pale golden. Drain and cool on absorbent kitchen paper.

Stir together the salad cream and single (light) cream in a large basin. Add the cooked mixed vegetables, chopped onion and mushrooms. Season, stir well, turn into a salad bowl and serve chilled, garnished with watercress sprigs.

French (Green) Bean and Mushroom Salad

METRIC/IMPERIAL
3 tablespoons vegetable oil
2 tablespoons lemon juice
1 tablespoon chopped fresh mint
salt and freshly ground black
*   pepper*
225 g/8 oz button mushrooms,
*   wiped and thinly sliced*
500 g/1 lb French beans, trimmed
TO FINISH:
lettuce leaves
2 teaspoons snipped chives

AMERICAN
3 tablespoons vegetable oil
2 tablespoons lemon juice
1 tablespoon chopped fresh mint
salt and freshly ground black
*   pepper*
2 cups button mushrooms, wiped
*   and thinly sliced*
1 lb green beans, trimmed
TO FINISH:
lettuce leaves
2 teaspoons chopped chives

To make the dressing, mix together the oil, lemon juice and chopped mint and seasoning to taste.

Place the mushrooms in a small bowl, pour over the dressing, cover and allow to marinate for several hours, or overnight if time permits.

Cook the beans, whole, in boiling lightly salted water for about 4 minutes, or until just tender but still slightly crisp. Drain and cool.

Combine the beans with the mushrooms and stir lightly with a fork to coat the beans with the dressing. Serve on a bed of lettuce leaves in a salad dish and scatter over the snipped chives.

Rosy Coleslaw

METRIC/IMPERIAL
3–4 tablespoons cranberry sauce
4 tablespoons mayonnaise
1 tablespoon white vinegar
salt and freshly ground black
*   pepper*
1 lb white cabbage, core removed
*   and finely shredded*
chopped chives to garnish

AMERICAN
3–4 tablespoons whole berry
*   cranberry sauce*
¼ cup mayonnaise
1 tablespoon white vinegar
salt and freshly ground black
*   pepper*
6 cups finely shredded white
*   cabbage*
chopped chives for garnish

Combine the cranberry sauce, mayonnaise and vinegar in a bowl and season to taste.

Add the shredded cabbage gradually, tossing it to coat well with the dressing. Cover and chill for at least 2 hours.

Spoon the coleslaw into a glass salad bowl and serve sprinkled with chopped chives.

Patio Salad

METRIC/IMPERIAL
50 g/2 oz canned tuna
50 g/2 oz Edam cheese, diced
50 g/2 oz button mushrooms, wiped and cut in quarters
1 large stalk celery, scrubbed and chopped
25 g/1 oz black olives
few lettuce leaves, shredded, to finish

FOR THE DRESSING:
pinch each of salt, pepper and sugar
good pinch of dry mustard
2 teaspoons vinegar
1 tablespoon salad oil

AMERICAN
2 oz canned tuna
½ cup diced Edam cheese
½ cup quartered button mushrooms
1 large celery stick, scrubbed and chopped
¼ cup ripe olives
few lettuce leaves, shredded, to finish

FOR THE DRESSING:
pinch each of salt, pepper and sugar
good pinch of dry mustard
2 teaspoons vinegar
1 tablespoon salad oil

Prepare the dressing by shaking together the seasonings, vinegar and oil. Drain the oil from the fish and break into chunks. Place this and all the other ingredients, except the lettuce leaves, in a bowl. Pour over the dressing and mix well. Allow to stand for at least 30 minutes in a cold place. Serve on a bed of shredded lettuce.
Serves 2

Sweet Winter Salad

METRIC/IMPERIAL
100 g/4 oz seedless raisins
50 g/2 oz shelled walnuts
100 g/4 oz carrots, peeled
2 stalks celery, scrubbed
1 sweet green pepper
2 small heads chicory, trimmed

FOR THE DRESSING:
2 teaspoons lemon juice
salt and black pepper
1 teaspoon clear honey
3 tablespoons salad oil

AMERICAN
¾ cup seedless raisins
½ cup shelled walnuts
¼ lb carrots, peeled
2 celery sticks, scrubbed
1 sweet green pepper
2 small heads endive, trimmed

FOR THE DRESSING:
2 teaspoons lemon juice
salt and black pepper
1 teaspoon honey
3 tablespoons salad oil

Mix all the ingredients for the dressing except the oil, and gradually beat in the oil so that it emulsifies the dressing. Allow to stand for at least 1 hour.

Chop the raisins and walnuts roughly. Grate the carrot. Remove coarse strings from the celery and chop. Remove seeds, core and white pith from the green pepper and cut into thin strips. Separate the chicory (endive) heads into the leaves. Toss all the salad ingredients lightly in the dressing, and serve chilled with assorted cold meats, or with hot roast beef or pork.

Melon in Curry Cream

METRIC/IMPERIAL

1 medium melon, preferably
    honeydew, peeled and quartered

FOR THE CURRY CREAM:

50 g/2 oz butter

1 small onion, peeled and finely
    chopped

2 inner stalks celery, scrubbed and
    chopped

3 tablespoons flour

1 tablespoon curry powder

1 teaspoon soft brown sugar

½ teaspoon ground bay leaves

3 tablespoons lemon juice

150 ml/¼ pint milk

150 ml/¼ pint chicken stock

4 tablespoons single cream

salt

pinch of curry powder to garnish
    (optional)

AMERICAN

1 medium-size melon, preferably
    honeydew, peeled and quartered

FOR THE CURRY CREAM:

¼ cup butter

1 small onion, peeled and finely
    chopped

2 inner celery sticks, scrubbed and
    chopped

3 tablespoons flour

1 tablespoon curry powder

1 teaspoon firmly packed light
    brown sugar

½ teaspoon ground bay leaves

3 tablespoons lemon juice

⅔ cup milk

⅔ cup chicken stock

¼ cup light cream

salt

pinch of curry powder for garnish
    (optional)

Place the melon quarters on a large dish and carefully remove the seeds, reserving the juice. Discard the seeds. Dice the melon flesh neatly, and place in a glass serving dish.

To make the curry cream, melt the butter in a saucepan with a heavy base. Add the chopped onion and celery and cook gently until limp. Stir in the flour and curry powder and cook over low heat for 2 minutes, stirring all the time. Add the sugar, ground bay leaves, lemon juice, reserved melon juice, milk and stock and bring to the boil, stirring constantly. Lower the heat, cover and simmer for 15 minutes. Cool, stir in the cream and add salt to taste. Chill well.

Pour the curry cream over the melon dice and, if liked, garnish with a pinch of curry powder. Serve very cold.

Cottage Cheese and Parsley Quiche

METRIC/IMPERIAL
175 g/6 oz quantity shortcrust
    pastry (page 246)
25 g/1 oz butter
1 large onion, chopped
500 g/1 lb cottage cheese
4 tablespoons chopped parsley
2 eggs, beaten
salt and pepper
TO GARNISH:
watercress
grated carrot

AMERICAN
1½ cup quantity pie pastry
    (page 246)
2 tablespoons butter
1 large onion, chopped
1 lb (2 cups) cottage cheese
¼ cup chopped parsley
2 eggs, beaten
salt and pepper
FOR GARNISH:
watercress
grated carrot

Roll out the dough and use to line a 20 cm/8 inch flan or quiche pan or ring placed on top of a lightly buttered baking sheet.

Melt the butter in a frying pan, add the onion and fry gently until softened. Put the cottage cheese through a fine sieve and mix with the parsley, eggs and fried onion. Season to taste with salt and pepper. Beat well and pour into the pastry case.

Bake in a preheated moderately hot oven (190°C/375°F, Gas Mark 5) for 15 minutes, then reduce the heat to moderate (160°C/325°F, Gas Mark 3) and bake for a further 45 minutes or until the filling has set and the top is golden.

If baked in a flan ring, remove the ring and place the quiche on a warmed serving dish. Garnish with watercress and small piles of grated carrot.

Quiche Lorraine

METRIC/IMPERIAL
175 g/6 oz quantity shortcrust
pastry (page 246)
100 g/4 oz streaky bacon, derinded
and cut into strips
150 ml/¼ pint single cream
150 ml/¼ pint milk
3 eggs, beaten
salt and pepper
large pinch of grated nutmeg

AMERICAN
1 ½ cup quantity pie pastry
(page 246)
¼ lb slab bacon, cut into strips
¾ cup light cream
¾ cup milk
3 eggs, beaten
salt and pepper
large pinch of grated nutmeg

Roll out the dough and use to line a 20 cm/8 inch flan or quiche pan, or flan ring resting on a lightly buttered baking sheet. Fry the bacon in a frying pan until crisp. Drain on paper towels and spread over the bottom of the pastry case.

Warm the cream and milk until just below boiling point. Mix with the eggs. Season to taste with salt and pepper and add the nutmeg. Pour into the pastry case.

Bake in a preheated moderately hot oven (200°C/400°F, Gas Mark 6) for 10 minutes, then lower the heat to moderate (160°C/325°F, Gas Mark 3) and bake for a further 35 to 45 minutes, or until the filling is set.

Corned Beef Pie

METRIC/IMPERIAL
175 g/6 oz corned beef, chopped
50 g/2 oz fresh breadcrumbs
2 teaspoons finely grated onion
50 g/2 oz cheese, grated
2 tablespoons finely chopped
parsley
½ teaspoon Worcestershire sauce
salt and pepper
225 g/8 oz quantity shortcrust
pastry (page 246)
3 tablespoons milk

AMERICAN
¾ cup chopped corned beef
1 cup soft bread crumbs
2 teaspoons finely grated onion
½ cup grated cheese
2 tablespoons finely chopped
parsley
½ teaspoon Worcestershire sauce
salt and pepper
2 cup quantity pie pastry (page
246)
3 tablespoons milk

Mix the beef with the breadcrumbs, onion, cheese, parsley, Worcester-shire sauce and salt and pepper to taste.

Cut the dough into two equal pieces. Roll out one piece and use to line a buttered 20 cm/8 inch pie plate or pan. Pile the beef filling into the middle and moisten the edges of the dough with a little water.

Roll out the remaining dough and lay over the pie. Press the edges well together and ridge with a fork. Brush with a little milk.

Bake in a preheated moderately hot oven (200°C/400°F, Gas Mark 6) for 45 minutes.

Corned Beef and Vegetable Tarts

METRIC/IMPERIAL
*175 g/6 oz quantity shortcrust
    pastry (page 246)*
100 g/4 oz corned beef, chopped
50 g/2 oz peas, cooked
50 g/2 oz potato, cooked and diced
15 g/½ oz butter
15 g/½ oz flour
4 tablespoons milk
1 egg, beaten
salt and pepper

AMERICAN
*1½ cup quantity pie pastry
    (page 246)*
½ cup chopped corned beef
½ cup cooked peas
½ cup diced cooked potato
1 tablespoon butter
2 tablespoons flour
¼ cup milk
1 egg, beaten
salt and pepper

Roll out the dough and cut into 12 rounds using a 7.5 cm/3 inch biscuit (cookie) cutter. Use to line 12 lightly buttered bun (muffin) tins.

Mix the corned beef with the peas and potato. Melt the butter in a saucepan, stir in the flour and cook for 2 minutes without browning. Slowly stir in the milk and cook, stirring, until thickened. Remove from the heat and stir in the beef mixture and egg. Season to taste with salt and pepper.

Spoon equal amounts of the filling into the lined tins. Bake in a preheated moderately hot oven (200°C/400°F, Gas Mark 6) for 10 minutes, then lower the heat to 190°C/375°F, Gas Mark 5 and bake for a further 12 to 15 minutes.
Makes 12

Bacon Batter Pudding

METRIC/IMPERIAL
50 g/2 oz butter
*225–350 g/8–12 oz lean bacon,
    derinded and chopped*
*1 quantity pancake batter (page
    133)*

AMERICAN
¼ cup butter
½–¾ lb Canadian bacon, chopped
1 quantity crêpe batter (page 133)

Put the butter into a 25 x 30 cm/10 x 12 inch baking pan and melt in a preheated hot oven (220°C/425°F, Gas Mark 7). Scatter the bacon over the bottom of the pan, then pour over the batter.

Return the pan to the oven and bake for 30 minutes, then lower the heat to moderately hot (200°C/400°F, Gas Mark 6) and bake for a further 15 to 20 minutes.

VARIATIONS:
Corned Beef Batter Pudding – make as above, using corned beef, cut into 2.5 cm/1 inch cubes, instead of bacon.
Meatball Batter Pudding – melt the butter as above and pour the batter into the pan, then add 500 g/1 lb minced (ground) beef, well seasoned and shaped into small balls. Bake as above.

Cheese and Ham Pudding

METRIC/IMPERIAL
2 eggs, separated
75 g/3 oz Derby or Cheshire
  cheese, grated
300 ml/½ pint lukewarm milk
50 g/2 oz fresh white breadcrumbs
25–50 g/1–2 oz cooked ham, finely
  chopped
½ teaspoon salt
½ teaspoon dry mustard
watercress to garnish

AMERICAN
2 eggs, separated
¾ cup grated cheese
1¼ cups lukewarm milk
1 cup soft white bread crumbs
¼–½ cup finely chopped cooked
  ham
½ teaspoon salt
½ teaspoon dry mustard
watercress for garnish

Beat the egg yolks with the cheese and milk. Mix the breadcrumbs with the ham, salt and mustard. Slowly stir the milk mixture into the crumb mixture. Leave to stand for 30 minutes.

Beat the egg whites to a stiff snow and fold into the mixture. Pour into a buttered 600 ml/1 pint (2½ cup) baking dish. Bake in a preheated moderately hot oven (200°C/400°F, Gas Mark 6) for 25 to 30 minutes or until golden brown. Garnish with watercress and serve immediately.

VARIATION:
Cheese and Parsley Pudding – make as above, using 2 tablespoons finely chopped parsley instead of the ham.

Fish Pudding

METRIC/IMPERIAL
500 g/1 lb cod fillet, cooked and
  flaked
1 tablespoon lemon juice
25 g/1 oz butter, melted
salt and pepper
300 ml/½ pint hot milk
225 g/8 oz dry breadcrumbs
2 eggs, separated

AMERICAN
1 lb cod fillet, cooked and flaked
1 tablespoon lemon juice
2 tablespoons butter, melted
salt and pepper
1¼ cups hot milk
4 cups dry bread crumbs
2 eggs, separated

Mix the fish with the lemon juice, butter, and salt and pepper to taste. Pour the milk over the breadcrumbs and leave until cool, then mix with the fish. Beat in the egg yolks.

Beat the egg whites until stiff and fold into the fish mixture. Pour into a buttered 1.8 litre/3 pint pudding basin (2 quart steaming mold). Cover tightly with buttered greaseproof (parchment) paper and steam for 1½ hours.

Steamed Bacon Pudding

METRIC/IMPERIAL
500 g/1 lb streaky bacon rashers,
   derinded
350 g/12 oz self-raising flour
pepper
100 g/4 oz butter
1 medium onion, grated
½ teaspoon dried mixed herbs
1 tablespoon finely chopped
   parsley
2 large eggs, beaten
4 to 5 tablespoons cold milk

AMERICAN
1 lb bacon slices
3 cups self-rising flour
pepper
½ cup butter
1 medium-size onion, grated
½ teaspoon dried Italian seasoning
1 tablespoon finely chopped
   parsley
2 large eggs, beaten
4 to 5 tablespoons cold milk

Line a lightly-buttered 1.2 litre/2 pint pudding basin (1 quart steaming mold) with 8 to 10 of the bacon rashers (slices). Finely chop the rest of the bacon.

Sift the flour and pepper to taste into a mixing bowl. Rub in the butter until the mixture resembles fine crumbs. Add the chopped bacon, onion, herbs and parsley. Mix to a soft batter with the eggs and milk, stirring briskly without beating.

Pour into the basin (mold) and cover with buttered greaseproof (parchment) paper or foil. Steam steadily for 2 hours.

Turn out onto a warm dish and serve hot.

Cheese and Onion Pudding

METRIC/IMPERIAL
25 g/1 oz butter
2 medium onions, peeled and finely
   sliced
600 ml/1 pint milk
100 g/4 oz fresh white
   breadcrumbs
100 g/4 oz Cheddar cheese, grated
salt and freshly ground black
   pepper
3 large eggs, lightly beaten

AMERICAN
2 tablespoons butter
2 medium-size onions, peeled and
   finely sliced
2½ cups milk
2 cups soft white bread crumbs
1 cup grated Cheddar cheese
salt and freshly ground black
   pepper
3 large eggs, lightly beaten

Heat the butter in a pan. Add the onions and fry gently until golden. Add the milk and bring just to boiling point. Pour over the breadcrumbs, stir well. Fold in the cheese, seasoning and beaten eggs. Turn into a greased pie dish and bake in a fairly hot oven (190°C/375°F, Gas Mark 5) for 30 minutes or until golden-brown and well risen. Serve immediately.

Leek and Bacon Gratin

METRIC/IMPERIAL
8 large leeks, white and pale green
   part washed and sliced into
   5 cm/2 inch lengths
1 large carrot, peeled and sliced
   into 5 cm/2 inch lengths
12 rashers streaky bacon
FOR THE SAUCE:
25 g/1 oz butter
25 g/1 oz flour
300 ml/½ pint milk
salt and freshly ground black
   pepper
50 g/2 oz Cheddar cheese, grated
TO FINISH:
50 g/2 oz Cheddar cheese, grated
50 g/2 oz fresh white breadcrumbs

AMERICAN
8 large leeks, white and pale green
   part washed and sliced into
   2 inch lengths
1 large carrot, peeled and sliced
   into 2 inch lengths
12 slices streaky bacon
FOR THE SAUCE:
2 tablespoons butter
¼ cup flour
1¼ cups milk
salt and freshly ground black
   pepper
½ cup grated Cheddar cheese
TO FINISH:
½ cup grated Cheddar cheese
1 cup soft white bread crumbs

Cook the sliced leeks and carrots in boiling, salted water to cover for 10 to
15 minutes or until tender. Drain, reserving the liquid, and turn into a
buttered flameproof casserole.

Meanwhile prepare the sauce. Melt the butter in a pan, stir in the flour
and cook for 2 to 3 minutes, stirring constantly. Remove the pan from the
heat and gradually add the milk and 150 ml/¼ pint (⅔ cup) of the liquid
from the vegetables, stirring constantly. Return the pan to the heat. Bring
slowly to the boil stirring all the time. Lower the heat, add the seasoning to
taste and simmer gently until the sauce thickens. Stir in the 50 g/2 oz
(½ cup) cheese.

Grill the bacon rashers, arrange on top of the leeks and carrots and
cover with the sauce. Sprinkle thickly with the mixed cheese and
breadcrumbs. Pour over the drippings from the grilled bacon and place the
dish under a hot grill until the surface is golden-brown and crisp. Serve
immediately.

Toad-in-the-Hole

METRIC/IMPERIAL
500 g/1 lb pork sausages
1 quantity pancake batter
   (page 133)

AMERICAN
1 lb pork link sausages
1 quantity crêpe batter (page 133)

Place the sausages in a 25 x 30 cm/10 x 12 inch baking pan. Cook in a
preheated hot oven (220°C/425°F, Gas Mark 7) for 10 minutes.

Pour the batter over the sausages and return to the oven. Bake for
30 minutes, then reduce the heat to moderately hot (200°C/400°F, Gas
Mark 6) and bake for a further 15 to 20 minutes.

Egg Croquettes

METRIC/IMPERIAL
4 hard-boiled eggs, shelled and
  chopped
1 egg yolk
salt and freshly ground pepper
FOR THE PANADA:
250 ml/8 fl oz milk
1 slice of onion
3 peppercorns
1 blade of mace
1 small bay leaf
50 g/2 oz butter
50 g/2 oz flour
FOR COATING:
seasoned flour
1 egg, beaten
dry white breadcrumbs
vegetable oil for frying

AMERICAN
4 hard-cooked eggs, shelled and
  chopped
1 egg yolk
salt and freshly ground pepper
FOR THE PANADA:
1 cup milk
1 slice of onion
3 peppercorns
1 blade of mace
1 small bay leaf
¼ cup butter
½ cup flour
FOR COATING:
seasoned flour
1 egg, beaten
dry white bread crumbs
vegetable oil for frying

First make the panada. Put the milk into a saucepan. Add the onion, peppercorns, mace and bay leaf. Bring slowly to the boil then remove from the heat, cover and allow to stand for 10 minutes. Strain and discard the flavourings.

Melt the butter in a clean saucepan over low heat. Stir in the flour and allow to cook for 3 minutes stirring constantly. Gradually add the flavoured milk and bring to the boil, stirring all the time. The mixture should be very thick. Remove from the heat and add the chopped hard-boiled (hard-cooked) eggs, egg yolk and seasoning to taste. Turn the mixture out on a plate to cool then chill well.

Shape into 8 croquettes and coat with the seasoned flour. Dip into the beaten egg and cover evenly with breadcrumbs.

Heat the oil in a deep-fat fryer or saucepan until it is hot enough to turn a stale bread cube golden-brown in 30 seconds (190°C/375°F). Fry the croquettes, 4 at a time, in the hot oil, until golden-brown and crisp. Drain on absorbent kitchen paper and serve hot with a tomato sauce.
Makes 8

Spanish Omelette

METRIC/IMPERIAL
25 g/1 oz butter
2 teaspoons olive or corn oil
1 large onion, thinly sliced
1 large potato, cooked and diced
2 medium tomatoes, skinned and
  chopped
1 red or green pepper, cored,
  seeded and chopped
3 large eggs
2 teaspoons cold water
salt and pepper

AMERICAN
2 tablespoons butter
2 teaspoons olive or corn oil
1 large onion, thinly sliced
1 large potato, cooked and diced
2 medium-size tomatoes, peeled
  and chopped
1 red or green pepper, cored,
  seeded and chopped
3 large eggs
2 teaspoons cold water
salt and pepper

Heat the butter and oil in a frying pan, add the onion and potato and fry until pale gold, turning fairly often. Add the tomatoes and red or green pepper and fry for a further 2 to 3 minutes.

Beat the eggs together with the water, and season to taste with a little salt and pepper. Pour into the frying pan with the vegetables. Cook gently until the base of the omelette is firm. Place the pan under a hot grill (broiler) to cook the top until just set. Slide onto a warmed plate without folding, and cut in half to serve.

Omelette

METRIC/IMPERIAL
3 large eggs
4 teaspoons cold water
salt and pepper
25 g/1 oz butter

AMERICAN
3 large eggs
4 teaspoons cold water
salt and pepper
2 tablespoons butter

Beat the eggs and water together and season to taste with salt and pepper.

Melt the butter in a frying pan until very hot (do not let it brown). Pour in the egg mixture. Cook for about 5 seconds, then move the edges of the setting omelette to the middle of the pan, using a knife or spatula. At the same time, tilt the pan so that the uncooked egg can flow to the edges. Cook for a further minute or until the underside is set and the top is only slightly moist.

Remove from the heat, fold in half and slide out onto a warmed dish. Serve immediately.
Serves 1

VARIATIONS:
Bacon, Mushroom and Onion Omelette – melt 15 g/½ oz (1 tablespoon) butter in a frying pan, add 1 tablespoon each of finely chopped bacon, mushroom and onion and fry until softened. Add to the beaten egg mixture and cook the omelette as above.
Cheese Omelette – make as above, stirring 40 to 50 g/1½ to 2 oz (about ½ cup) finely grated cheese into the egg mixture before cooking as above.
Bacon Omelette – melt 15 g/½ oz (1 tablespoon) butter in a frying pan, add 100 g/4 oz coarsely chopped lean (Canadian) bacon and fry until golden. Make the omelette as above and add the bacon just before folding in half.
Chicken Omelette – make as above, adding 100 g/4 oz (½ cup) diced cooked chicken just before folding the omelette in half.
Croûton Omelette – melt 25 g/1 oz (2 tablespoons) butter, add 1 slice of bread, cut into 5 mm/¼ inch cubes, and fry until golden brown. Make the omelette as above, and add the croûtons just before folding in half.
French Omelette – make as above, and sprinkle with chopped parsley before serving.
Fried Onion Omelette – melt 15 g/½ oz (1 tablespoon) butter in a frying pan, add 1 tablespoon finely chopped onion and fry until golden. Make the omelette as above, adding the onion to the egg mixture.
Ham Omelette – melt 15 g/½ oz (1 tablespoon) butter in a frying pan, add 100 g/4 oz (½ cup) chopped cooked ham and fry until golden. Make the omelette as above, and add the ham just before folding in half.
Tomato Omelette – melt 25 g/1 oz (2 tablespoons) butter in a frying pan, add 100 g/4 oz (½ cup) skinned and chopped tomatoes and heat through. Make the omelette as above and add the tomatoes just before folding.

Ham and Potato Omelette – melt 15 g/½ oz (1 tablespoon) butter in a frying pan, add 2 tablespoons each diced cooked ham and diced potato and fry until soft and golden. Add to the egg mixture before cooking as above.

Kidney Omelette – melt 25 g/1 oz (2 tablespoons) butter in a frying pan, add 100 g/4 oz thinly sliced kidneys and fry until browned. Make the omelette as above and add the kidneys just before folding in half.

Leek and Mushroom Omelette – melt 15 g/½ oz (1 tablespoon) butter in a frying pan, add 1 tablespoon each finely chopped leek, onion and mushroom and fry until softened. Add to the egg mixture before cooking as above.

Mushroom Omelette – melt 25 g/1 oz (2 tablespoons) butter in a frying pan, add 100 g/4 oz (1 cup) sliced mushrooms and fry until tender. Make the omelette as above and add the mushrooms just before folding in half.

Onion Omelette – melt 15 g/½ oz (1 tablespoon) butter in a frying pan, add 1 thinly sliced small onion and fry until pale gold. Make the omelette as above and add the onion just before folding in half.

Parsley Omelette – add 1 tablespoon finely chopped parsley to the beaten egg mixture, then make the omelette as above.

Pancakes (Crêpes)

METRIC/IMPERIAL	AMERICAN
100 g/4 oz flour	*1 cup flour*
large pinch of salt	*large pinch of salt*
1 egg	*1 egg*
300 ml/½ pint milk	*1½ cups milk*
15 g/½ oz butter, melted	*1 tablespoon butter, melted*
melted butter for frying	*melted butter for frying*

Sift the flour and salt into a bowl. Add the egg, half the milk and the melted butter and beat to a smooth, creamy batter. Stir in the remaining milk. Use as required.

To make pancakes (crêpes), brush the bottom of a 15 cm/6 inch frying pan very lightly with melted butter and heat. When hot, pour in just enough of the batter to cover the bottom of the pan thinly and evenly.

Fry until golden brown, then turn over with a spatula, or toss, and cook the other side until golden. Slide out onto a plate and repeat with the remaining batter.

Makes 8 to 10

Bacon and Pineapple Pancakes (Crêpes)

METRIC/IMPERIAL
16 streaky bacon rashers, derinded
1 quantity pancake batter (page 133)
8 canned pineapple rings, halved

AMERICAN
16 bacon slices
1 quantity crêpe batter (page 133)
8 canned pineapple rings

Grill (broil) or fry the bacon and drain on paper towels. Make the pancakes (crêpes). Place two rashers (slices) of bacon on each, roll up and top each with half a canned pineapple ring.

Bacon and Parsley Pancakes (Crêpes)

METRIC/IMPERIAL
350 g/12 oz bacon, derinded and chopped
½ quantity parsley coating sauce (page 242)
1 quantity pancake batter (see page 133)
butter

AMERICAN
¾ lb slab bacon, chopped
½ quantity parsley coating sauce (page 242)
1 quantity crêpe batter (see page 133)
butter

Grill (broil) or fry the bacon and drain on paper towels. Mix with the sauce.
Make the pancakes (crêpes). Stuff with the bacon sauce, roll up and arrange in a baking dish. Top each with a pat of butter. Cover the dish with foil and heat in a preheated moderate oven (180°C/350°F, Gas Mark 4) for 20 minutes.

Ham and Cheese Pancakes (Crêpes)

METRIC/IMPERIAL
1 quantity pancake batter (page 133)
225 g/8 oz lean cooked ham, chopped
½ quantity mornay sauce (page 238)
butter

AMERICAN
1 quantity crêpe batter (page 133)
1 cup chopped lean cooked ham
½ quantity mornay sauce (page 238)
butter

Make the pancakes (crêpes). Mix the ham with the sauce and use to stuff the pancakes (crêpes). Roll up and arrange in a baking dish. Top each with a pat of butter and cover with a lid or foil.
Heat in a preheated moderate oven (180°C/350°F, Gas Mark 4) for 20 minutes.

Brittany Pancakes (Crêpes)

METRIC/IMPERIAL
225 g/8 oz minced beef
1 tablespoon tomato ketchup
1 teaspoon Worcestershire sauce
1 quantity pancake batter (see page 133)
1 x 298 g/10½ oz can condensed cream of tomato, mushroom or other flavour soup

AMERICAN
½ lb ground beef
1 tablespoon tomato ketchup
1 teaspoon Worcestershire sauce
1 quantity crêpe batter (see page 133)
1 x 10½ oz can condensed cream of tomato, mushroom or other flavor soup

Fry the beef until browned and crumbly. Drain off the fat, then mix the ketchup and Worcestershire sauce into the beef.

Make the pancakes (crêpes). Stuff with the beef mixture, roll up and arrange in a baking dish. Pour over the soup (undiluted). Heat in a preheated moderate oven (180°C/350°F, Gas Mark 4) for 20 minutes.

Country Pancakes (Crêpes)

METRIC/IMPERIAL
25 g/1 oz butter
100 g/4 oz mushrooms, chopped
4 large tomatoes, skinned and chopped
1 quantity pancake batter (see page 133)
1 quantity cheese coating sauce (page 242)
150 ml/¼ pint natural yogurt
25 g/1 oz Lancashire cheese, crumbled

AMERICAN
2 tablespoons butter
1 cup chopped mushrooms
4 large tomatoes, peeled and chopped
1 quantity crêpe batter (see page 133)
1 quantity cheese coating sauce (page 242)
⅔ cup plain yogurt
¼ cup grated cheese

Melt the butter in a frying pan, add the mushrooms and tomatoes and fry until the mushrooms are tender.

Make the pancakes (crêpes). Stuff with the mushroom mixture, roll up and arrange in a flameproof dish. Mix the cheese sauce with the yogurt and pour over the pancakes (crêpes). Sprinkle the cheese on top. Brown under a hot grill (broiler) and serve.

Kidney Pancakes (Crêpes)

METRIC/IMPERIAL
1 quantity pancake batter (page 133)
350 g/12 oz kidney, cooked and
chopped
½ quantity hot brown sauce
(page 240)

AMERICAN
1 quantity crêpe batter (page 133)
¾ lb kidney, cooked and chopped
½ quantity hot brown sauce
(page 240)

Make the pancakes (crêpes). Mix the kidney with the sauce and use to stuff the pancakes (crêpes). Roll up and serve.

Miniature Party Pancakes (Crêpes)

METRIC/IMPERIAL
1 quantity pancake batter (page 133)
cottage cheese

AMERICAN
1 quantity crêpe batter (page 133)
cottage cheese

Make the pancakes (crêpes), using only 1 tablespoon batter for each. Spread with cottage cheese, roll up and spear with cocktail sticks.

VARIATION:
Party Pancake (Crêpe) Kebabs – make miniature party pancakes (crêpes) as above, then wrap around cooked cocktail sausages, small grilled (broiled) tomatoes, grilled (broiled) bacon rolls, grilled (broiled) mushrooms and slices of cooked kidney. Spear on to cocktail sticks and serve hot.

Toreador Pancakes (Crêpes)

METRIC/IMPERIAL
15 g/½ oz butter
1 small onion, chopped
225 g/8 oz corned beef, chopped
1 quantity pancake batter (page 133)
1 x 298 g/10½ oz can condensed
tomato soup
crushed potato crisps

AMERICAN
1 tablespoon butter
1 small onion, chopped
1 cup chopped corned beef
1 quantity crêpe batter (page 133)
1 x 10½ oz can condensed tomato
soup
crushed potato chips

Melt the butter in a frying pan, add the onion and fry until pale gold. Mix in the corned beef and keep hot.

Make the pancakes (crêpes). Stuff with the corned beef mixture, roll up and arrange in a baking dish. Coat with the undiluted soup and sprinkle the crisps (potato chips) on top.

Heat in a preheated moderately hot oven (190°C/375°F, Gas Mark 5) for 15 to 20 minutes.

Tuna and Cucumber Pancakes (Crêpes)

METRIC/IMPERIAL
1 x 200 g/7 oz can tuna fish,
    drained
4 tablespoons natural yogurt
1 quantity pancake batter
    (page 133)
1 quantity cucumber sauce
    (page 238)
toasted breadcrumbs

AMERICAN
1 x 7 oz can tuna fish, drained
1/4 cup plain yogurt
1 quantity crêpe batter (page 133)
1 quantity cucumber sauce
    (page 238)
toasted bread crumbs

Mash the tuna with the yogurt. Make the pancakes (crêpes), stuff with the tuna mixture and roll up. Arrange in a baking dish. Coat with the sauce and sprinkle breadcrumbs on top.

Heat in a preheated moderate oven (180°C/350°F, Gas Mark 4) for 20 minutes.

Basic Savoury Fritters

METRIC/IMPERIAL
50 g/2 oz plain flour
1/4 teaspoon salt
1 egg
15 g/1/2 oz butter, melted
100 ml/4 fl oz flat beer
1 egg white
vegetable oil for frying

AMERICAN
1/2 cup all-purpose flour
1/4 teaspoon salt
1 egg
1 tablespoon butter, melted
1/2 cup flat beer
1 egg white
vegetable oil for frying

Sift the flour and salt into a bowl. Beat the egg lightly and stir in the melted butter. Pour this mixture into the flour with the beer and beat until just smooth. Allow the batter to stand at room temperature for 1 hour if you have time. Stiffly whisk the egg white and fold into the batter.

Heat the oil in a deep-fat fryer or saucepan until it is hot enough to turn a stale bread cube golden in 30 seconds (190°C/375°F). Drop tablespoonfuls of the mixture into the hot oil, a few at a time, and fry until crisp and golden-brown. Remove and drain on absorbent kitchen paper. Transfer to a warm serving dish and serve hot, sprinkled with crumbled Danish blue or grated hard cheese.

VARIATIONS:
Salami Fritters – remove the rind and finely chop 75 g/3 oz continental sausage (Salami, Mortadella or Cervelat). Stir this into the basic batter, drop by spoonfuls and fry as Basic savoury fritters.
Chicken Fritters – very finely chop 100 g/4 oz cooked chicken. Stir into the basic batter with 1 tablespoon grated mild onion and a little freshly ground black pepper. Drop by spoonfuls and fry as Basic savoury fritters.

Cheese and Rice Hot Pot

METRIC/IMPERIAL
225–350 g/8–12 oz rice
salt and pepper
25 g/1 oz butter
1 medium onion, chopped
1 quantity white coating sauce
  (page 242)
2 tablespoons tomato purée
225 g/8 oz cottage cheese
50 g/2 oz hazelnuts, chopped
50 g/2 oz Lancashire cheese,
  crumbled
1 tomato, sliced
parsley to garnish

AMERICAN
1–1½ cups rice
salt and pepper
2 tablespoons butter
1 medium-size onion, chopped
1 quantity white coating sauce
  (page 242)
2 tablespoons tomato paste
1 cup cottage cheese
½ cup chopped hazelnuts
½ cup grated cheese
1 tomato, sliced
parsley for garnish

Cook the rice in boiling salted water until tender. Drain if necessary. Melt the butter in a frying pan, add the onion and fry until softened. Stir the rice and fried onion into the sauce and add the tomato purée (paste), cottage cheese and hazelnuts. Mix well together and season to taste with salt and pepper.

Pour into a buttered 1.2 litre/2 pint (5 cup) baking dish and sprinkle the cheese on top. Bake in a preheated moderately hot oven (190°C/375°F, Gas Mark 5) for 25 to 30 minutes or until golden. Arrange the tomato slices on top and garnish with parsley. Serve hot.

Welsh Rarebit

METRIC/IMPERIAL
4 large slices of bread
25 g/1 oz butter, softened
¼ teaspoon salt
pinch of cayenne pepper
1 teaspoon made mustard
175 g/6 oz Cheddar cheese, grated
2 tablespoons milk
¼ teaspoon Worcestershire sauce

AMERICAN
4 large slices of bread
2 tablespoons butter, softened
¼ teaspoon salt
pinch of cayenne
1 teaspoon prepared mustard
1½ cups grated Cheddar cheese
2 tablespoons milk
¼ teaspoon Worcestershire sauce

Toast the bread on one side only. Cream the butter well, then beat in the salt, cayenne pepper, mustard, cheese, milk and Worcestershire sauce.

Spread equal amounts of the mixture thickly over the untoasted sides of the bread. Put under a preheated hot grill (broiler) and cook until brown.

VARIATIONS:
Buck Rarebit – top each serving with a hot poached egg.
Tomato Rarebit – top each serving with 3 to 4 slices of fried or grilled (broiled) tomatoes.
Bacon Rarebit – top each serving with 2 grilled (broiled) or fried bacon rashers (slices).

Cheese Roll Puffs

METRIC/IMPERIAL
50 g/2 oz luncheon meat, chopped
1 small celery stalk, chopped
1 large hard-boiled egg, chopped
2 tablespoons sweet pickle
4 tablespoons double cream
4 large soft rolls
175 g/6 oz Cheddar cheese, grated
1 teaspoon made mustard
1 egg, beaten
salt and pepper

AMERICAN
½ cup chopped luncheon meat
1 small celery stalk, chopped
1 large hard-cooked egg, chopped
2 tablespoons pickle relish
¼ cup heavy cream
4 large soft rolls
1½ cups grated Cheddar cheese
1 teaspoon prepared mustard
1 egg, beaten
salt and pepper

Mix together the luncheon meat, celery and egg with the sweet pickle (relish) and 2 tablespoons of the cream. Cut each of the rolls in half and spread with the meat mixture. Arrange on a lightly buttered baking sheet.

Mix the cheese with the rest of the cream, the mustard and egg. Season to taste with salt and pepper. Spoon carefully over the roll halves on top of the meat mixture. Bake in a preheated moderately hot oven (200°C/400°F, Gas Mark 6) for 10 to 15 minutes or until golden brown and fluffy. Serve immediately.

Gloucester Pie

METRIC/IMPERIAL
150 g/5 oz butter
8 slices of bread, crusts removed
100 g/4 oz double Gloucester
   cheese, thinly sliced
225 g/8 oz tomatoes, skinned and
   thinly sliced
1 egg
150 ml/¼ pint milk
1 teaspoon made mustard
salt and pepper

AMERICAN
10 tablespoons butter
8 slices of bread, crusts removed
¼ lb cheese, thinly sliced
½ lb tomatoes, peeled and thinly
   sliced
1 egg
¾ cup milk
1 teaspoon prepared mustard
salt and pepper

Butter the bread thickly, using 100 g/4 oz (½ cup) of the butter. Sandwich together in pairs, with the cheese and tomatoes. Cut each sandwich into four triangles and arrange in a shallow buttered baking dish.

Beat the egg with the milk, mustard and salt and pepper to taste. Pour over the sandwiches in the dish and leave to stand for 30 minutes or until the bread has absorbed all the milky liquid. Dot the top of the sandwiches with the remaining butter.

Bake in a preheated moderately hot oven (190°C/375°F, Gas Mark 5) for 25 to 30 minutes or until the top is crisp and golden.

Cheese Soufflé

METRIC/IMPERIAL
40 g/1½ oz butter
2 tablespoons flour
300 ml/½ pint hot milk
4 eggs, separated
100 g/4 oz Cheddar cheese, grated
salt and freshly ground black
   pepper
pinch of grated nutmeg

AMERICAN
3 tablespoons butter
2 tablespoons flour
1¼ cups hot milk
4 eggs, separated
1 cup grated Cheddar cheese
salt and freshly ground black
   pepper
pinch of grated nutmeg

Melt the butter in a saucepan. Add the flour and stir over moderate heat for 1 minute. Gradually add the milk and bring to the boil, stirring constantly. Cook for 2 minutes. Remove from the heat, and beat in the egg yolks one at a time. Stir in the cheese and the seasonings. Replace over heat and stir constantly for 1 minute. Stiffly whisk the egg whites, remove the pan from the heat and fold a little egg white into the cheese mixture. Quickly but thoroughly fold in the rest of the egg white, making sure that all the cheese mixture at the bottom of the saucepan is blended in. Have ready a 15 cm/6 inch soufflé dish, well buttered. If liked, sprinkle a little extra grated cheese into the base of the soufflé dish. Turn the mixture into it and bake in a fairly hot oven (200°C/400°F, Gas Mark 6) for about 25 minutes, or until golden-brown and just firm.

Macaroni Cheese

METRIC/IMPERIAL
75 g/3 oz broken macaroni
salt and pepper
20 g/¾ oz butter
20 g/¾ oz flour
½ teaspoon dry mustard
300 ml/½ pint milk
175 g/6 oz Cheddar cheese, grated
parsley to garnish

AMERICAN
3 oz broken macaroni — 9 ozs.
salt and pepper
1½ tablespoons butter 2¼ ozs.
3 tablespoons flour 2¼ ozs.
½ teaspoon dry mustard
1¼ cups milk 1½ PTS.
1½ cups grated Cheddar cheese ABOUT 1 POUND.
parsley for garnish

Cook the macaroni in boiling salted water for 15 minutes or until tender.
Meanwhile, melt the butter in a saucepan. Add the flour and mustard and cook gently for 2 minutes, stirring all the time. Do not let the mixture brown. Gradually stir in the milk and cook, stirring, until the sauce boils and thickens. Simmer for 2 minutes, then remove from the heat and stir in 100 g/4 oz (1 cup) of the cheese. Season to taste with salt and pepper.
Drain the macaroni. Add it to the sauce and mix well. Pour into a buttered 900 ml/1½ pint (1 quart) flameproof dish and sprinkle with the rest of the cheese. Place under a preheated hot grill (broiler) and cook until the cheese is melted and golden brown. Garnish with parsley and serve.

Marrow (Squash) Cheese

METRIC/IMPERIAL
1 medium marrow, peeled, seeded
   and cubed
2 large onions, sliced into rings
salt
100 g/4 oz Lancashire cheese,
   crumbled
1 quantity white coating sauce
   (page 242)
2 tablespoons toasted
   breadcrumbs
25 g/1 oz butter

AMERICAN
1 medium-size summer squash,
   peeled, seeded and cubed
2 large onions, sliced into rings
salt
1 cup grated cheese
1 quantity white coating sauce
   (page 242)
2 tablespoons toasted bread
   crumbs
2 tablespoons butter

Steam the marrow (squash) cubes over boiling water until they are only just tender. Cook the onion rings in boiling salted water until soft. Drain.
Arrange half the marrow (squash) over the bottom of a buttered 1.2 litre/2 pint (1 quart) baking dish. Cover with all the onions and half the cheese and top with the rest of the marrow (squash). Coat with the sauce and sprinkle the rest of the cheese and all the breadcrumbs over the top. Dot with the butter.
Bake in a preheated hot oven (220°C/425°F, Gas Mark 7) for 15 minutes or until the top is light brown.

Cheese and Potato Pasties

METRIC/IMPERIAL
225 g/8 oz flour
pinch of salt
100 g/4 oz lard, cut into pieces
2–3 tablespoons cold water
FOR THE FILLING:
2 medium potatoes, peeled and
   chopped
1 teaspoon grated onion
100 g/4 oz Cheddar cheese, diced
salt and freshly ground black
   pepper
pinch of dried sage (optional)

AMERICAN
2 cups flour
pinch of salt
½ cup shortening
2–3 tablespoons cold water
FOR THE FILLING:
2 medium-size potatoes, peeled
   and chopped
1 teaspoon grated onion
⅔ cup diced Cheddar cheese
salt and freshly ground black
   pepper
pinch of dried sage (optional)

Sift the flour and salt into a bowl. Rub in the lard (shortening) until the mixture resembles fine breadcrumbs. Stir in just sufficient water to hold the mixture together, then form into a smooth ball. Wrap in foil or greaseproof (waxed) paper and chill in the refrigerator for 30 minutes.

Roll out the pastry on a floured surface and cut out 4 rounds using a saucer. Mix the filling ingredients together and place an equal amount in the centre of each circle. Dampen the edges, draw the opposite edges together over the centres and pinch firmly together to seal.

Place the pasties on a greased baking sheet and bake in a fairly hot oven (200°/400°F, Gas Mark 6) for 30 minutes. Serve hot or cold.

Potato, Cheese and Onion Pie

METRIC/IMPERIAL
750 g/1½ lb potatoes
salt and pepper
4 tablespoons milk
1 egg, beaten
175 g/6 oz cheese, grated
1 teaspoon dry mustard
1 medium onion, boiled and finely
   chopped
3 tablespoons finely chopped
   parsley
½ teaspoon yeast extract

AMERICAN
1½ lb potatoes
salt and pepper
¼ cup milk
1 egg, beaten
1½ cups grated cheese
1 teaspoon dry mustard
1 medium-size onion, boiled and
   finely chopped
3 tablespoons finely chopped
   parsley
½ teaspoon brewer's yeast

Cook the potatoes in boiling salted water until tender. Drain and mash well with the milk, egg, 100 g/4 oz (1 cup) of the cheese, the mustard, onion, parsley and yeast extract (brewer's yeast). Season to taste.

Pour into buttered 1.2 litre/2 pint (1 quart) baking dish and sprinkle the rest of the cheese on top. Bake in a preheated hot oven (220°C/425°F, Gas Mark 7) for 15 minutes or until the top is light brown.

Macaroni Cheese Balls with Spanish Sauce

METRIC/IMPERIAL
225 g/8 oz short-cut macaroni
50 g/2 oz butter
50 g/2 oz plain flour
300 ml/½ pint milk
½ teaspoon salt
½ teaspoon dry mustard
225 g/8 oz cheese, grated
2 eggs, beaten
vegetable oil for frying
FOR THE COATING:
2 eggs, beaten
175 g/6 oz dry breadcrumbs
FOR THE SAUCE:
4 tablespoons vegetable oil
1 onion, peeled and finely chopped
2 cloves of garlic, crushed
1 small green pepper, cored,
  seeded and chopped
1 x 396 g/14 oz can tomatoes
1 teaspoon dried mixed herbs
salt and freshly ground black
  pepper
2 teaspoons cornflour

AMERICAN
2 cups elbow macaroni
¼ cup butter
½ cup all-purpose flour
1¼ cups milk
½ teaspoon salt
½ teaspoon dry mustard
2 cups grated cheese
2 eggs, beaten
vegetable oil for frying
FOR THE COATING:
2 eggs, beaten
1½ cups dried bread crumbs
FOR THE SAUCE:
4 tablespoons vegetable oil
1 onion, peeled and finely chopped
2 cloves garlic, crushed
1 small green pepper, seeded and
  chopped
1 can (16 oz) tomatoes
1 teaspoon dried mixed herbs
salt and freshly ground black
  pepper
2 teaspoons cornstarch

Cook the macaroni in plenty of boiling lightly salted water. Drain well. Place the butter, flour, milk, salt and mustard together in a saucepan and whisk over moderate heat until the mixture comes to the boil. Cook for 2 minutes. Remove from the heat and add the cheese. Stir in the beaten eggs and the macaroni. Allow to become almost cold and then divide the mixture into 12 to 16 equal portions. With clean wet hands shape each portion into a ball and coat with the beaten eggs and then the breadcrumbs. The balls must be completely coated so repeat the process if necessary.

To make the sauce, heat the oil in a saucepan. Add the chopped onion and the crushed garlic and fry until the onion is soft but not browned. Add the chopped pepper, tomatoes and their liquid and the herbs. Season to taste. Moisten the cornflour (cornstarch) with a little cold water and stir into the tomato mixture. Bring to the boil, stirring constantly, reduce the heat and simmer for 15 minutes.

To fry the macaroni cheese balls, heat the oil in a deep-fat fryer or saucepan until it is hot enough to turn a stale bread cube golden-brown in 45 seconds (185°C/360°F). Fry the balls, a few at a time, until golden-brown. Pile up on a warm serving dish and hand the sauce separately.

143

Apple Fritters

METRIC/IMPERIAL
3 medium cooking apples, peeled,
    cored and cut into 5 mm/¼ inch
    thick rings
1 quantity sweet fritter batter
    (page 253)
oil for deep frying
sifted icing sugar

AMERICAN
3 medium-size tart apples, peeled,
    cored and cut into ¼ inch thick
    rings
1 quantity sweet fritter batter
    (page 253)
oil for deep frying
sifted confectioners' sugar

Coat the apple rings with the batter and deep fry for 2 to 3 minutes. Drain
on paper towels. Dredge with icing (confectioners') sugar and serve hot.

Apple Charlotte

METRIC/IMPERIAL
grated rind of 1 medium lemon
100 g/4 oz caster sugar
100 g/4 oz fresh white
    breadcrumbs
500 g/1 lb cooking apples, peeled,
    cored and sliced
75 g/3 oz butter, melted

AMERICAN
grated rind of 1 medium-size lemon
½ cup sugar
2 cups soft white bread crumbs
1 lb tart apples, peeled, cored and
    sliced
6 tablespoons butter, melted

Mix the lemon rind, sugar and breadcrumbs together well. Fill a buttered
1.2 litre/2 pint (5 cup) baking dish with layers of the breadcrumb mixture
and apples, beginning and ending with a layer of the breadcrumb mixture
and sprinkling the melted butter between the layers.
    Bake in a preheated moderately hot oven (190°C/375°F, Gas Mark 5) for
45 minutes to 1 hour or until the top is golden brown and the apples are
tender.

Baked Apple Dumplings

METRIC/IMPERIAL
40 g/1½ oz granulated sugar
½ teaspoon grated lemon rind
4 medium cooking apples, peeled
    and cored
225 g/8 oz quantity shortcrust
    pastry (page 246)
milk
sifted icing sugar

AMERICAN
3 tablespoons granulated sugar
½ teaspoon grated lemon rind
4 medium-size tart apples, peeled
    and cored
2 cup quantity pie pastry
    (page 246)
milk
sifted confectioners' sugar

Mix the granulated sugar with the lemon rind and put equal amounts into the centre hole of each apple. Cut the dough (before rolling) into four pieces and roll out each into a round big enough to enclose an apple.

Place the apples on the middle of the dough rounds, dampen the edges and wrap the dough around the apples, pressing the edges well together. Arrange on a lightly buttered baking sheet, brush with the milk and make a small slit in the top of each dumpling.

Bake in a preheated hot oven (220°C/425°F, Gas Mark 7) for 15 minutes, then reduce the heat to moderate (180°C/350°F, Gas Mark 4) and bake for a further 30 minutes. Remove from the oven and dredge with icing sugar.

Apple Batter Pudding

METRIC/IMPERIAL
50 g/2 oz butter
500 g/1 lb cooking apples, peeled,
    cored and sliced
100 g/4 oz caster sugar
1 teaspoon ground cinnamon
1 quantity pancake batter
    (page 133)

AMERICAN
¼ cup butter
1 lb tart apples, peeled, cored and
    sliced
½ cup sugar
1 teaspoon ground cinnamon
1 quantity crêpe batter (page 133)

Place the butter in a baking pan and melt in a preheated hot oven (220°C/425°F, Gas Mark 7). Scatter the apples over the bottom of the pan and sprinkle with the sugar and cinnamon. Pour in the batter.

Return to the oven and bake for 30 minutes, then reduce the heat to moderately hot (200°C/400°F, Gas Mark 6) and bake for a further 15 to 20 minutes.

VARIATIONS:
Dried Fruit Batter Pudding – make as above, using 100 g/4 oz (⅔ cup) mixed dried fruit instead of the apples, and sprinkling the fruit with 50 g/ 2 oz (¼ cup) caster sugar and 1 teaspoon finely grated lemon rind.
Rhubarb Batter Pudding – make as above, using 500 g/1 lb rhubarb, cut into 5 cm/2 inch pieces, instead of the apples, and ground ginger instead of cinnamon.

Apple Turnovers

METRIC/IMPERIAL
225 g/8 oz quantity rough puff
    pastry (page 247)
225 g/8 oz cooking apples, peeled,
    cored and sliced
50 g/2 oz caster sugar
little egg white, lightly beaten
extra caster sugar for sprinkling

AMERICAN
2 cup quantity rough puff pastry
    (page 247)
½ lb tart apples, peeled, cored and
    sliced
¼ cup sugar
little egg white, lightly beaten
extra sugar for sprinkling

Roll out the dough and cut into six 10 cm/4 inch squares. Mix the apples with the sugar and spread equal amounts onto the middle of each dough square. Dampen the edges of the dough and fold each square in half to make a triangle. Press the edges down firmly and ridge using the back of a knife. Brush the tops with the beaten egg white and sprinkle extra sugar on top.

    Put on a lightly buttered baking sheet and bake in a preheated hot oven (220°C/425°F, Gas Mark 7) for 20 minutes. Reduce the heat to moderate (180°C/350°F, Gas Mark 4) and bake for a further 20 minutes.
Makes 6

Apple Amber

METRIC/IMPERIAL
500 g/1 lb cooking apples, peeled,
    cored and sliced
1 tablespoon water
25 g/1 oz butter
2 egg yolks
25–75 g/2–3 oz caster sugar
1 teaspoon ground cinnamon
3 tablespoons stale cake crumbs
1 quantity meringue topping
    (page 250)

AMERICAN
1 lb tart apples, peeled, cored and
    sliced
1 tablespoon water
2 tablespoons butter
2 egg yolks
4–6 tablespoons sugar
1 teaspoon ground cinnamon
3 tablespoons stale cake crumbs
1 quantity meringue topping
    (page 250)

Place the apples in a saucepan with the water and butter and cook until pulpy and soft. Beat until quite smooth. Add the egg yolks, sugar, cinnamon and cake crumbs and mix well together.

    Put into a 600 ml/1 pint (2½ cup) baking dish and cover with the meringue topping. Bake in a preheated cool oven (150°/300°F, Gas Mark 2) for 30 minutes or until the meringue is a light gold.

Baked Apples with Syrup and Lemon

METRIC/IMPERIAL
4 cooking apples, cored
½ teaspoon finely grated lemon
  rind
1 tablespoon golden syrup
25 g/1 oz butter
3 tablespoons warm water

AMERICAN
4 tart apples, cored
½ teaspoon finely grated lemon
  rind
1 tablespoon corn syrup
2 tablespoons butter
3 tablespoons warm water

With a sharp knife, score a line around each of the apples about one-third of the way down. Stand the apples in a baking dish.

Mix the lemon rind and syrup together well and spoon equal amounts into the centre hole in each apple. Top with a large knob of butter and pour the water into the dish.

Bake in a preheated moderate oven (180°C/350°F, Gas Mark 4) for 45 minutes to 1 hour or until the apples are puffed up and tender. Using the water in the dish, baste the apples at least three times during baking or they may split open.

Apple Charlotte with Brown Breadcrumbs

METRIC/IMPERIAL
500 g/1 lb cooking apples, peeled,
  cored and sliced
2 tablespoons water
100 g/4 oz soft brown sugar
100 g/4 oz fresh brown
  breadcrumbs
2 tablespoons demerara sugar
½ teaspoon ground cinnamon
2 tablespoons shredded beef suet

AMERICAN
1 lb tart apples, peeled, cored and
  sliced
2 tablespoons water
⅔ cup firmly packed light brown
  sugar
2 cups soft brown bread crumbs
2 tablespoons brown or raw sugar
½ teaspoon ground cinnamon
2 tablespoons shredded beef suet

Put the sliced apples into a saucepan with the water and simmer for 10 to 15 minutes until tender. Sweeten with the soft (light) brown sugar.

Mix breadcrumbs, demerara (brown or raw) sugar and cinnamon.

Place half the sweetened apple in a greased pie dish. Cover with half the crumb mixture, then the rest of the apple and finally top with the remaining crumb mixture. Sprinkle the surface with the shredded suet.

Cover the dish with greased greaseproof (waxed) paper or foil and bake in a moderate oven (180°C/350°F, Gas Mark 4) for 30 to 40 minutes. Serve very hot with custard or cream.

Fresh Fruit Suet Pudding

METRIC/IMPERIAL
750 g/1 ½ lb fresh fruit
225 g/8 oz quantity suet crust
  pastry (page 248)
100–150 g/4–5 oz soft brown sugar
1 tablespoon fresh white
  breadcrumbs
1 tablespoon water

AMERICAN
1 ½ lb fresh fruit
2 cup quantity suet crust pastry
  (page 248)
½–⅔ cup firmly packed brown
  sugar
1 tablespoon soft white bread
  crumbs
1 tablespoon water

Prepare the fruit according to type. Roll out two-thirds of the pastry dough and use to line a buttered 1.2 litre/2 pint pudding basin (5 cup steaming mold). Fill with alternate layers of sugar, breadcrumbs and fruit, beginning and ending with breadcrumbs. Pour in the water.

Dampen the edges of the dough. Roll out the remaining dough, place on top of the basin (mold) and press the edges firmly together.

Cover firmly with buttered greaseproof (parchment) paper or foil. Steam steadily for 2½ to 3 hours. Serve from the basin (mold), with a table napkin wrapped around it.

Queen of Puddings

METRIC/IMPERIAL
25 g/1 oz caster sugar
1 teaspoon finely grated lemon rind
75 g/3 oz fresh white breadcrumbs
450 ml/¾ pint milk
25 g/1 oz butter
2 egg yolks
2 tablespoons warmed raspberry
  jam
1 quantity meringue topping
  (page 250)

AMERICAN
2 tablespoons sugar
1 teaspoon finely grated lemon rind
1 ½ cups soft white bread crumbs
2 cups milk
2 tablespoons butter
2 egg yolks
2 tablespoons warmed raspberry
  jam
1 quantity meringue topping
  (page 250)

Put the suger, lemon rind and breadcrumbs in a mixing bowl and toss lightly to mix. Pour the milk into a saucepan, add the butter and heat slowly until the butter melts. Pour over the breadcrumb mixture and leave to stand for about 30 minutes.

Beat the egg yolks into the crumb mixture and spread in a buttered 900 ml/1½ pint (1 quart) baking dish. Bake in a preheated moderate oven (160°C/325°F, Gas Mark 3) for 30 minutes, or until the base is firm and set.

Remove from the oven and spread over the warmed jam. Cover with whirls of the meringue topping. Return to the oven and bake for a further 30 to 40 minutes or until pale gold.

Cabinet Pudding

METRIC/IMPERIAL
6 trifle sponge cakes
50 g/2 oz glacé cherries, chopped
25 g/1 oz caster sugar
1 teaspoon vanilla essence
2 large eggs
600 ml/1 pint milk

AMERICAN
6 individual dessert sponge shells
⅓ cup chopped glacé cherries
2 tablespoons sugar
1 teaspoon vanilla extract
2 large eggs
2½ cups milk

Cut each of the sponge cakes into 6 cubes. Put the cake cubes and cherries in a bowl and add the sugar. Toss lightly to mix well. Beat the vanilla essence (extract), eggs and milk together well and slowly stir into the cake mixture. Leave to stand for 30 minutes.

Pour into a buttered 900 ml/1½ pint pudding basin (1 quart steaming mold) and cover well with greaseproof (parchment) paper or buttered foil. Steam for 1 hour. Turn out very carefully onto a warmed serving plate to serve.

Roly-Poly Pudding

METRIC/IMPERIAL
225 g/8 oz quantity suet crust
   pastry (page 248)
3–4 tablespoons jam, golden syrup
   or treacle
1 teaspoon finely grated lemon rind

AMERICAN
2 cup quantity suet crust pastry
   (page 248)
3–4 tablespoons jam, maple syrup
   or molasses
1 teaspoon finely grated lemon rind

Roll out the pastry dough into an oblong, about 25 x 20 cm/10 x 8 inches. Spread with the jam, syrup or treacle (molasses) to within 2.5 cm/1 inch of the edges. Sprinkle the lemon rind on top. Dampen the edges with a little water and roll up loosely like a Swiss (jelly) roll, starting at one of the shorter sides. Press the edges well together.

With the join underneath, wrap loosely in foil. Twist the ends of the foil so that they stay closed. Steam for 2½ to 3 hours.

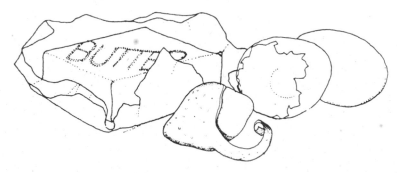

Baked Rice Pudding

METRIC/IMPERIAL	AMERICAN
50 g/2 oz pudding rice	¼ cup short-grain rice
600 ml/1 pint milk	2½ cups milk
25 g/1 oz caster sugar	2 tablespoons sugar
1 strip of lemon rind	1 strip of lemon rind
grated nutmeg	grated nutmeg
15 g/½ oz butter	1 tablespoon butter

Put the rice into a buttered 900 ml/1½ pint (1 quart) baking dish and stir in the milk. Leave for 30 minutes.

Add the sugar and lemon rind and stir well. Sprinkle the top with nutmeg and dot with the butter.

Bake in a preheated cool oven (150°C/300°F, Gas Mark 2) for 2 to 2½ hours. Stir the skin into the pudding at least three times during the first hour.

Sago Pudding

METRIC/IMPERIAL	AMERICAN
600 ml/1 pint milk	2½ cups milk
40 g/1½ oz sago	¼ cup pearl sago
25 g/1 oz caster sugar	2 tablespoons sugar
15 g/½ oz butter	1 tablespoon butter

Pour the milk into a saucepan and heat until lukewarm. Sprinkle in the sago and cook gently, stirring, until the mixture comes to the boil and thickens.

Add the sugar and butter and cook very gently for a further 5 to 7 minutes, stirring frequently.

VARIATION:
Semolina Pudding – make as above using semolina (or cream of wheat) instead of sago.

Sponge Pudding

METRIC/IMPERIAL	AMERICAN
100 g/4 oz self-raising flour	*1 cup self-rising flour*
pinch of salt	*pinch of salt*
100 g/4 oz butter	*½ cup butter*
½ teaspoon vanilla essence	*½ teaspoon vanilla extract*
100 g/4 oz caster sugar	*½ cup sugar*
2 large eggs	*2 large eggs*
2 tablespoons cold milk	*2 tablespoons cold milk*

Sift the flour and salt into a mixing bowl. Cream the butter, vanilla essence (extract) and sugar together until light and fluffy. Beat the eggs into the creamed mixture one at a time, adding a tablespoon of the flour mixture with each. Fold in the rest of the flour mixture and slowly mix in the milk.

Pour the mixture into a buttered 1.2 litre/2 pint (5 cup) pie dish and bake in a preheated moderate oven (180°F/350°F, Gas Mark 4) for 45 minutes to 1 hour or until a skewer inserted into the pudding comes out clean.

VARIATIONS:
Chocolate Sponge Pudding – make as above, sifting 15 g/½ oz (2 tablespoons) each cocoa powder and cornflour (cornstarch) with the flour.
Fruit Sponge Pudding – make as above, stirring in 50 g/2 oz (⅓ cup) dried fruit after the milk and egg.
Jam Sponge Pudding – make as above, placing 2 tablespoons jam in the bottom of the dish before adding the mixture.

Bread and Butter Pudding

METRIC/IMPERIAL	AMERICAN
6 thin slices of white bread, crusts removed	*6 thin slices of white bread, crusts removed*
50 g/2 oz butter	*¼ cup butter*
40 g/1½ oz caster sugar	*3 tablespoons sugar*
50 g/2 oz dried fruit	*⅓ cup dried fruit*
600 ml/1 pint milk	*2½ cups milk*
2 large eggs	*2 large eggs*

Spread the bread thickly with the butter and cut into small squares. Put half the squares into a buttered 1.2 litre/2 pint (5 cup) baking dish and sprinkle with half the sugar and all the fruit. Cover with the rest of the buttered bread, putting the buttered sides facing upwards. Sprinkle with the rest of the sugar.

Beat the milk and eggs well together and strain into the dish over the bread. Leave to stand for 30 minutes.

Bake in a preheated moderate oven (160°C/325°F, Gas Mark 3) for 45 minutes to 1 hour or until set and the top is golden and crisp.

Baked Egg Custard

METRIC/IMPERIAL	AMERICAN
3 large eggs	3 large eggs
600 ml/1 pint milk	2½ cups milk
25 g/1 oz caster sugar	2 tablespoons sugar
grated nutmeg	grated nutmeg

Beat the eggs with the milk and strain into a buttered 900 ml/1½ pint (1 quart) baking dish. Stir in the sugar. Sprinkle the grated nutmeg on top. Place the dish in a roasting pan containing enough water to come halfway up the sides of the dish.

Bake in a preheated moderate oven (160°C/325°F, Gas Mark 3) for 45 minutes to 1 hour or until the egg custard has set and is firm to touch.

Eve's Pudding

METRIC/IMPERIAL	AMERICAN
500 g/1 lb cooking apples, peeled, cored and thinly sliced	1 lb tart apples, peeled, cored and thinly sliced
75–100 g/3–4 oz caster sugar	6–8 tablespoons sugar
1 quantity sponge pudding mixture (see page 151)	1 quantity sponge pudding batter (see page 151)

Arrange the apples in layers in a buttered 1.5 litre/2½ pint (1½ quart) pie dish, sprinkling the sugar between the layers. Cover with the sponge pudding mixture.

Bake in a preheated moderate oven (180°C/350°F, Gas Mark 4) for 1 to 1¼ hours or until a skewer inserted into the middle comes out clean.

Fruit Crumble

METRIC/IMPERIAL	AMERICAN
500 g/1 lb fresh fruit	1 lb fresh fruit
175–250 g/6–9 oz caster sugar	¾–1 cup sugar
175 g/6 oz flour	1½ cups flour
75 g/3 oz butter	6 tablespoons butter

Prepare the fruit according to type. Put into a 1.2 litre/2 pint (5 cup) baking dish in layers with 100 to 175 g/4 to 6 oz (½ to ¾ cup) of the sugar.

Sift the flour into a mixing bowl and rub in the butter finely. Add the remaining sugar and toss together to mix well. Sprinkle the crumble mixture over the fruit and press down tightly using the back of a knife.

Bake in a preheated moderately hot oven (190°C/375°F, Gas Mark 5) for 15 minutes, then lower the heat to moderate (180°C/350°F, Gas Mark 4) and bake for a further 45 minutes or until the top is light brown.

Popovers

METRIC/IMPERIAL
50 g/2 oz flour
pinch of salt
1 small egg
150 ml/¼ pint milk
40 g/1½ oz butter, melted

AMERICAN
½ cup flour
pinch of salt
1 small egg
¾ cup milk
3 tablespoons butter, melted

Sift the flour and salt into a mixing bowl. Add the egg and milk and beat to a smooth, creamy batter.

Pour a small amount of the melted butter into 12 deep bun (muffin) tins. Heat in a preheated hot oven (220°C/425°F, Gas Mark 7) for about 4 minutes, then spoon about 1 tablespoon of the batter into each tin. Bake for about 20 minutes and serve hot.

VARIATION:
Fruit Popovers – make as above, adding ½ teaspoon currants to each tin before pouring in the batter.

Chocolate Pudding

METRIC/IMPERIAL
150 g/5 oz self-raising flour
15 g/½ oz cocoa powder
pinch of salt
15 g/½ oz cornflour
75 g/3 oz butter
75 g/3 oz caster sugar
5–6 tablespoons cold milk
1 large egg, beaten

AMERICAN
1¼ cups self-rising flour
2 tablespoons cocoa powder
pinch of salt
2 tablespoons cornstarch
6 tablespoons butter
6 tablespoons sugar
5–6 tablespoons cold milk
1 large egg, beaten

Sift the flour, cocoa powder, salt and cornflour (cornstarch) into a mixing bowl. Rub in the butter finely. Stir in the sugar. Mix to a soft mixture using the milk and egg.

Pour into a buttered 1.2 litre/2 pint pudding basin (5 cup steaming mold) and cover well with buttered greaseproof (parchment) paper or foil. Steam for 1½ to 2 hours or until the pudding has risen well and is firm. Turn out onto a warmed serving plate to serve.

VARIATIONS:
Coconut Pudding – make as above, omitting the cocoa powder and cornflour (cornstarch). Add 40 to 50 g/1½ to 2 oz desiccated coconut (½ cup shredded coconut) with the sugar, and 1 teaspoon vanilla essence (extract) with the milk and egg.
Plain Family Pudding – make as above, omitting the cocoa powder and cornflour (cornstarch) and increasing the flour to 175 g/6 oz (1½ cups).

Steamed Suet Pudding

METRIC/IMPERIAL
100 g/4 oz flour
1½ teaspoons baking powder
¼ teaspoon salt
100 g/4 oz fresh white
*   breadcrumbs*
75 g/3 oz shredded suet
75 g/3 oz caster sugar
6–8 tablespoons cold milk
1 large egg, beaten

AMERICAN
1 cup flour
1½ teaspoons baking powder
¼ teaspoon salt
2 cups soft white bread crumbs
⅓ cup shredded suet
6 tablespoons sugar
6–8 tablespoons cold milk
1 large egg, beaten

Sift the flour, baking powder and salt into a mixing bowl. Add the breadcrumbs, suet and sugar and stir well. Mix to a soft batter with the milk and egg.

Pour into a lightly buttered 1.2 litre/2 pint pudding basin (5 cup steaming mold) and cover well with buttered greaseproof (parchment) paper or foil. Steam for 2½ to 3 hours. Turn out onto a warmed serving plate to serve.

VARIATIONS:
College Pudding – make as above, adding 100 g/4 oz (⅔ cup) dried mixed fruit with the sugar.
Fair Lady Pudding – make as above, adding the finely grated rind of 1 orange with the sugar.
Four-Fruit Pudding – make as above, adding 25 g/1 oz (3 tablespoons) each chopped dates, figs, prunes and mixed candied peel with the sugar.
Spotted Dick – make as above, adding 75 g/3 oz (½ cup) currants and 25 g/1 oz (3 tablespoons) chopped mixed candied peel with the sugar.
Syrup Pudding – make as above, pouring 2 tablespoons golden (maple) syrup into the basin (mold) before adding the batter.
Treacle (Molasses) Pudding – make as above, pouring 2 tablespoons treacle (molasses) into the basin (mold) before adding the batter.

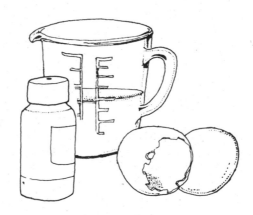

Baked Jam Roll

METRIC/IMPERIAL
225 g/8 oz quantity shortcrust
  pastry (page 246)
225 g/8 oz jam
milk
caster sugar

AMERICAN
2 cup quantity pie pastry
  (page 246)
⅔ cup jam
milk
sugar

Roll out the dough into an oblong about 25 x 20 cm/10 x 8 inches. Spread the jam over to within 1 cm/½ inch of the edges. Dampen the edges with a little cold water, then roll up like a Swiss (jelly) roll, starting from one of the longest sides. Press the edges together well.

Place on a lightly buttered baking sheet, taking care not to break the roll when lifting. Brush with milk and sprinkle the top with sugar.

Bake in a preheated hot oven (220°C/425°F, Gas Mark 7) for 20 minutes, then lower the heat to moderately hot (190°C/375°F, Gas Mark 5) and bake for a further 20 minutes.

Delicate Orange Pudding

METRIC/IMPERIAL
100 g/4 oz glacé cherries
50 g/2 oz angelica
100 g/4 oz unsalted butter
100 g/4 oz caster sugar
grated rind and juice of 1 orange
2 eggs, beaten
75 g/3 oz self-raising flour
50 g/2 oz fresh white breadcrumbs
3 tablespoons lemon jelly
  marmalade
1 orange, peeled and thinly sliced

AMERICAN
½ cup candied cherries
¼ cup angelica
½ cup sweet butter
½ cup sugar
grated rind and juice of 1 orange
2 eggs, beaten
¾ cup self-rising flour
1 cup soft white bread crumbs
3 tablespoons lemon jelly
  marmalade
1 orange, peeled and thinly sliced

Roughly chop the glacé (candied) cherries and angelica. Soften the butter slightly and cream with the sugar until light and fluffy. Add the orange rind. Gradually beat in the eggs. Sift the flour, mix with the breadcrumbs and fold·into the creamed mixture. Stir in the orange juice, cherries and angelica to distribute the fruit evenly through the mixture.

Coat the base and sides of a 1 kg/2 lb loaf tin (9 x 5 inch loaf pan) with the jelly marmalade and cover with overlapping orange slices. Pour the pudding mixture into the tin. Stand it in a roasting tin, half filled·with water, and bake in a fairly hot oven (200°C/400°F, Gas Mark 6) for 45 minutes.

Turn out on a serving dish and serve hot with custard or lightly whipped cream.

Rhubarb Pudding

METRIC/IMPERIAL
100 g/4 oz self-raising flour
pinch of salt
50 g/2 oz butter or margarine, cut into pieces
100 g/4 oz sugar
500 g/1 lb young rhubarb, trimmed, cleaned and cut into 2.5 cm/ 1 inch slices
150 ml/¼ pint milk

AMERICAN
1 cup self-rising flour
pinch of salt
¼ cup butter or margarine, cut into pieces
½ cup sugar
1 lb young rhubarb, trimmed, cleaned and cut into 1 inch slices
⅔ cup milk

Sift the flour and salt into a mixing bowl. Add the fat and rub (cut) into the flour until the mixture resembles fine breadcrumbs. Stir in the sugar and rhubarb and beat in the milk to make a thick batter. Turn into a buttered 1 litre/1¾ pint (4½ cup) baking dish and bake in a fairly hot oven (200°C/400°F, Gas Mark 6) for 30 to 40 minutes. Serve at once with caster sugar.

Sweet Soufflé Omelette

METRIC/IMPERIAL
3 large eggs, separated
25 g/1 oz caster sugar
½ teaspoon vanilla essence
25 g/1 oz butter
4 teaspoons icing sugar, sifted

AMERICAN
3 large eggs, separated
2 tablespoons granulated sugar
½ teaspoon vanilla extract
2 tablespoons butter
4 tablespoons confectioners' sugar, sifted

Beat the egg yolks with the caster (granulated) sugar and vanilla essence (extract) until very thick and pale. Beat the egg whites until stiff and gently fold into the egg yolk mixture.

Melt the butter in a large frying pan. Pour in the egg mixture and cook for 2 to 2½ minutes or until the base is set. Place the pan under a hot grill (broiler) and cook until the top is well puffed up and golden.

Slide the omelette onto a sheet of greaseproof (parchment) paper dusted with the icing (confectioners') sugar. Score down the centre, fold in half and serve immediately.

VARIATIONS:
Apple Soufflé Omelette – spread 2 to 3 tablespoons warm sweetened apple purée (sauce) over the omelette before folding in half.
Apricot Soufflé Omelette – spread 3 tablespoons warmed apricot jam over the omelette before folding in half.
Raspberry or Strawberry Soufflé Omelette – spread 3 tablespoons warmed raspberry or strawberry jam over the omelette before folding in half.

Lemon Pancakes (Crêpes)

METRIC/IMPERIAL
1 quantity pancake batter (page 133)
caster sugar
lemon juice

AMERICAN
1 quantity crêpe batter (page 133)
sugar
lemon juice

Make the pancakes (crêpes). Sprinkle with sugar and lemon juice, roll up and serve.

VARIATION:
Orange Pancakes (Crêpes) – make as above, using orange juice instead of lemon juice.

Mandarin Cream Pancakes (Crêpes)

METRIC/IMPERIAL
1 quantity pancake batter (page 133)
1 x 300 g/11 oz can mandarin
   oranges, well drained and syrup
   reserved
300 ml/½ pint double cream, stiffly
   whipped

AMERICAN
1 quantity crêpe batter (page 133)
1 x 12 oz can mandarin oranges,
   well drained and syrup reserved
1¼ cups heavy cream, stiffly
   whipped

Make the pancakes (crêpes). Mix the oranges into the cream and spread over the pancakes. Roll up and serve, with the syrup from the oranges.

Party Layer Pancakes (Crêpes)

METRIC/IMPERIAL
1 quantity pancake batter (page 133)
6 tablespoons apricot jam
1 tablespoon lemon juice
1 quantity meringue topping
   (page 250)
8 glacé cherries, halved

AMERICAN
1 quantity crêpe batter (page 133)
6 tablespoons apricot jam
1 tablespoon lemon juice
1 quantity meringue topping
   (page 250)
8 glacé cherries, halved

Make the pancakes (crêpes).
   Put the jam and lemon juice into a saucepan and warm gently over a low heat. Put one pancake (crêpe) on a serving dish and spread with a little of the jam and lemon juice mixture. Add another on top and spread with the jam mixture. Repeat with the rest of the pancakes (crêpes).
   Cover the top pancake (crêpe) with the meringue topping and decorate with the glacé cherries. Bake in a preheated hot oven (230°C/450°F, Gas Mark 8) for 1 to 2 minutes or until the meringue is golden brown. Cut into slices like a cake and serve immediately.

Spiced Apple Pancakes (Crêpes)

METRIC/IMPERIAL
1 quantity pancake batter
(page 133)
5–6 tablespoons hot, thick,
sweetened apple purée
large pinch of ground cinnamon

AMERICAN
1 quantity crêpe batter (page 133)
5–6 tablespoons hot thick,
sweetened apple sauce
large pinch of ground cinnamon

Make the pancakes (crêpes). Mix the apple purée (sauce) with the cinnamon and spread over the pancakes (crêpes). Roll up and serve.

Syrup and Orange Pancakes (Crêpes)

METRIC/IMPERIAL
1 quantity pancake batter
(page 133)
5–6 tablespoons golden syrup,
warmed
1 teaspoon finely grated orange
rind

AMERICAN
1 quantity crêpe batter (page 133)
5–6 tablespoons maple syrup,
warmed
1 teaspoon finely grated orange
rind

Make the pancakes (crêpes). Spread with the syrup and sprinkle with the orange rind. Roll up and serve.

Raspberry Pancakes (Crêpes)

METRIC/IMPERIAL
1 quantity pancake batter
(page 133)
5–6 tablespoons raspberry jam,
melted

AMERICAN
1 quantity crêpe batter (page 133)
5–6 tablespoons raspberry jam,
melted

Make the pancakes (crêpes). Spread with the jam, roll up and serve.

VARIATION:
Strawberry Pancakes (Crêpes) – make as above, using strawberry jam instead of raspberry.

Lemon and Apricot Pancakes (Crêpes)

METRIC/IMPERIAL
*1 quantity pancake batter
 (page 133)
5–6 tablespoons apricot jam,
 melted
1 teaspoon finely grated lemon rind
1–2 tablespoons lemon juice*

AMERICAN
*1 quantity crêpe batter (page 133)
5–6 tablespoons apricot jam,
 melted
1 teaspoon finely grated lemon rind
1–2 tablespoons lemon juice*

Make the pancakes (crêpes). Mix the jam with the lemon rind and juice and spread over the pancakes (crêpes). Roll up and serve.

Apricot Pancake (Crêpe) Layer

METRIC/IMPERIAL
*1 quantity pancake batter
 (page 133)*
FOR THE FILLING:
*1 x 425 g/15 oz can apricot halves
2 teaspoons arrowroot
3 tablespoons orange jelly
 marmalade
1 tablespoon flaked almonds*

AMERICAN
1 quantity crêpe batter (page 133)
FOR THE FILLING:
*1 can (16 oz) apricot halves
2 teaspoons arrowroot
3 tablespoons orange jelly
 marmalade
1 tablespoon slivered almonds*

Fry the pancakes and keep them warm while you prepare the filling.
   Drain the apricot halves and cut each one into 4 neat slices. Moisten the arrowroot with 1 tablespoon of the apricot syrup and put the remaining syrup in a saucepan with the marmalade. Stir over gentle heat until the marmalade has melted. Add the moistened arrowroot and bring to the boil, stirring constantly. Cook gently until the mixture thickens and clears, stirring all the time. Fold in the apricot slices.
   Place one pancake (crêpe) on an ovenproof plate and cover with a little of the apricot filling. Continue in layers arranging a few good slices on top of the last pancake. Scatter with the flaked (slivered) almonds and place in a moderate oven (180°C/350°F, Gas Mark 4) for about 15 minutes. Serve warm, cut into wedges. For special occasions, decorate with extra apricot slices.

Cottage Cheese Blintzes

METRIC/IMPERIAL
1 quantity pancake batter (page 133)
350 g/12 oz cottage cheese
1 egg yolk
50 g/2 oz caster sugar
1 teaspoon vanilla essence
50 g/2 oz butter
1 teaspoon ground cinnamon
150 ml/¼ pint soured cream or natural yogurt

AMERICAN
1 quantity crêpe batter (page 133)
1½ cups cottage cheese
1 egg yolk
¼ cup sugar
1 teaspoon vanilla extract
¼ cup butter
1 teaspoon ground cinnamon
¾ cup sour cream or plain yogurt

Make 8 pancakes (crêpes), cooking on one side only. Turn them out onto a clean tea (dish) towel.

Mix the cottage cheese well with the egg yolk, 2 tablespoons of the sugar and the vanilla essence (extract). Spread equal amounts of this mixture onto the centres of the cooked sides of the pancakes (crêpes). Fold over the edges, envelope-style.

Melt the butter in a large frying pan until hot and sizzling. Put four pancakes (crêpes) in, joins underneath, and fry on all sides until golden. Drain on paper towels and keep hot while frying the remaining pancakes (crêpes). Add more butter to the pan if needed.

Sprinkle with the remaining sugar and the cinnamon and serve with the soured cream or yogurt.

VARIATIONS:
Cottage Cheese and Banana Blintzes – make as above, adding 3 mashed medium bananas to the cottage cheese filling.
Cottage Cheese and Peach Blintzes – make as above, adding 6 tablespoons chopped canned peaches to the cottage cheese filling.
Cottage Cheese and Raisin Blintzes – make as above, adding 50 to 75 g/2 to 3 oz (½ cup) raisins and 1 teaspoon finely grated lemon or orange rind to the cottage cheese filling.
Cottage Cheese and Strawberry Blintzes – make as above, then cover the finished blintzes with 5 to 6 tablespoons warmed strawberry jam instead of sugar and cinnamon.

Spiced Apple Whip

METRIC/IMPERIAL
225 g/8 oz cooking apples, peeled,
  cored and thinly sliced
3 tablespoons cold water
1 clove
½ teaspoon finely grated lemon
  rind
¼ teaspoon mixed spice
25–40 g/1–1½ oz sugar
2 teaspoons gelatine
4 tablespoons hot water
red food colouring
2 teaspoons milk
4 tablespoons double cream
1 egg white
TO DECORATE:
whipped cream
8 glacé cherries

AMERICAN
½ lb cooking apples, peeled, cored
  and thinly sliced
3 tablespoons cold water
1 clove
½ teaspoon finely grated lemon
  rind
¼ teaspoon apple pie spice
2–3 tablespoons sugar
2 teaspoons unflavored gelatin
¼ cup hot water
red food coloring
2 teaspoons milk
¼ cup heavy cream
1 egg white
FOR DECORATION:
whipped cream
8 glacé cherries

Place the apples in a saucepan with the cold water, clove, lemon rind and spice. Bring slowly to the boil, then cover and simmer until the fruit is soft and tender. Remove from the heat and take out the clove. Sweeten to taste with the sugar. Purée in a blender or food processor or rub through a fine sieve.

Dissolve the gelatine in the hot water. Add to the apple purée and stir well. Chill until it is just beginning to thicken. Tint with a few drops of food colouring.

Whip the milk and cream together until thick. Fold into the apple mixture. Beat the egg white to a stiff snow and fold in. Spoon into a serving dish and chill until set. Just before serving, decorate with cream and glacé cherries.

Peach Mousse

METRIC/IMPERIAL
1 tablespoon gelatine
6 tablespoons hot water
1 tablespoon sugar
150 ml/¼ pint peach purée (made
    from drained canned peaches)
2 tablespoons lemon juice
2 egg whites
TO DECORATE:
150 ml/¼ pint double cream,
    whipped
chopped almonds

AMERICAN
1 tablespoon unflavored gelatin
6 tablespoons hot water
1 tablespoon sugar
¾ cup peach purée (made from
    drained canned peaches)
2 tablespoons lemon juice
2 egg whites
FOR DECORATION:
¾ cup heavy cream, whipped
chopped almonds

Dissolve the gelatine in the hot water. Add the sugar and stir in the peach purée and lemon juice. Leave until cold and just beginning to thicken.

Beat the egg whites until stiff and fold into the peach mixture. Pour into four glass dishes and chill until set.

Just before serving, decorate with the whipped cream sprinkled with chopped almonds.

VARIATION:
Apricot Mousse – make as above, using canned apricots instead of peaches to make the purée.

Cold Rice Crème

METRIC/IMPERIAL
75 g/3 oz round-grain rice
600 ml/1 pint milk
25 g/1 oz sugar
1 egg, separated
15 g/½ oz butter
1 packet orange jelly
few glacé cherries, halved, to
    decorate

AMERICAN
6 tablespoons short-grain rice
2½ cups milk
2 tablespoons sugar
1 egg, separated
1 tablespoon butter
1 package orange-flavored gelatin
few candied cherries, halved, for
    decoration

Put the rice, milk and sugar in a saucepan. Bring to the boil, stir well, reduce the heat, cover and simmer for 30 minutes, stirring occasionally. Lightly beat the egg yolk, stir into the rice mixture with the butter, then remove from the heat. Dissolve the jelly in 150 ml/¼ pint (⅔ cup) boiling water and allow to cool. Stir into the rice mixture. Whisk the egg white until stiff and fold into the rice and jelly mixture, then pour into an oiled ring mould. Chill well until set. Turn out on a serving dish and decorate with halved glacé (candied) cherries.

Mocha Mousse

METRIC/IMPERIAL
1 tablespoon gelatine
2 tablespoons cold water
2 tablespoons instant coffee
1 tablespoons cocoa powder
2 tablespoons sugar
300 ml/½ pint boiling water
200 ml/7 fl oz evaporated milk,
    chilled
TO DECORATE:
4 tablespoons double cream,
    whipped (optional)
chocolate curls (optional)

AMERICAN
1 tablespoon unflavored gelatin
2 tablespoons cold water
2 tablespoons instant coffee
1 tablespoons unsweetened cocoa
2 tablespoons sugar
1¼ cups boiling water
⅞ cup evaporated milk, chilled
FOR DECORATION:
4 tablespoons heavy cream,
    whipped (optional)
chocolate curl (optional)

Sprinkle the gelatine over the cold water in a cup and allow to soften for 5 minutes.

Place the instant coffee, cocoa and sugar in a measuring jug and gradually add the boiling water, stirring all the time until dissolved. Add the softened gelatine and stir well until completely melted. Allow to cool until mixture is on the point of setting.

Place the evaporated milk in a bowl and whisk steadily until it is thick and fluffy. Gradually whisk in the coffee mixture and pour into a rinsed 1 litre/1¾ pint (4¼ cup) fluted mould. Chill until set then turn out on a serving dish. If liked, decorate with rosettes of whipped cream and chocolate curls.

Chocolate Curls – these can be made quickly by scraping a clean potato peeler across the bottom of a block of plain chocolate.

Oranges Che Yang

METRIC/IMPERIAL
1 x 311 g/11 oz can mandarin
    oranges
300 ml/½ pint sweetened apple
    purée
25 g/1 oz stem ginger, chopped
1 teaspoon grated nutmeg
1 tablespoon clear honey
2 teaspoons lemon juice
2 tablespoons ginger syrup

AMERICAN
1 can (11 oz) mandarin oranges
1¼ cups sweetened applesauce
1 tablespoon chopped preserved
    ginger
1 teaspoon grated nutmeg
1 tablespoon honey
2 teaspoons lemon juice
2 tablespoons ginger syrup

Drain the mandarin segments from the syrup. Mix the fruit with the apple purée (applesauce), chopped ginger, grated nutmeg, honey, lemon juice and ginger syrup.

Serve in small glasses with Crème Chantilly (page 251).

Unbaked Apricot Cheesecake

METRIC/IMPERIAL
FOR THE BISCUIT CRUST:
50 g/2 oz butter or margarine
100 g/4 oz digestive biscuits,
crushed
½ teaspoon ground cinnamon
FOR THE FILLING:
1 x 425 g/15 oz can apricot halves
350 g/12 oz cottage cheese, sieved
75 g/3 oz caster sugar
grated zest and juice of 1 large
lemon
1 tablespoon gelatine
150 ml/¼ pint whipping cream
flaked almonds (optional)

AMERICAN
FOR THE BISCUIT CRUST:
¼ cup butter or margarine
1½ cups crushed Graham crackers
½ teaspoon ground cinnamon
FOR THE FILLING:
1 can (16 oz) apricot halves
1½ cups cottage cheese, sieved
6 tablespoons sugar
grated zest and juice of 1 large
lemon
1 tablespoon unflavored gelatin
⅔ cup heavy cream
slivered almonds (optional)

Place the butter or margarine in a saucepan. Stir over moderate heat until just melted, but do not allow it to colour. Remove from the heat, stir in the biscuit crumbs and ground cinnamon and mix well. Press the crumb mixture into the base of a greased loose-bottomed 17.5 cm/7 inch cake tin (springform pan), smoothing well with the back of a metal spoon. Chill in the refrigerator while preparing the filling.

Drain the apricot halves, reserve the syrup, and liquidize in an electric blender or pass through a sieve. Place the apricot purée, sieved cottage cheese, sugar and lemon zest and juice together in a bowl and beat until smooth. Measure 2 tablespoons of the reserved apricot syrup in a small basin, sprinkle on the gelatine and stir well. Place the basin in a pan of hot water and stir until the gelatine has completely dissolved. Cool and add to the cheese mixture. Whip the cream until thick and fold into the cheese mixture. Turn on to the chilled biscuit base and allow to set. Remove the cake tin (springform pan) and serve the cheesecake on its base on a plate. If liked, sprinkle with flaked almonds.

Peach Melba

METRIC/IMPERIAL
French custard ice cream
(page 172)
4 canned peach halves
175–225 g/6–8 oz fresh raspberries
sifted icing sugar

AMERICAN
French custard ice cream
(page 172)
4 canned peach halves
¾–1 cup fresh raspberries
sifted confectioners' sugar

Put scoops of ice cream into four glass dishes and top each serving with a peach half.

Crush the raspberries with the back of a spoon and sweeten to taste. Spoon the raspberry purée over the peach halves and serve.

Meringue Basket

METRIC/IMPERIAL
1 quantity meringue mixture
   (page 193)
whipped cream
fresh fruit

AMERICAN
1 quantity meringue mixture
   (page 193)
whipped cream
fresh fruit

Using a 20 cm/8 inch plate as a guide, draw a circle in the middle of an oiled and lined baking sheet. Spread some of the meringue mixture over the circle to fill it in, and raise the edges by piping or spooning the meringue upwards.

Dry out on a preheated very cool oven (110°C/225°F, Gas Mark ¼) for 1½ hours.

Remove from the oven. Peel the lining paper away, then turn the meringue basket upside-down on the sheet. Put back in the oven and continue baking for 45 minutes. When cold, fill with whipped cream and fruit.

Pineapple Cheese Cream

METRIC/IMPERIAL
1 tablespoon gelatine
2 tablespoons hot water
1 x 425 g/15 oz can pineapple
   chunks
2 eggs, separated
100 g/4 oz caster sugar
1 tablespoon lemon juice and
   grated zest of ½ lemon
350 g/12 oz cottage cheese, sieved
150 ml/¼ pint double cream
angelica leaves to decorate

AMERICAN
1 tablespoon unflavored gelatin
2 tablespoons hot water
1 can (16 oz) pineapple chunks
2 eggs, separated
½ cup sugar
1 tablespoon lemon juice and
   grated zest of ½ lemon
1½ cups cottage cheese, sieved
⅔ cup heavy cream
angelica leaves for decoration

Soften the gelatine in the water. Drain the syrup from the pineapple chunks. Whisk the egg yolks and sugar together until thick and creamy. Slowly whisk in 150 ml/¼ pint (⅔ cup) pineapple syrup.

Put the mixture into a saucepan, add the softened gelatine and stir over low heat until dissolved. Add the grated lemon zest and leave to cool. Stir in the sieved cottage cheese and lemon juice. Leave until beginning to set. Beat until smooth.

Lightly whip the cream and fold into the mixture. Beat the egg whites until stiff, and finely chop half the pineapple chunks. Fold the chopped pineapple and the beaten egg whites into the mixture. Put into a serving dish or individual glasses, and decorate with the remaining pineapple chunks and angelica leaves. Chill before serving.

Christmas Crumble

METRIC/IMPERIAL	AMERICAN
100 g/4 oz mincemeat	½ cup mincemeat
150 ml/¼ pint cold water	⅔ cup cold water
finely grated zest of 1 orange	finely grated zest of 1 orange
2 teaspoons cornflour	2 teaspoons cornstarch
1 tablespoon rum or brandy	1 tablespoon rum or brandy
2 teaspoons sugar	2 teaspoons sugar
FOR THE TOPPING:	FOR THE TOPPING:
100 g/4 oz butter	½ cup butter
50 g/2 oz demerara sugar	⅓ cup brown or raw sugar
100 g/4 oz quick cook oats	¼ lb quick cook oats
TO DECORATE:	FOR DECORATION:
150 ml/¼ pint double cream	⅔ cup heavy cream
25 g/1 oz chopped walnuts	¼ cup chopped walnuts

Place the mincemeat with the cold water and orange zest in a saucepan. Bring to the boil, reduce the heat and simmer for 5 minutes. Moisten the cornflour (cornstarch) with 1 tablespoon of water and stir it into the mincemeat, then add the rum or brandy and the sugar. Bring to the boil, stirring constantly. Cook for 1 minute then allow to become quite cold.

To make the topping, melt the butter in a saucepan and stir in the demerara (brown or raw) sugar and oats until well coated. Place half the oat mixture in the bottom of a trifle dish, cover with the mincemeat sauce and top with the remaining oat mixture.

Whip the cream until just holding its shape then spread lightly over the centre of the crumble and sprinkle with the chopped walnuts.

Junket

METRIC/IMPERIAL	AMERICAN
2 teaspoons caster sugar	2 teaspoons sugar
600 ml/1 pint milk	2½ cups milk
1 teaspoon rennet	1 teaspoon rennet

Put the sugar and milk into a saucepan and heat until blood hot (tepid). Pour into a serving dish, stir in the rennet and leave for 1½ to 2 hours at room temperature.

After the junket has set, it can be chilled and served very cold.

VARIATIONS:
Coffee Junket – make as above, adding 2 teaspoons instant coffee powder with the sugar.
Fresh Lemon Junket – make as above, adding 1 teaspoon finely grated lemon rind with the sugar, and tinting the mixture pale yellow with food colouring before adding the rennet.

Banana Splits

METRIC/IMPERIAL	AMERICAN
150 ml/¼ pint double cream	¾ cup heavy cream
4 large bananas, split lengthways	4 large bananas, split lengthwise
French custard ice cream (page 172)	French custard ice cream (page 172)
25 g/1 oz walnuts, chopped	¼ cup chopped walnuts
4 glacé cherries	4 glacé cherries
hot chocolate or fudge sauce (pages 239 or 233)	hot chocolate or fudge sauce (pages 239 or 233)

Whip the cream until thick. Sandwich the banana halves together with the ice cream. Place on four small plates and cover with the whipped cream. Sprinkle with the nuts and put a whole cherry in the middle of each. Serve immediately, with the sauce.

Gooseberry Whip

METRIC/IMPERIAL	AMERICAN
225 g/8 oz gooseberries, topped and tailed	½ lb gooseberries, trimmed
3 tablespoons cold water	3 tablespoons cold water
25–50 g/1–2 oz sugar	2–4 tablespoons sugar
2 teaspoons gelatine	2 teaspoons unflavored gelatin
4 tablespoons hot water	¼ cup hot water
½ teaspoon finely grated lemon rind	½ teaspoon finely grated lemon rind
green food colouring	green food coloring
4 tablespoons double cream	¼ cup heavy cream
2 teaspoons milk	2 teaspoons milk
1 egg white	1 egg white
TO DECORATE:	FOR DECORATION:
whipped cream	whipped cream
candied angelica leaves	candied angelica leaves

Put the gooseberries in a saucepan with the 3 tablespoons of cold water. Bring slowly to the boil, then cover the pan and simmer until soft. Remove from the heat and sweeten to taste with the sugar. Purée in a blender or food processor or rub through a sieve.

Dissolve the gelatine in the hot water. Add to the gooseberry purée with the lemon rind and a few drops of food colouring. Chill until the mixture just begins to thicken.

Whip the cream and milk together until thick. Fold into the gooseberry mixture. Beat the egg white until stiff and fold in. Spoon into a serving dish and chill until firm and set.

Just before serving, decorate with whipped cream and angelica leaves.

Banana and Ginger Dessert

METRIC/IMPERIAL
1 x 33 g/1⅓ oz packet vanilla
  blancmange powder
2 tablespoons sugar
600 ml/1 pint milk
100 g/4 oz apricot jam
4 bananas
75 g/3 oz stem ginger, finely
  chopped
150 ml/¼ pint double cream
1 teaspoon caster sugar
½ teaspoon vanilla essence

AMERICAN
1 package (1⅓ oz) vanilla
  blancmange powder
2 tablespoons sugar
2½ cups milk
¼ cup apricot jam
4 bananas
⅓ cup finely chopped preserved
  ginger
⅔ cup heavy cream
1 teaspoon sugar
½ teaspoon vanilla

Make up the vanilla blancmange using the sugar and milk, according to the directions on the packet. Pour into a shallow serving dish and allow to set.

Heat the jam and rub through a sieve. Peel the bananas, cut into halves lengthwise, then scoop out a little 'trough' down the centre of each half. Fill this with pieces of the very finely chopped ginger, reserving larger pieces for the decoration, and brush the sides of the bananas thickly with the jam. Arrange on the set blancmange.

Whip the cream, add the sugar and vanilla essence and pipe down the centres of the banana halves over the ginger. Decorate with the remaining pieces of ginger.

Orange Snow Creams

METRIC/IMPERIAL
1 orange jelly tablet
5 tablespoons boiling water
150 ml/¼ pint double cream
2 egg whites
fresh mint leaves to decorate

AMERICAN
1 package orange-flavored gelatin
⅓ cup boiling water
¾ cup heavy cream
2 egg whites
fresh mint leaves for decoration

Dissolve the jelly (gelatin) in the boiling water. Pour into a measuring jug and make up to 450 ml/¾ pint (2 cups) with cold water. Leave in a cool place until just beginning to thicken.

Whip the cream until light and fluffy. Beat the egg whites to a stiff snow. Put the jelly (gelatin) in a large bowl and whisk until quite foamy. Fold in the whipped cream alternately with the egg whites. When quite smooth and blended pour into four glass dishes. Chill until firm. Just before serving decorate with fresh mint leaves.

Rich Fruit Fool

METRIC/IMPERIAL
500 g/1 lb fresh fruit
3 tablespoons water
75–175 g/3–6 oz caster sugar
300 ml/½ pint double cream
2 tablespoons milk
red or green food colouring
TO DECORATE:
whipped cream
25 g/1 oz toasted almonds, finely
chopped

AMERICAN
1 lb fresh fruit
3 tablespoons water
⅓–¾ cup sugar
1¼ cups heavy cream
2 tablespoons milk
red or green food coloring
FOR DECORATION:
whipped cream
¼ cup finely chopped toasted
almonds

Prepare the fruit according to type. Put into a saucepan with the water and bring slowly to the boil. Cover and simmer until the fruit is soft. Remove from the heat and stir in sugar to taste. Purée in a blender or food processor or rub through a fine sieve. Leave until cold.

Whip the cream and milk together until thick. Fold into the fruit purée. Tint with the food colouring. Pour into four glass dishes and chill.

Just before serving, decorate with whipped cream and almonds.

VARIATIONS:
Custard Cream Fruit Fool – make as above, using only 150 ml/¼ pint (¾ cup) cream and 1 tablespoon milk. Fold in 150 ml/¼ pint (¾ cup) cold custard with the whipped cream.
Custard Fruit Fool – make as above, using 300 ml/½ pint (1¼ cups) cold custard instead of the cream and milk mixture.

Pots-au-Chocolat

METRIC/IMPERIAL
75 g/3 oz plain chocolate
25 g/1 oz butter
3 eggs, separated
1 tablespoon warm water
whipped cream to decorate

AMERICAN
3 squares (1 oz each) semisweet
chocolate
2 tablespoons butter
3 eggs, separated
1 tablespoon warm water
whipped cream for decoration

Break up the chocolate and put it in a heatproof bowl over a saucepan of boiling water or in a double boiler. Add the butter and heat until both have melted. Beat in the egg yolks. When smooth, remove from the heat and stir in the warm water. Cool slightly.

Beat the egg whites to a stiff snow and fold gently into the chocolate mixture. Pour into four glass dishes and chill. Just before serving, decorate with whipped cream.

Trifle Alexandra

METRIC/IMPERIAL
1 x 411 g/14½ oz can peach halves
slices of stale sponge cake
1 tablespoon milk
150 ml/¼ pint double cream
1 tablespoon sifted icing sugar
1 egg white
100 g/4 oz fresh or frozen
    strawberries
extra sifted icing sugar

AMERICAN
1 x 14½ oz can peach halves
slices of stale sponge cake
1 tablespoon milk
¾ cup heavy cream
1 tablespoon sifted confectioners'
    sugar
1 egg white
¼ lb fresh or frozen strawberries
    (about 1 cup)
extra sifted confectioners' sugar

Drain the peaches, reserving the syrup. Line the bottom of a small serving dish with the sponge cake. Moisten with 4 to 5 tablespoons of the peach syrup, then arrange the peach halves on top.

Whip the milk and cream together until thick. Stir in the sugar. Beat the egg white to a stiff snow and fold into the cream mixture. Pile over the peaches and chill.

Just before serving, crush the strawberries using the back of a spoon. Sweeten to taste with the extra icing (confectioners') sugar and trickle over the cream.

Lemon Cream Snow

METRIC/IMPERIAL
300 ml/½ pint double cream
2 tablespoons milk
5 tablespoons sifted icing sugar
2 teaspoons finely grated lemon
    rind
1 egg white

AMERICAN
1¼ cups heavy cream
2 tablespoons milk
⅓ cup confectioners' sugar, sifted
2 teaspoons finely grated lemon
    rind
1 egg white

If using the freezing compartment of the refrigerator, set the refrigerator at the coldest setting at least 1 hour before beginning.

Pour the cream and milk into a well-chilled bowl and beat well together until thick. Stir in the sugar and lemon rind and pour into an ice cube tray. Place the tray in the freezer (or freezing compartment) and freeze for 45 minutes.

Pour the mixture back into the chilled bowl and break up with a fork. Stir gently until smooth. Beat the egg white to a stiff snow and fold into the cream mixture. Return to the washed and dried ice cube tray and freeze for a further 2 hours or until firm.

Dairy Ice Cream

METRIC/IMPERIAL
300 ml/½ pint double cream
2 tablespoons milk
5 tablespoons sifted icing sugar
1 teaspoon vanilla essence

AMERICAN
1¼ cups heavy cream
2 tablespoons milk
⅓ cup confectioners' sugar, sifted
1 teaspoon vanilla extract

If using the freezer compartment of the refrigerator, set the refrigerator at the coldest setting at least 1 hour before beginning.

Pour the cream and milk into a well-chilled bowl and beat well together until thick. Stir in the sugar and vanilla essence (extract) and pour into an ice cube tray. Place the tray in the freezer (or freezing compartment) and freeze for 45 minutes.

Pour the mixture back into the chilled bowl and break up with a fork. Stir gently until smooth. Return to the washed and dried ice cube tray and freeze for a further 2 hours or until firm.

VARIATIONS:

Raspberry Dairy Ice Cream – make as above, adding 75 to 100 g/ 3 to 4 oz (½ cup) lightly crushed raspberries after the initial freezing.

Tutti-Frutti Dairy Ice Cream – make as above, adding 2 chopped canned pineapple rings, 1 small sliced banana and 2 tablespoons chopped canned mandarin oranges after the initial freezing.

Peach Dairy Ice Cream – make as above, omitting the vanilla and reducing the sugar to 3 tablespoons. Add canned peach halves, coarsely chopped, 1 teaspoon finely grated lemon rind and 2 tablespoons rosehip syrup after the initial freezing.

Almond Dairy Ice Cream – make as above, using almond essence (extract) instead of vanilla, and adding 25 g/1 oz (¼ cup) chopped toasted almonds after the initial freezing.

Apricot Dairy Ice Cream – make as above, omitting the vanilla and reducing the sugar to 3 tablespoons. Add 8 canned apricot halves, coarsely chopped, 1 teaspoon finely grated orange rind and 2 tablespoons rose hip syrup after the initial freezing.

Coffee Dairy Ice Cream – make as above, using 2 to 3 teaspoons instant coffe powder dissolved in 2 teaspoons water instead of the vanilla.

Chocolate Dairy Ice Cream – make as above, adding 2 tablespoons cocoa powder dissolved in 3 tablespoons water after the initial freezing.

Chocolate Chip Dairy Ice Cream – make as above, adding 50 g/2 oz (¼ cup) coarsely grated plain (sweet) chocolate after the initial freezing.

Lemon Dairy Ice Cream – make as above, omitting the vanilla and stirring in 2 teaspoons finely grated lemon rind after the initial freezing.

Orange Dairy Ice Cream – make as above, omitting the vanilla and reducing the sugar to 4 tablespoons. Add 1 teaspoon finely grated orange rind and 1 tablespoon orange liqueur after the initial freezing.

French Custard Ice Cream

METRIC/IMPERIAL
300 ml/½ pint single cream
1 tablespoon sugar
2 large eggs, beaten
2 teaspoons vanilla essence

AMERICAN
1¼ cups light cream
1 tablespoon sugar
2 large eggs, beaten
2 teaspoons vanilla extract

If using the frozen food compartment of the refrigerator, at least 1½ to 2 hours before starting to prepare the ice cream, set the refrigerator to its coldest setting.

Place the cream, sugar and eggs in a double boiler or a heatproof bowl standing over a saucepan of simmering water. Cook, stirring, until the custard becomes thick enough to coat the back of a spoon. Do not allow to boil. Pour the custard into a bowl, stir in the vanilla and leave to cool completely.

Pour the custard into a metal freezer tray and place in the freezer (or frozen food compartment of the refrigerator). Freeze for 1 hour or until the custard has frozen 1 cm/½ inch around the sides of the tray.

Turn into a chilled bowl and beat well until smooth. Put back into the freezer tray (after washing and drying it well) and freeze for 1½ to 2 hours longer or until firm.

Blancmange

METRIC/IMPERIAL
3 tablespoons cornflour
600 ml/1 pint milk
15 g/½ oz butter
40 g/1½ oz caster sugar
1 teaspoon vanilla essence

AMERICAN
3 tablespoons cornstarch
2½ cups milk
1 tablespoon butter
3 tablespoons sugar
1 teaspoon vanilla extract

Mix the cornflour (cornstarch) to a smooth paste with a little of the cold milk. Warm the remaining milk, then mix with the cornflour (cornstarch) paste. Cook, stirring, until it comes to the boil and thickens. Lower the heat and simmer for 3 minutes.

Remove from the heat and stir in the butter, sugar and vanilla essence (extract). Pour into a 600 ml/1 pint (2½ cup) mould that has been rinsed out with cold water, and leave to cool. Chill until set and firm. Turn out on to a chilled serving plate to serve.

VARIATIONS:
Extra Creamy Blancmange – make as above, using half single (light) cream and half milk.
Coffee Blancmange – make as above, adding 2 to 3 teaspoons instant coffee powder to the milk when it is being heated.
Honey Blancmange – make as above, using 1 tablespoon honey instead of the sugar.

BUDGET

Sweet Pies and Pastries

MEALS

Orange Treacle Tart

METRIC/IMPERIAL	AMERICAN
FOR THE PASTRY:	FOR THE PASTRY:
225 g/8 oz flour	2 cups flour
pinch of salt	pinch of salt
50 g/2 oz margarine, cut into pieces	¼ cup margarine, cut into pieces
50 g/2 oz lard, cut into pieces	¼ cup shortening, cut into pieces
2 tablespoons cold water	2 tablespoons cold water
FOR THE FILLING:	FOR THE FILLING:
225 g/8 oz golden syrup	⅔ cup light corn syrup
100 g/4 oz chunky marmalade	⅓ cup chunky marmalade
2 tablespoons lemon juice	2 tablespoons lemon juice
225 g/8 oz fresh white breadcrumbs	4 cups soft white bread crumbs

To make the pastry, sift the flour and salt into a bowl. Rub (cut) in the margarine and lard (shortening) and add just sufficient cold water to make a firm dough. Wrap in foil or greaseproof (waxed) paper and chill in the refrigerator for 30 minutes.

Roll out the pastry on a floured surface and use to line a 20 cm/8 inch sandwich tin or a flan dish or flan ring placed on a baking sheet.

To make the filling, mix together the syrup, marmalade and lemon juice until well blended. Add the breadcrumbs and stir until coated with the syrup mixture. Spoon the filling into the pastry case and smooth the top. Bake in a moderate oven (180°C/350°F, Gas Mark 4) for 25 to 30 minutes, or until golden-brown.

Black Treacle (Molasses) Tart

METRIC/IMPERIAL
225 g/8 oz quantity shortcrust
    pastry (page 246)
50 g/2 oz walnuts, chopped
225 g/8 oz sugar
1 tablespoon flour
3 eggs, beaten
350 g/12 oz black treacle
25 g/1 oz butter, melted
pinch of salt
whipped cream to serve

AMERICAN
2 cup quantity pie pastry
    (page 246)
½ cup chopped walnuts
1 cup sugar
1 tablespoon flour
3 eggs, beaten
1 cup molasses
2 tablespoons melted butter
pinch of salt
whipped cream for serving

Roll out the pastry dough and use to line a 20 cm/8 inch flan or quiche tin. Sprinkle the chopped walnuts on the bottom of the pastry case.

Beat the sugar, flour and eggs together well. Add the black treacle (molasses), melted butter and salt and mix well. Pour over the nuts in the pastry case.

Bake in a preheated hot oven (230°C/450°F, Gas Mark 8) for 10 minutes, then reduce the heat to cool (150°C/300°F, Gas Mark 2) and continue baking for 30 minutes.

Allow to cool before serving, with whipped cream.

Fruit Pie

METRIC/IMPERIAL
1 kg/2 lb fresh fruit
175–225 g/6–8 oz granulated sugar
225 g/8 oz quantity shortcrust
    pastry (page 246)
beaten egg for brushing
caster sugar for sprinkling

AMERICAN
2 lb fresh fruit
¾–1 cup sugar
2 cup quantity pie pastry
    (page 246)
beaten egg for brushing
extra sugar for sprinkling

Prepare the fruit according to type. Fill a 1.2 litre/2 pint (5 cup deep) pie dish with layers of fruit and sugar, beginning and ending with fruit. Dome the fruit up in the centre, so that it will support the pastry.

Roll out the dough and cut to fit the top of the pie. Moisten the edges of the dish with water and line with a strip of dough made from the trimmings. Moisten the strip with water, then cover with the dough lid. Press the edges well together and flute with the back of a fork. Brush with beaten egg and make two slits in the top.

Bake in a preheated hot oven (220°C/425°F, Gas Mark 7) for 15 minutes. Lower the heat to moderate (180°C/350°F, Gas Mark 4) and bake for a further 30 to 35 minutes. Sprinkle the top lightly with sugar before serving.

Fruit Slices

METRIC/IMPERIAL
FOR THE PASTRY:
225 g/8 oz flour
pinch of salt
150 g/5 oz butter or margarine, cut
 into pieces
2 teaspoons caster sugar
2–3 tablespoons cold water
FOR THE FILLING:
1 tablespoon cornflour
150 ml/¼ pint water
75 g/3 oz sugar
350 g/12 oz mixed dried fruit
 (sultanas, raisins, currants)
1 teaspoon ground cinnamon
TO GLAZE:
cold water
caster sugar

AMERICAN
FOR THE PASTRY:
4 cups flour
pinch of salt
½ cup plus 2 tablespoons butter or
 margarine, cut into pieces
2 teaspoons sugar
2–3 tablespoons cold water
FOR THE FILLING:
1 tablespoon cornstarch
⅔ cup water
6 tablespoons sugar
¾ lb mixed dried fruit (golden
 raisins, raisins, currants)
1 teaspoon ground cinnamon
TO GLAZE:
cold water
sugar

Sift the flour and salt into a bowl. Rub (cut) in the fat until the mixture resembles fine breadcrumbs. Stir in the sugar and add just sufficient water to hold the mixture together, then form into a smooth ball. Wrap in foil or greaseproof (waxed) paper and chill in the refrigerator for 30 minutes.

To make the filling, blend the cornflour (cornstarch) to a smooth paste with a little of the water. Stir in the remaining water and place in a saucepan. Add the sugar, fruit and cinnamon and bring to the boil, stirring constantly, until the mixture thickens. Cook for 1 minute then allow to cool.

Divide the pastry into 2 equal portions. Roll out one half to line a greased 30 x 22.5 cm/12 x 9 inch Swiss roll tin (jelly roll pan). Cover the base with the fruit mixture and spread evenly. Roll the remaining pastry to cover. Lay this over the filling, dampen the edges and press together to seal. Flute with your finger and thumb or press with the back of a fork. Brush with a little water and dredge with caster sugar. Bake in a fairly hot oven (190°C/375°F, Gas Mark 5) for about 25 minutes, or until pale golden.

Cut into 5 x 11 cm/2 x 4½ inch slices and allow to cool before removing from the tin.
Makes 12

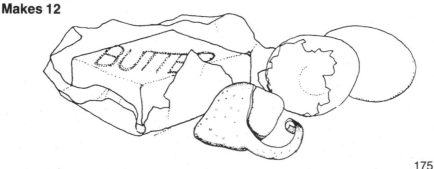

Glazed Apple Flan

METRIC/IMPERIAL

100 g/4 oz quantity sweet flan
  pastry (page 248)
1 egg yolk
25 g/1 oz caster sugar
15 g/½ oz flour
½ teaspoon vanilla essence
150 ml/¼ pint + 1 tablespoon milk
100 g/4 oz granulated sugar
4 tablespoons water
1 medium cooking apple, peeled,
  cored and sliced
little extra caster sugar for
  sprinkling
150 ml/¼ pint double cream
1 tablespoon sifted icing sugar
2 teaspoons orange juice

AMERICAN

1 cup quantity sweet flan pastry
  (page 248)
1 egg yolk
½ cup + 2 tablespoons granulated
  sugar
2 tablespoons flour
½ teaspoon vanilla extract
¾ cup + 1 tablespoon milk
¼ cup water
1 medium cooking apple, peeled,
  cored and sliced
little extra sugar for sprinkling
¾ cup heavy cream
1 tablespoon sifted confectioners'
  sugar
2 teaspoons orange juice

Roll out the dough and use to line a 15 to 18 cm/6 to 7 inch fluted flan or quiche pan, or a flan ring placed on a lightly buttered baking sheet. Prick well all over and line with foil. Bake in a preheated moderately hot oven (200°C/400°F, Gas Mark 6) for 15 minutes. Remove the foil and continue baking for 15 minutes. Remove from the oven and leave to cool.

Beat the egg yolk and caster sugar (2 tablespoons of the granulated sugar) together until light and creamy. Sift in the flour and add the vanilla and 150 ml/¼ pint (¾ cup) of the milk. Pour into a small saucepan and cook, stirring, until the mixture comes to the boil and thickens. Leave to cool.

Dissolve the granulated (remaining) sugar in the water in a saucepan. Add the apples and poach until tender. Drain well and cool.

Spread the cold custard over the bottom of the pastry case. Cover with the apple slices and sprinkle with a little extra caster (granulated) sugar. Place under a preheated grill (broiler) and cook until the sugar melts and begins to turn golden brown. Cool, then chill.

Whip the cream and remaining milk together until thick. Fold in the icing (confectioners') sugar and orange juice. Pipe or spoon over the apples and chill for at least 30 minutes before serving.

Jam Tart

METRIC/IMPERIAL
175 g/6 oz quantity shortcrust
*   pastry (page 246)*
2 tablespoons fresh breadcrumbs
3 tablespoons jam

AMERICAN
1 ½ cup quantity pie pastry
*   (page 246)*
2 tablespoons soft bread crumbs
3 tablespoons jam

Roll out the dough and use to line a 20 to 23 cm/8 to 9 inch pie pan.
Sprinkle the bottom of the case with the breadcrumbs and place the pan
on a baking sheet. Spread the jam in the case.

Bake in a preheated hot oven (230°C/450°F, Gas Mark 8) for 10 minutes,
then reduce the heat to cool (150°C/300°F, Gas Mark 2) and continue
baking for 30 minutes. Leave to cool before serving.

Lattice Jam Tart

METRIC/IMPERIAL
225 g/8 oz quantity shortcrust
*   pastry (page 246)*
6 tablespoons jam

AMERICAN
2 cup quantity pie pastry (page
*   246)*
6 tablespoons jam

Roll out the pastry dough and use three-quarters to line an 18 cm/7 inch
tart tin. Spread the jam evenly over the bottom of the pastry case. Use the
remaining dough in strips, to make a lattice on top of the jam.

Bake in a preheated hot oven (220°C/425°F, Gas Mark 7) for 15 to
20 minutes. Leave to cool before serving.

Mince Pie

METRIC/IMPERIAL
225 g/8 oz quantity shortcrust
*   pastry (page 246)*
500 g/1 lb mincemeat
beaten egg
sifted icing sugar

AMERICAN
2 cup quantity pie pastry (page
*   246)*
1 lb (about 2 cups) mincemeat
beaten egg
sifted confectioners' sugar

Cut the pastry into two pieces. Roll out one portion and use to line a lightly
buttered 18 to 20 cm/7 to 8 inch pie pan or plate. Spread the mincemeat
over the dough to within 1 cm/½ inch of the edge. Moisten the edges with
a little water.

Roll out the remaining dough and lay over the pie pan. Press the edges
well together. Brush with a little beaten egg and place on a baking sheet.

Bake in a preheated hot oven (220°C/425°F, Gas Mark 7) for 15 minutes.
Lower the heat to moderately hot (200°C/400°F, Gas Mark 6) and bake for
a further 30 minutes. Dredge with sifted icing (confectioners') sugar before
serving.

Berry Flan

METRIC/IMPERIAL
*100 g/4 oz quantity sweet flan
  pastry (page 248)*
1 egg yolk
25 g/1 oz caster sugar
15 g/½ oz flour
½ teaspoon vanilla essence
150 ml/¼ pint + 1 tablespoon milk
*500 g/1 lb raspberries, strawberries
  or loganberries*
*2 tablespoons redcurrant jelly,
  melted*
150 ml/¼ pint double cream
1 tablespoon sifted icing sugar
2 teaspoons orange juice

AMERICAN
*1 cup quantity sweet flan pastry
  (page 248)*
1 egg yolk
2 tablespoons granulated sugar
2 tablespoons flour
½ teaspoon vanilla extract
¾ cup + 1 tablespoon milk
*1 lb raspberries, strawberries or
  loganberries*
*2 tablespoons red currant jelly,
  melted*
¾ cup heavy cream
*1 tablespoon sifted confectioners'
  sugar*
2 teaspoons orange juice

Roll out the dough and use to line a 15 to 18 cm/6 to 7 inch fluted flan or quiche pan, or a flan ring placed on a lightly buttered baking sheet. Prick well all over and line with foil. Bake in a preheated moderately hot oven (200°C/400°F, Gas Mark 6) for 15 minutes. Remove the foil and continue baking for 15 minutes. Remove from the oven and leave to cool.

Beat the egg yolk and caster (granulated) sugar together until light and thick. Sift in the flour and add the vanilla and 150 ml/¼ pint (¾ cup) of the milk. Pour into a small saucepan and cook, stirring, until the mixture comes to the boil and thickens. Leave to cool.

Spread the cold custard over the bottom of the pastry case. Cover with the berries and brush with the redcurrant jelly.

Whip the cream and remaining milk together until thick. Fold in the icing (confectioners') sugar and orange juice. Pipe or spoon over the berries and chill for at least 30 minutes before serving.

VARIATIONS:
Apricot Flan – make as above, using well-drained canned apricot halves instead of berries, and apricot jam instead of redcurrant jelly.
Peach Flan – make as above, using well-drained canned peach halves instead of berries.

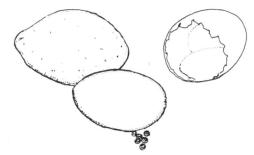

Custard Tart

METRIC/IMPERIAL
175 g/6 oz quantity shortcrust
  pastry (page 246)
1 tablespoon fresh white
  breadcrumbs
2 eggs
25 g/1 oz caster sugar
300 ml/½ pint lukewarm milk
1 egg yolk
grated nutmeg

AMERICAN
1 ½ cup quantity pie pastry (page
  246)
1 tablespoon soft white bread
  crumbs
2 eggs
2 tablespoons sugar
1 ¼ cups lukewarm milk
1 egg yolk
grated nutmeg

Roll out the dough and use to line a 20 to 23 cm/8 to 9 inch pie pan.
Sprinkle the bottom of the case with the breadcrumbs and place the pan
on a baking sheet.
    Beat the eggs with the sugar, milk and egg yolk and strain into the pastry
case. Sprinkle with grated nutmeg.
    Bake in a preheated moderately hot oven (200°C/400°F, Gas Mark 6) for
15 minutes. Lower the heat to moderate (160°C/325°F, Gas Mark 3) and
bake for a further 30 to 45 minutes, or until the filling is set.

Double Crust Fruit Pie

METRIC/IMPERIAL
500 g/1 lb fresh fruit
225 g/8 oz quantity shortcrust
  pastry (page 246)
100–150 g/4–5 oz granulated sugar
beaten egg for brushing
caster sugar for sprinkling

AMERICAN
1 lb fresh fruit
2 cup quantity pie pastry
  (page 246)
½–⅔ cup sugar
beaten egg for brushing
extra sugar for sprinkling

Prepare the fruit according to type.
    Divide the dough in half. Roll out one portion and use to line a lightly
buttered pie plate or pan. Cover the dough with layers of fruit and sugar,
leaving about 2.5 cm/1 inch clear around the edge. Moisten the edges of
the pastry with a little water. Roll out the second portion of dough and lay
over the pie. Press the edges well together, and flake using a fork.
    Brush the top with beaten egg and make two slits in the top of the pie.
Bake in a preheated hot oven (220°C/425°F, Gas Mark 7) for 20 minutes.
Lower the heat to moderate (180°C/350°F, Gas Mark 4) and bake for a
further 30 to 40 minutes. Sprinkle the top with sugar before serving.

Lemon Meringue Pie

METRIC/IMPERIAL

175 g/6 oz quantity shortcrust
  pastry (page 246)
2 tablespoons cornflour
50 g/2 oz caster sugar
finely grated rind and juice of
  2 large lemons
50 ml/¼ pint water
15 g/½ oz butter
2 egg yolks
1 quantity meringue topping
  (page 250)

AMERICAN

1½ cup quantity pie pastry
  (page 246)
2 tablespoons cornstarch
¼ cup sugar
finely grated rind and juice of
  2 large lemons
¾ cup water
1 tablespoon butter
2 egg yolks
1 quantity meringue topping
  (page 250)

Roll out the dough and use to line an 18 to 20 cm/7 to 8 inch fluted flan or quiche pan, or a flan ring placed on a lightly buttered baking sheet.

Prick all over with a fork and line with foil. Bake in a preheated moderately hot oven (200°C/400°F, Gas Mark 6) for 15 minutes. Remove the foil and bake for a further 15 minutes.

Meanwhile, put the cornflour (cornstarch) into a bowl and mix in the sugar and lemon rind. Mix to a smooth paste with a little of the cold water. Heat the rest of the water in a saucepan with the lemon juice. Mix with the cornflour (cornstarch) paste, then return to the saucepan. Cook, stirring, until the mixture comes to the boil and thickens. Simmer for 3 minutes. Beat in the butter and egg yolks and cook gently for a further minute. Pour into the pastry case.

Pile the meringue topping on top and spread well to the edges. Reduce the oven heat to very cool (110°C/225°F, Gas Mark ¼) and bake the pie for 1½ to 2 hours or until the meringue is crisp and golden.

Family Sponge

METRIC/IMPERIAL
175 g/6 oz butter or margarine
175 g/6 oz sugar
3 eggs
225 g/8 oz self-raising flour
pinch of salt
2 tablespoons milk
4 tablespoons jam
caster sugar to sprinkle

AMERICAN
¾ cup butter or margarine
1½ cups sugar
3 eggs
2 cups self-rising flour
pinch of salt
2 tablespoons milk
¼ cup jam
sugar to sprinkle

Cream the butter and sugar together until pale and fluffy. Add the eggs one at a time beating well after each addition. Fold in the flour and salt with the milk.

Turn the mixture into a greased 20 cm/8 inch square cake tin lined with greased greaseproof (waxed) paper. Bake in a moderate oven (180°C/350°F, Gas Mark 4) for 30 to 35 minutes, or until well risen and golden-brown. The cake will have shrunk slightly from the sides of the tin.

Turn the cake out on a wire rack to cool. When cold split into 2 layers and sandwich together with the jam and sprinkle with caster sugar. Serve cut into squares.

VARIATIONS:
Fruit Cake – add the grated zest of 1 orange to the creamed mixture and 75 g/3 oz (½ cup) mixed dried fruit, (sultanas (golden raisins), raisins, currants) with the flour. Bake for 40 to 45 minutes.
Cup Cakes – the mixture may be baked in paper cases in well-greased bun tins (muffin pans) for about 15 minutes. Top with glacé icing or brush with melted redcurrant jelly, sprinkle with coconut and top with half a glacé cherry.

Dripping Gingerbread

METRIC/IMPERIAL
350 g/12 oz wholewheat flour
pinch of salt
2 teaspoons ground ginger
100 g/4 oz beef dripping
100 g/4 oz golden syrup
100 g/4 oz black treacle
75 g/3 oz soft brown sugar
1 teaspoon bicarbonate of soda
150 ml/¼ pint milk, warmed

AMERICAN
3 cups wholewheat flour
pinch of salt
2 teaspoons ground ginger
½ cup beef dripping
⅓ cup corn syrup
⅓ cup molasses
½ cup firmly packed light brown
  sugar
1 teaspoon baking soda
⅔ cup milk, warmed

Sift the flour, salt and ground ginger together into a large mixing bowl. Melt the dripping, golden syrup (corn syrup), treacle (molasses) and brown sugar gently in a saucepan over low heat. Add to the flour and beat well. Dissolve the bicarbonate of soda (baking soda) in the warm milk. Add to the beaten mixture and mix thoroughly.

Pour into a greased 25 x 20 cm/10 x 8 inch tin, lined with greased greaseproof (waxed) paper. Bake in a cool oven (150°C/300°F, Gas Mark 2) for about 1 hour, or until a fine skewer inserted in the centre comes out clean. Leave the gingerbread to cool in the tin, then turn out and strip off the lining paper. Store in an airtight tin to keep the cake moist.

Gingerbread

METRIC/IMPERIAL
225 g/8 oz flour
½ teaspoon bicarbonate of soda
2 teaspoons ground ginger
1 teaspoon mixed spice
100 g/4 oz golden syrup
25 g/1 oz soft brown sugar
25 g/1 oz butter
1 egg, beaten
2 tablespoons milk
1 teaspoon black treacle

AMERICAN
2 cups flour
½ teaspoon baking soda
2 teaspoons ground ginger
1 teaspoon apple pie spice
⅓ cup light corn syrup
2½ tablespoons brown sugar
2 tablespoons butter
1 egg, beaten
2 tablespoons milk
1 teaspoon molasses

Sift the flour, soda and spices into a mixing bowl. Make a well in the middle. Put the syrup, sugar and butter into a saucepan and heat gently until the butter has melted. Mix well, then pour into the well in the flour with the egg, milk and treacle (molasses). Stir without beating until well mixed.

Pour into a greased and lined 15 cm/6 inch round deep cake pan. Bake in a preheated moderate oven (180°C/350°F, Gas Mark 4) for 1 hour or until a wooden cocktail stick inserted in the centre comes out clean. Turn out onto a wire rack and peel away the lining paper when the cake is cold.

Swiss (Jelly) Roll

METRIC/IMPERIAL
3 eggs
75 g/3 oz caster sugar
75 g/3 oz self-raising flour
4 tablespoons warmed jam

AMERICAN
3 eggs
6 tablespoons sugar
¾ cup self-rising flour
¼ cup warmed jam

Put the eggs into a large heatproof bowl placed over a saucepan of hot water and whisk for 2 minutes. Add the sugar and continue whisking for 10 minutes or until thick and creamy. Remove the bowl from the saucepan and whisk for a further 5 minutes or until cool. (If using an electric mixer, no heat is needed.) Fold in the flour with a metal spoon.

Pour the cake mixture into a greased and lined 30 x 20 cm/12 x 8 inch Swiss (jelly) roll pan. Bake in a preheated moderately hot oven (100°C/400°F, Gas Mark 6) for 10 to 12 minutes.

Turn out onto a sugared sheet of greaseproof (parchment) paper placed on a tea (dish) towel. Peel off the lining paper, and trim away the crusty edges from the cake.

Spread quickly with the jam, roll up and hold rolled up for at least 1 minute. Cool on a wire rack.

VARIATION:
Chocolate Swiss (Jelly) Roll – make as above, using only 65 g/2½ oz (½ cup + 2 tablespoons) flour and adding 2 tablespoons cocoa powder.

Family Fruit Cake

METRIC/IMPERIAL
225 g/8 oz self-raising flour
100 g/4 oz butter
1 teaspoon finely grated lemon rind
100 g/4 oz mixed dried fruit
100 g/4 oz caster sugar
1 egg
5 tablespoons milk

AMERICAN
2 cups self-rising flour
½ cup butter
1 teaspoon finely grated lemon rind
⅔ cup mixed dried fruit
½ cup sugar
1 egg
5 tablespoons milk

Sift the flour into a bowl. Rub in the butter well, then stir in the lemon rind, fruit and sugar. Mix to a batter with the egg and milk. Stir with a metal spoon until everything is well mixed; do not beat.

Pour into a greased and lined 15 cm/6 inch round deep cake pan. Bake in a preheated moderate oven (180°C/350°F, Gas Mark 4) for 1¼ to 1½ hours or until a wooden cocktail stick inserted in the centre comes out clean. Leave to cool in the pan for at least 5 minutes, then turn out onto a wire rack.

VARIATION:
Plain Family Cake – make as above, omitting the fruit.

Parkin

METRIC/IMPERIAL
225 g/8 oz flour
1 teaspoon mixed spice
1 teaspoon ground cinnamon
1 teaspoon ground ginger
½ teaspoon salt
1 teaspoon bicarbonate of soda
225 g/8 oz oatmeal
150 ml/¼ pint milk
175 g/6 oz black treacle
100 g/4 oz soft brown sugar
150 g/5 oz butter
1 egg, beaten

AMERICAN
2 cups flour
1 teaspoon apple pie spice
1 teaspoon ground cinnamon
1 teaspoon ground ginger
½ teaspoon salt
1 teaspoon baking soda
1⅓ cups oatmeal
¾ cup milk
½ cup molasses
½ cup firmly packed light brown
  sugar
½ cup + 2 tablespoons butter
1 egg, beaten

Sift the flour, spices, salt and soda into a bowl. Add the oatmeal and make a well in the middle.

Put the milk, treacle (molasses), sugar and butter in a saucepan. Heat gently, stirring, until the butter has melted. Pour into the well in the flour with the egg and stir, without beating, until the mixture is smooth and creamy.

Pour into a greased and lined 18 cm/7 inch square cake pan. Bake in a preheated moderate oven (180°C/350°F, Gas Mark 4) for 1 hour or until a wooden cocktail stick inserted in the centre comes out clean. Cool on a wire rack and store, without taking the lining paper off, in a tin for about 1 week before cutting.

Orange, Carrot and Nut Cake

METRIC/IMPERIAL
100 g/4 oz butter
175 g/6 oz caster sugar
1 teaspoon ground cinnamon
1 teaspoon grated orange zest
2 eggs, lightly beaten
75 g/3 oz raw carrot, finely grated
50 g/2 oz walnuts, finely chopped
1 tablespoon orange juice
225 g/8 oz self-raising flour
pinch of salt

AMERICAN
½ cup butter
¾ cup sugar
1 teaspoon ground cinnamon
1 teaspoon grated orange zest
2 eggs, lightly beaten
½ cup raw carrot, finely grated
½ cup finely chopped walnuts
1 tablespoon orange juice
2 cups self-rising flour
pinch of salt

Cream the butter and sugar together in a bowl until pale and fluffy. Beat in the ground cinnamon and orange zest. Gradually add the eggs, beating well after each addition. Stir in the grated carrot, chopped nuts and orange juice. Sift the flour and salt together and fold into the creamed mixture.

Turn into a greased 20 cm/8 inch cake tin lined with greased greaseproof (waxed) paper and smooth the top. Bake in a warm oven (160°C/325°F, Gas Mark 3) for 45 to 55 minutes, or until the centre of the cake springs back when lightly pressed with a fingertip. Turn out on a wire rack to cool. If liked, the cake can be decorated with orange glacé icing, butter icing, or sifted icing (confectioners') sugar.

Oat Crisps

METRIC/IMPERIAL
150 g/5 oz butter
50 g/2 oz golden syrup
100 g/4 oz demerara sugar
75 g/3 oz quick cook oats
50 g/2 oz desiccated coconut
100 g/4 oz plain flour
1 teaspoon bicarbonate of soda
1 teaspoon hot water

AMERICAN
½ cup plus 2 tablespoons butter
4 tablespoons corn syrup
⅔ cup brown or raw sugar
3 tablespoons quick cook oats
⅔ cup shredded coconut
1 cup all-purpose flour
1 teaspoon baking soda
1 teaspoon hot water

Place the butter, syrup and sugar in a large saucepan. Heat gently until the butter has melted and the sugar dissolved. Mix together the oats, coconut and flour, then stir into the melted mixture. Dissolve the bicarbonate of soda (baking soda) in the hot water and stir into the oat mixture. Allow to cool for a few minutes then form into 18 balls.

Place the balls well apart on greased baking sheets. Leave plenty of space for spreading. Bake in a warm oven (160°C/325°F, Gas Mark 3) for 15 to 20 minutes, or until evenly browned. Leave to cool slightly and set before removing them with a palette knife. Cool on a wire rack. Store in an airtight container.

Cherry Cake

METRIC/IMPERIAL
100 g/4 oz glacé cherries,
quartered
225 g/8 oz self-raising flour
50 g/2 oz semolina
150 g/5 oz butter
100 g/4 oz caster sugar
1 teaspoon finely grated lemon rind
2–3 tablespoons milk
2 eggs, beaten
½ teaspoon vanilla essence

AMERICAN
⅔ cup quartered glacé cherries
2 cups self-rising flour
½ cup semolina flour
½ cup + 2 tablespoons butter
½ cup sugar
1 teaspoon finely grated lemon rind
2–3 tablespoons milk
2 eggs, beaten
½ teaspoon vanilla extract

Rinse the cherries to remove the syrup and dry well. Mix with 1 tablespoon of the flour. Sift the rest of the flour and the semolina into a bowl and rub in the butter well. Stir in the cherries, sugar and lemon rind. Add the milk, eggs and vanilla and mix to a stiff mixture without beating.

Pour into a greased and lined 18 cm/7 inch round cake pan. Bake in a preheated moderate oven (180°C/350°F, Gas Mark 4) for 1 hour or until a wooden cocktail stick inserted in the centre comes out clean. Leave to cool in the pan for 5 minutes, then turn out onto a wire rack.

Genoese Sandwich (Layer) Cake

METRIC/IMPERIAL
50 g/2 oz butter
3 eggs
75 g/3 oz caster sugar
75 g/3 oz flour

AMERICAN
¼ cup butter
3 eggs
6 tablespoons sugar
¾ cup flour

Melt the butter over a very low heat. Strain into a clean bowl, using a coffee filter paper, muslin or cheesecloth. Leave to cool.

Put the eggs in a large heatproof bowl placed over a saucepan of boiling water and whisk for 2 minutes. Add the sugar and whisk for a further 8 to 10 minutes or until pale and fairly thick. Remove the bowl from the saucepan and continue to whisk for 5 minutes or until cool. (If using an electric mixer, no heat is needed.)

Using a metal spoon, fold in half the cooled butter and half the flour, then fold in the rest of the flour and butter. Pour into two greased and lined 18 cm/7 inch round sandwich (layer) cake pans. Bake in a preheated moderate oven (180°C/350°F, Gas Mark 4) for 25 to 35 minutes. Leave to cool in the pans for 1 minute, then turn out onto a clean tea (dish) towel. Peel away the lining paper. When cold, sandwich together with whipped cream or buttercream (page 250).

Sponge Sandwich (Layer) Cake

METRIC/IMPERIAL	AMERICAN
3 eggs	3 eggs
75 g/3 oz caster sugar	6 tablespoons sugar
75 g/3 oz self-raising flour	¾ cup self-rising flour

Put the eggs into a large heatproof bowl placed over a saucepan of hot water and whisk for 2 minutes. Add the sugar and continue whisking for 10 minutes or until thick and creamy. Remove the bowl from the saucepan and whisk for a further 5 minutes or until cool. (If using an electric mixer no heat is needed.) Fold in the flour with a metal spoon.

Divide between two greased and lined 18 cm/7 inch sandwich tins (layer cake pans). Bake in a preheated moderate oven (180°C/350°F, Gas Mark 4) for 20 minutes. Turn out onto a sheet of sugared greaseproof (parchment) paper placed on top of a tea (dish) towel and leave to cool.

VARIATIONS:
Deep Sponge Cake – make the cake mixture as above, using plain (all-purpose) flour instead of self-raising. Pour into a greased and lined 18 cm/7 inch round deep cake pan. Bake as above, allowing 45 to 55 minutes or until a skewer inserted into the centre comes out clean. Cool, then cut into two layers and sandwich together with buttercream (page 250). Dredge the top of the cake with sifted icing (confectioners' sugar).
Jam and Cream Sponge Sandwich (Layer) Cake – make as above. When cold, sandwich the layers together with 2-3 tablespoons jam and 4-6 tablespoons whipped cream.

Butterfly Cakes

METRIC/IMPERIAL	AMERICAN
100 g/4 oz butter, softened	½ cup butter, softened
100 g/4 oz caster sugar	½ cup sugar
2 eggs	2 eggs
100 g/4 oz self-raising flour, sifted	1 cup self-rising flour, sifted
1 quantity buttercream (page 250)	1 quantity buttercream (page 250)

Cream the butter and sugar together until light and fluffy. Beat in the eggs one at a time, adding a tablespoon of the flour with each. Fold in the rest of the flour.

Divide the cake mixture between 18 small paper cake cases. Bake in a preheated moderately hot oven (190°C/375°F, Gas Mark 5) for 15 to 20 minutes. Cool on a wire rack.

Cut off a slice from the top of each cake. Cut each slice in half. Put a blob of buttercream on top of each cake and replace the halved slices to resemble wings.
Makes 18

Rich Butter Cake

METRIC/IMPERIAL
175 g/6 oz butter, softened
175 g/6 oz caster sugar
3 eggs
225 g/8 oz flour
1 ½ teaspoons baking powder
2 tablespoons milk

AMERICAN
¾ cup butter, softened
¾ cup sugar
3 eggs
2 cups flour
1 ½ teaspoons baking powder
2 tablespoons milk

Cream the butter with the sugar until light and fluffy. Beat in the eggs one at a time, adding a tablespoon of flour with each. Beat in the rest of the flour with the baking powder and milk.

Pour into a greased and lined 20 cm/8 inch round cake pan and smooth the top. Bake in a preheated moderate oven (160°C/325°F, Gas Mark 3) for 1 ½ to 1 ¾ hours or until a wooden cocktail stick inserted in the centre comes out clean.

Leave to cool in the pan for 5 minutes, then turn out onto a wire rack. Peel off the paper when the cake is cold.

VARIATIONS:
Almond and Raisin Cake – make as above, adding ½ teaspoon almond essence (extract) to the creamed mixture, 50 g/2 oz (½ cup) ground almonds with the flour, and 100 g/4 oz (⅔ cup) raisins after the eggs.
Coconut Cake – make as above, adding 1 teaspoon vanilla essence (extract) to the creamed mixture, 50 g/2 oz desiccated coconut (⅓ cup shredded coconut) after the eggs, and increasing the milk to 4 tablespoons.
Currant Cake – make as above, adding 1 teaspoon finely grated lemon rind to the creamed mixture, and 175 g/6 oz (1 cup) currants after the eggs.
Ginger Cake – make as above, adding 1 teaspoon ground ginger with the flour, and 75 g/3 oz (½ cup) chopped preserved ginger after the eggs.
Madeira Cake – make as above, adding the finely grated rind of 1 medium lemon to the creamed mixture. Before baking, place 2 strips of lemon rind on the top of the cake.
Orange cake – make as above, adding 2 teaspoons finely grated orange rind to the creamed mixture.
Seed Cake – make as above, adding 1 tablespoon caraway seeds after the eggs.
Sultana (Raisin) Cake – make as above, adding 1 teaspoon finely grated lemon rind and ½ teaspoon vanilla essence (extract) to the creamed mixture, and 175 g/6 oz sultanas (1 cup golden raisins) after the eggs.

Dundee Cake

METRIC/IMPERIAL	AMERICAN
175 g/6 oz butter, softened	¾ cup butter, softened
175 g/6 oz caster sugar	¾ cup sugar
finely grated rind of 1 small orange	finely grated rind of 1 small orange
3 eggs	3 eggs
225 g/8 oz flour	2 cups flour
1½ teaspoons baking powder	1½ teaspoons baking powder
50 g/2 oz ground almonds	½ cup ground almonds
100 g/4 oz currants	⅔ cup currants
100 g/4 oz sultanas	⅔ cup golden raisins
100 g/4 oz raisins	⅔ cup raisins
50 g/2 oz chopped mixed peel	⅓ cup chopped mixed candied peel
2 tablespoons milk	2 tablespoons milk
25–50 g/1–2 oz blanched almonds, split	¼–½ cup split blanched almonds

Cream the butter with the sugar until light and fluffy. Beat in the orange rind, then the eggs one at a time, adding a tablespoon of flour with each. Beat in the remaining flour and baking powder. Stir in the ground almonds, fruit and mixed peel. Beat in the milk.

Pour into a greased and lined 20 cm/8 inch round deep cake pan and smooth the top. Cover the top with the split almonds. Bake in a preheated cool oven (150°C/300°F, Gas Mark 2) for 2½ to 3 hours or until a wooden cocktail stick inserted in the centre comes out clean. Cool on a wire rack.

VARIATION:
Genoa Cake – make as above, using lemon rind instead of orange rind. Omit the raisins, and increase the mixed candied peel to 100 g/4 oz (⅔ cup). Use 25 g/1 oz (¼ cup) chopped almonds instead of the ground almonds, and add 50 g/2 oz (⅓ cup) chopped glacé cherries.

Madeleines

METRIC/IMPERIAL	AMERICAN
1 quantity Victoria sandwich mixture (page 194)	1 quantity Victoria layer cake batter (page 194)
apricot jam, melted	apricot jam, melted
desiccated coconut	shredded coconut
6–7 glacé cherries, halved	6–7 glacé cherries, halved

Pour the cake mixture into 12 to 14 well-greased dariole moulds. Bake in a preheated moderate oven (180°C/350°F, Gas Mark 4) for 25 to 30 minutes. Turn out onto a wire rack to cool.

When cold, cut a slice off the bottoms of the cakes (the widest part) so that they have flat bases. Brush the jam all over them, then roll in the coconut. Put half a glacé cherry on the top of each.

Chocolate Layer Cake

METRIC/IMPERIAL
100 g/4 oz self-raising flour
pinch of salt
2 tablespoons cocoa powder
100 g/4 oz butter
25 g/1 oz golden syrup
100 g/4 oz caster sugar
½ teaspoon vanilla essence
2 eggs
4 teaspoons milk
whipped cream

AMERICAN
1 cup self-rising flour
pinch of salt
2 tablespoons cocoa powder
½ cup butter
2 tablespoons light corn syrup
½ cup sugar
½ teaspoon vanilla extract
2 eggs
4 teaspoons milk
whipped cream

Sift the flour and salt with the cocoa powder twice. Cream the butter, syrup, sugar and vanilla together until light and fluffy. Beat in the eggs one at a time, adding a tablespoon of the flour mixture with each. Fold in the rest of the flour mixture with a metal spoon alternately with the milk.

Pour into a greased and lined 20 cm/8 inch round deep cake pan. Smooth the top with a knife. Bake in a preheated moderate oven (180°C/350°F, Gas Mark 4) for 45 to 55 minutes or until a wooden cocktail stick inserted in the centre comes out clean. Turn out onto a wire rack, peel off the lining paper and leave to cool.

When cold, cut the cake into two or three layers. Sandwich back together with whipped cream and spread cream over the top of the cake. Chill before serving.

VARIATIONS:
Chocolate and Lime Layer Cake – make as above, but cover the top of the cake with 1 quantity lime velvet frosting (page 251).
Mocha Layer Cake – make as above, but sandwich the cake layers together and cover the top with a double quantity of coffee buttercream (page 250). Decorate the top of the cake with grated chocolate and glacé cherries.

Small Iced Cakes

METRIC/IMPERIAL
1 quantity Victoria sandwich
    mixture (page 194)
1 quantity glacé icing (page 251)

AMERICAN
1 quantity Victoria layer cake batter
    (page 194)
1 quantity glacé icing (page 251)

Divide the cake mixture between 18 paper cake cases. Bake in a
preheated moderately hot oven (190°C/375°F, Gas Mark 5) for 20 to
25 minutes. When cold, spread a little glacé icing on the top of each.
Makes 18

VARIATION:
Small Seed Cakes – make the Victoria sandwich (layer) cake mixture,
adding 2 teaspoons caraway seeds after the eggs. Bake as above, but do
not ice.

Caramel and Almond Gâteau

METRIC/IMPERIAL
1 x 18 cm/7 inch round deep
    sponge cake (page 187)
1 quantity caramel cream frosting
    (page 252)
50–75 g/2–3 oz toasted flaked
    almonds
12 toasted blanched almonds

AMERICAN
1 x 7 inch round deep sponge cake
    (page 187)
1 quantity caramel cream frosting
    (page 252)
½–¾ cup toasted sliced almonds
12 toasted blanched almonds

Cut the sponge cake into two layers, then sandwich together with some of
the frosting. Cover the top and sides with the remaining frosting.
    Roll the sides of the cake in the flaked almonds. Arrange the blanched
almonds on the top of the cake. Chill lightly before serving.

Coffee and Hazelnut Gâteau

METRIC/IMPERIAL
3 Victoria sandwich cake layers
    (page 194)
double quantity coffee buttercream
    (page 250)
50 g/2 oz hazelnuts, finely chopped
25 g/1 oz whole hazelnuts

AMERICAN
3 Victoria layer cake layers
    (page 194)
double quantity coffee buttercream
    (page 250)
½ cup finely chopped hazelnuts
¼ cup whole hazelnuts

Sandwich the cake layers together and cover the sides of the cake with
buttercream. Roll the sides in the chopped nuts, then cover the top of the
cake with buttercream. Decorate the top with the whole hazelnuts and chill
before serving.

Chocolate Cakes

METRIC/IMPERIAL
200 g/7 oz self-raising flour
25 g/1 oz cocoa powder
100 g/4 oz butter
75 g/3 oz caster sugar
1 egg, beaten
2–4 teaspoons milk
1 teaspoon vanilla essence

AMERICAN
1¾ cups self-rising flour
¼ cup cocoa powder
½ cup butter
6 tablespoons sugar
1 egg, beaten
2–4 teaspoons milk
1 teaspoon vanilla extract

Sift the flour and cocoa powder into a bowl. Rub in the butter. Add the sugar and mix to a stiff batter with the egg, milk and vanilla.

Put in 10 spoonfuls onto a lightly buttered baking sheet. Bake in a preheated moderately hot oven (200°C/400°F, Gas Mark 6) for 15 to 20 minutes. Cool on a wire rack.
Makes 10

Ginger and Peanut Loaf

METRIC/IMPERIAL
350 g/12 oz self-raising flour
pinch of salt
1 teaspoon ground ginger
50 g/2 oz soft brown sugar
75 g/3 oz sultanas
50 g/2 oz stem ginger, chopped
75 g/3 oz unsalted peanuts
75 g/3 oz butter
4 tablespoons black treacle
2 eggs
150 ml/¼ pint milk

AMERICAN
3 cups self-rising flour
pinch of salt
1 teaspoon ground ginger
¼ cup firmly packed light brown sugar
½ cup golden raisins
¼ cup chopped preserved ginger
¼ cup unsalted peanuts
6 tablespoons butter
¼ cup molasses
2 eggs
⅔ cup milk

Grease a 1 kg/2 lb loaf tin (9 x 5 inch loaf pan) and line the base with a piece of greased greaseproof (waxed) paper. Sift the flour, salt and ground ginger together into a bowl. Add the sugar, sultanas (golden raisins), ginger and peanuts.

Put the butter and treacle (molasses) into a saucepan and heat gently until melted. Add the treacle (molasses) mixture to the dry ingredients, and gradually beat in the eggs and the milk until well blended. Pour the mixture into the prepared loaf tin and bake in a warm oven (160°C/325°F, Gas Mark 3) for 1¼ hours.

Allow the loaf to cool slightly and then turn out on a wire rack and strip off the lining paper. The loaf can be topped with glacé icing and extra ginger and peanuts, if liked.

Meringues

METRIC/IMPERIAL
2 egg whites
100 g/4 oz caster sugar
25 g/1 oz granulated sugar

AMERICAN
2 egg whites
½ cup superfine sugar
2 tablespoons granulated sugar

Brush a large baking sheet with oil and cover with a double thickness of greaseproof (parchment) paper.

Place the egg whites in a large dry bowl and beat until very stiff and peaky. Add half the caster (superfine) sugar and continue beating until the mixture is shiny and stiff. Beat in the rest of the caster (superfine) sugar, then fold in the granulated sugar.

Spoon in 18 mounds on the baking sheet. Dry out in a preheated very cool oven (110°C/225°F, Gas Mark ¼) for 1½ hours.

Remove from the oven. Press a small hole in the base of each meringue with your thumb, then turn upside-down on the baking sheet. Return to the oven and bake for a further 45 minutes to 1 hour. Cool on a wire rack.
Makes 18

VARIATIONS:
Chocolate Cream Meringues – make as above, adding 1½ teaspoons chocolate blancmange (dessert) powder with the granulated sugar. When cold, sandwich pairs of meringues together with whipped cream.
Coffee Meringues – make as above, adding 2 teaspoons instant coffee powder with the granulated sugar.
Cream Meringues – make as above, then sandwich together pairs of meringues with whipped cream.
Lemon Meringues – make as above, adding ½ teaspoon finely grated lemon rind with the granulated sugar.
Orange Meringues – make as above, adding ½ teaspoon finely grated orange rind with the granulated sugar.
Raspberry Cream Meringues – make as above, adding 1½ teaspoons raspberry blancmange (dessert) powder with the granulated sugar. Sandwich together pairs of meringues with whipped cream.
Chocolate Finger Meringues – make the meringue mixture as above, then pipe in 7.5 cm/3 inch lengths onto the baking sheet. Bake as above. When cold, sandwich together pairs of meringue fingers with 1 quantity chocolate buttercream (page 250).

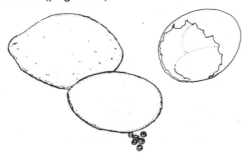

Victoria Sandwich (Layer) Cake

METRIC/IMPERIAL
100 g/4 oz caster sugar
100 g/4 oz butter, softened
2 eggs
100 g/4 oz self-raising flour

AMERICAN
½ cup sugar
½ cup butter, softened
2 eggs
1 cup self-rising flour

Cream the sugar and butter together until light and creamy. Beat in the eggs one at a time, adding a tablespoon of the flour with each. Slowly fold in the rest of the flour using a metal spoon.

Pour into two greased and lined 18 cm/7 inch sandwich tins (layer cake pans) and smooth the tops with a knife. Bake in a preheated moderate oven (180°C/350°F, Gas Mark 4) for 25 to 30 minutes. Leave to cool in the pans for 5 minutes, then turn out onto a wire rack. Peel off the paper and leave to cool.

VARIATIONS:

Chocolate Victoria Sandwich (Layer) Cake – make as above, then sandwich the two cake layers together with 1 quantity chocolate buttercream (page 250).

Strawberry Victoria Sandwich (Layer) Cake – make as above, then sandwich the two cake layers together and cover the top of the cake with about three-quarters of the double quantity of buttercream (page 250). Cover the buttercream on top with 100 to 175 g/4 to 6 oz (1 to 1½ cups) halved strawberries. Brush with 1 to 2 tablespoons melted apricot jam, then pipe the remaining buttercream around the edge of the top.

Jam Victoria Sandwich (Layer) Cake – make as above, then sandwich the two cake layers together with 2 to 3 tablespoons jam.

Lemon Victoria Sandwich (Layer) Cake – make as above, adding 1 teaspoon finely grated lemon rind to the creamed mixture. Sandwich the two cake layers together with 1 quantity lemon buttercream (page 250).

Mixed Fruit Victoria Sandwich (Layer) Cake – make as above, then sandwich the two cake layers together and cover the top of the cake with about three-quarters of a double quantity of buttercream (page 250). Arrange drained canned peach slices and halved black and green grapes on the top of the cake. Pipe the remaining buttercream around the edge of the top.

Rich Bran Fruit Loaf

METRIC/IMPERIAL
225 g/8 oz soft brown sugar
100 g/4 oz All Bran
225 g/8 oz mixed dried fruit
  (currants, raisins, sultanas)
1 tablespoons shredded dried
  orange peel
1 tablespoon golden syrup
250 ml/8 fl oz milk
1 egg, beaten
1 large banana, peeled and
  mashed
100 g/4 oz self-raising flour

AMERICAN
1⅓ cups firmly packed light brown
  sugar
1 cup All Bran
1⅓ cups mixed dried fruit (currants,
  raisins, golden raisins)
1 tablespoon shredded dried
  orange peel
1 tablespoon corn syrup
1 cup milk .
1 egg, beaten
1 large banana, peeled and
  mashed
1 cup self-rising flour

Place the sugar, All Bran, dried fruit, orange peel, syrup and milk in a bowl and stir well. Allow to soak overnight.

The next day, add the beaten egg, mashed banana and flour and mix thoroughly.

Turn the mixture into a greased 1 kg/2 lb loaf tin (9 x 5 inch loaf pan) and bake in a moderate oven (180°C/350°F, Gas Mark 4) for about 1 hour, until the cake is cooked, or until a skewer inserted in the centre comes out clean.

Turn out on a wire rack to cool slightly. Slice the loaf while still warm or very fresh, and serve with butter.

Fairy Cakes

METRIC/IMPERIAL
100 g/4 oz butter, softened
100 g/4 oz caster sugar
2 eggs
100 g/4 oz self-raising flour
50 g/2 oz currants

AMERICAN
½ cup butter, softened
½ cup sugar
2 eggs
1 cup self-rising flour
⅓ cup currants

Cream the butter and sugar together until light and fluffy. Beat in the eggs one at a time, adding a tablespoon of flour with each. Fold in the rest of the flour and the fruit.

Put into 18 small paper cases standing on a baking sheet. Bake in a preheated moderately hot oven (190°C/375°F, Gas Mark 5) for 20 to 25 minutes.
Makes 18

VARIATION:
Chocolate Chip Cakes – make as above, using 50 g/2 oz (¼ cup) chopped plain (sweet) chocolate instead of the currants.

Plain Biscuits (Cookies)

METRIC/IMPERIAL
225 g/8 oz self-raising flour
pinch of salt
150 g/5 oz butter
100 g/4 oz caster sugar
1 egg, beaten

AMERICAN
2 cups self-rising flour
pinch of salt
½ cup + 2 tablespoons butter
½ cup sugar
1 egg, beaten

Sift the flour and salt into a mixing bowl. Rub in the butter finely. Stir in the sugar. Mix to a very stiff dough with the egg. Turn onto a lightly floured board and knead gently until smooth and elastic. Put in a plastic bag and chill for 30 minutes.

Roll out the dough fairly thin. Using a 5 cm/2 inch biscuit (cookie) cutter, cut out about 30 rounds. Place on a lightly buttered baking sheet, and prick all over with a fork. Bake in a preheated moderate oven (180°C/350°F, Gas Mark 4) for 12 to 15 minutes. Leave on the baking sheet to cool.

Makes about 30

VARIATIONS:

Almond Biscuits (Cookies) – make as above, adding 50 g/2 oz (½ cup) ground almonds with the sugar, and ½ teaspoon vanilla essence (extract) with the egg.

Cherry Biscuits (Cookies) – make as above, adding 50 g/2 oz (⅓ cup) finely chopped glacé cherries with the sugar.

Chocolate Flake Biscuits (Cookies) – make as above, adding 50 g/2 oz (¼ cup) grated plain (sweet) chocolate with the sugar.

Coconut Biscuits (Cookies) – make as above, adding 50 g/2 oz desiccated coconut (⅓ cup shredded coconut) with the sugar, and ½ teaspoon vanilla essence (extract) with the egg.

Currant Biscuits (Cookies) – make as above, adding 50 g/2 oz (⅓ cup) currants with the sugar.

Jam Sandwich Biscuits (Cookies) – make as above. When cold, sandwich pairs of biscuits (cookies) together with raspberry jam, and sprinkle the tops with sifted icing (confectioners') sugar.

Lemon Biscuits (Cookies) – make as above, adding 1 teaspoon finely grated lemon rind with the sugar.

Spice Biscuits (Cookies) – make as above, adding 1½ teaspoons mixed spice (apple pie spice) or ground cinnamon with the flour.

Sugar-Topped Biscuits (Cookies) – make as above, but before baking brush with beaten egg and sprinkle with caster (granulated) sugar.

Walnut Biscuits (Cookies) – make as above, adding 40 g/1½ oz (⅓ cup) finely chopped walnuts with the egg.

Peanut Biscuits (Cookies)

METRIC/IMPERIAL
275 g/10 oz self-raising flour
½ teaspoon ground cinnamon
275 g/10 oz margarine
225 g/8 oz soft brown sugar
100 g/4 oz salted peanuts, finely
  chopped
100 g/¼ lb seedless raisins
1-2 tablespoons milk

AMERICAN
2½ cups self-rising flour
½ teaspoon ground cinnamon
1¼ cups margarine
1⅓ cups firmly packed light brown
  sugar
1 cup salted peanuts, finely
  chopped
⅔ cup seedless raisins
1-2 tablespoons milk

Sift the flour and cinnamon together. Cream the margarine and sugar together until light and fluffy. Fold in the flour with the chopped peanuts and raisins and sufficient milk to make a soft dough.

Using half the mixture, drop teaspoonfuls on to two baking sheets, allowing room to spread. Bake in a moderate oven (180°C/350°F, Gas Mark 4) for 10 minutes. Remove with a palette knife and cool on a wire rack while baking the second batch.
Makes about 48

Rich Shortbread

METRIC/IMPERIAL
100 g/4 oz butter, softened
50 g/2 oz caster sugar
150 g/5 oz flour
25 g/1 oz semolina
extra caster sugar for sprinkling

AMERICAN
½ cup butter, softened
¼ cup sugar
1¼ cups flour
¼ cup semolina flour
extra sugar for sprinkling

Cream the butter and sugar together until light and fluffy. Slowly mix in the flour and semolina. Draw together with your fingers and press into a lightly buttered 18 cm/7 inch sandwich tin (layer cake pan). Prick well all over, and mark the edges using a fork.

Bake in a preheated moderate oven (160°C/325°F, Gas Mark 3) for about 30 minutes. Leave to cool in the pan for 5 minutes, then cut into eight pieces. Dredge with extra sugar. Remove from the pan when cold.
Makes 8

VARIATIONS:
Lemon Shortbread – make as above, adding the finely grated rind of 1 lemon with the flour.
Orange Shortbread – make as above, adding 1 teaspoon grated orange rind with the flour.

Chocolate Drops

METRIC/IMPERIAL
50 g/2 oz caster sugar
100 g/4 oz butter, softened
½ teaspoon vanilla essence
90 g/3½ oz flour
15 g/½ oz cocoa powder

AMERICAN
¼ cup sugar
½ cup butter, softened
½ teaspoon vanilla extract
¾ cup + 2 tablespoons flour
2 tablespoons cocoa powder

Cream the sugar with the butter until light and fluffy. Add the vanilla and beat in well. Stir in the flour and cocoa powder.

Put in 18 to 20 teaspoons onto a lightly buttered and floured baking sheet, spacing them well apart from each other. Bake in a preheated moderately hot oven (190°C/375°F, Gas Mark 5) for 15 to 20 minutes. Cool on the baking sheet for 5 minutes, then transfer to a wire rack.
Makes 18 to 20

Flapjacks

METRIC/IMPERIAL
75 g/3 oz golden syrup
100 g/4 oz butter
75 g/3 oz soft brown sugar
225 g/8 oz rolled oats

AMERICAN
¼ cup light corn syrup
½ cup butter
½ cup firmly packed brown sugar
2¼ cups rolled oats

Put the syrup, butter and sugar in a saucepan and heat gently until melted. Stir in the oats and mix well together.

Spread into a lightly buttered Swiss (jelly) roll pan, about 20 x 30 cm/ 8 x 12 inches. Smooth the top with a knife. Bake in a preheated moderate oven (180°C/350°F, Gas Mark 4) for 25 to 35 minutes.

Leave to cool in the pan for 5 minutes, then cut into 24 fingers.
Makes 24

Golden Coconut Pyramids

METRIC/IMPERIAL
2 eggs
150 g/5 oz caster sugar
225 g/8 oz desiccated coconut

AMERICAN
2 eggs
½ cup + 2 tablespoons sugar
2⅔ cups shredded coconut

Beat the eggs well; stir in the sugar and coconut. Leave for 25 minutes.

Dip your hands in cold water and shape the coconut mixture into 24 pyramids. Place on baking sheets lined with edible rice paper. Bake in a preheated moderate oven (180°C/350°F, Gas Mark 4) for 25 to 35 minutes or until the pyramids are a pale gold. Remove from the sheets and cut away any extra rice paper, then put on a wire rack to cool.
Makes 24

Coconut Pyramids

METRIC/IMPERIAL
2 egg whites
175 g/6 oz desiccated coconut
150 g/5 oz caster sugar
10–12 glacé cherries, halved

AMERICAN
2 egg whites
1 cup shredded coconut
½ cup + 2 tablespoons sugar
10–12 glacé cherries, halved

Beat the egg whites to a fairly stiff snow. Fold in the coconut and sugar.
Drop in 20 to 24 mounds on a baking sheet lined with edible rice paper and
shape into pyramids.

Bake in a preheated cool oven (150°C/300°F, Gas Mark 2) for about
20 minutes. Remove from the oven, place a half glacé cherry on top of
each and return to the oven to bake for a further 15 to 25 minutes or until
pale gold. Cut away any extra rice paper and cool on a wire rack.
Makes 20 to 24

Butter Whirls

METRIC/IMPERIAL
175 g/6 oz butter, softened
50 g/2 oz icing sugar, sifted
½ teaspoon vanilla essence
175 g/6 oz flour
8-9 glacé cherries, halved

AMERICAN
¾ cup butter, softened
½ cup confectioners' sugar, sifted
½ teaspoon vanilla extract
1½ cups flour
8-9 glacé cherries, halved

Cream the butter, sugar and vanilla together until light and fluffy. Fold in
the flour. Put the mixture into a piping (pastry) bag fitted with a large
star-shaped nozzle (tube).

Pipe 16 to 18 flat whirls on a lightly buttered and floured baking sheet.
Put half a cherry on top of each whirl.

Bake in a preheated moderate oven (160°C/325°F, Gas Mark 3) for
20 minutes. Leave on the baking sheets to cool for about 5 minutes, then
transfer to a wire rack.
Makes 16 to 18

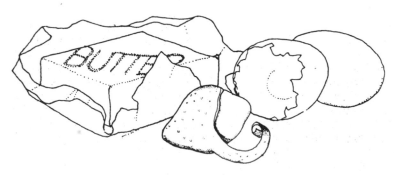

Gingersnaps

METRIC/IMPERIAL
100 g/4 oz self-raising flour
½ teaspoon mixed spice
1 teaspoon ground ginger
50 g/2 oz butter
40 g/1½ oz caster sugar
1 tablespoon black treacle, warmed
milk

AMERICAN
1 cup self-rising flour
½ teaspoon apple pie spice
1 teaspoon ground ginger
¼ cup butter
3 tablespoons sugar
1 tablespoon molasses, warmed
milk

Sift the flour and spices into a mixing bowl. Rub in the butter well. Add the sugar, and mix to a stiff paste with the black treacle (molasses) and milk.

Roll out thinly and, using a 5 cm/2 inch biscuit (cookie) cutter, cut out 26 to 30 rounds. Place on a lightly buttered baking sheet. Bake in a preheated moderate oven (180°C/350°F, Gas Mark 4) for about 10 minutes. Leave to cool on the sheet for at least 3 minutes, then transfer to a wire rack.
Makes 26 to 30

Chocolate Éclairs

METRIC/IMPERIAL
65 g/2½ oz quantity choux pastry
  (page 245)
300 ml/½ pint double cream
2 tablespoons milk
sifted icing sugar
1 quantity chocolate glacé icing
  (page 251)

AMERICAN
½ cup + 2 tablespoon quantity
  choux pastry (page 245)
1¼ cups heavy cream
2 tablespoons milk
sifted confectioners' sugar
1 quantity chocolate glacé icing
  (page 251)

Fit a piping (pastry) bag with a large plain nozzle (tube) and fill with the choux pastry. Pipe twelve 10 cm/4 inch lengths on a lightly buttered baking sheet. Bake in a preheated moderately hot oven (200°C/400°F, Gas Mark 6) for 10 minutes, then lower the heat to moderate (180°C/350°F, Gas Mark 4) and bake for a further 20 to 25 minutes or until the éclairs are puffed and golden.

Remove from the oven and make a slit along the side of each éclair. Return to the oven and bake for a further 5 minutes to dry out the insides. Cool on a wire rack.

Whip the cream and milk together until thick. Sweeten to taste with icing (confectioners') sugar and use to fill the éclairs. Cover the tops with the glacé icing and leave to set.
Makes 12

Cream Horns

METRIC/IMPERIAL
225 g/8 oz quantity flaky pastry
(page 249)
milk for brushing
caster sugar
4 tablespoons red jam
300 ml/½ pint double cream
sifted icing sugar

AMERICAN
2 cup quantity flaky pastry
(page 249)
milk for brushing
granulated sugar
¼ cup red jam
1¼ cups heavy cream
sifted confectioners' sugar

Brush 12 cream horn tins with a little melted butter. Roll out the pastry dough thinly and cut into 12 strips, 2.5 cm/1 inch wide and 30 cm/ 12 inches long. Dampen one side with a little water. Starting at the pointed end of each tin, wrap the dough strips around, with the dampened side towards the tin. Place on a damp baking sheet and leave for 30 minutes.

Bake in a preheated hot oven (230°F/450°F, Gas Mark 8)) for 10 minutes. Remove from the oven. Brush with milk and sprinkle with a little caster (granulated) sugar. Return to the oven and bake for a further 7 to 10 minutes.

Place on a wire rack. Cool for 5 minutes, then remove the tins very carefully. Leave until completely cold.

Pour a teaspoon of jam into the bottom of each pastry horn. Whip the cream until thick and sweeten to taste with icing (confectioners') sugar. Fill the horns with the cream.

Makes 12

Rock Cakes

METRIC/IMPERIAL
225 g/8 oz self-raising flour
100 g/4 oz butter
75 g/3 oz caster sugar
100 g/4 oz mixed dried fruit
1 egg, beaten
2–4 tablespoons milk

AMERICAN
2 cups self-rising flour
½ cup butter
6 tablespoons sugar
⅔ cup mixed dried fruit
1 egg, beaten
2–4 tablespoons milk

Sift the flour into a bowl. Rub in the butter. Add the sugar and fruit and mix to a stiff batter with the egg and milk.

Put 10 spoonfuls onto a lightly buttered baking sheet. Bake in a preheated moderately hot oven (200°C/400°F, Gas Mark 6) for 15 to 20 minutes. Cool on a wire rack.

Makes 10

VARIATION:
Walnut and Orange Cakes — make as above, omitting the fruit, and adding 50 to 75 g/2 to 3 oz (½ to ¾ cup) chopped walnuts and 1 teaspoon finely grated orange rind with the sugar.

Eccles Cakes

METRIC/IMPERIAL
15 g/½ oz butter
¼ teaspoon mixed spice
2 teaspoons soft brown sugar
25 g/1 oz currants
25 g/1 oz chopped mixed peel
225 g/8 oz quantity flaky pastry
(page 249)
milk for brushing
caster sugar

AMERICAN
1 tablespoon butter
¼ teaspoon apple pie spice
2 teaspoons brown sugar
3 tablespoons currants
3 tablespoons chopped mixed
candied peel
2 cup quantity flaky pastry
(page 249)
milk for brushing
granulated sugar

Melt the butter in a saucepan. Stir in the spice, brown sugar, fruit and peel and mix well together.

Roll out the dough to 5 mm/¼ inch thick and cut into eight rounds using a 7.5 cm/3 inch biscuit (cookie) cutter. Put a heaped teaspoon of the fruit mixture onto the middle of each pastry round. Dampen the edges with a little water, and, using the fingertips, draw up the edges so that they meet in the centre. Press well together. Turn upside down (join underneath) and roll out to 1 cm/½ inch thick. Cut three slits in the top of each with a sharp knife. Brush with milk and sprinkle caster (granulated) sugar on top.

Arrange on a baking sheet. Bake in a preheated hot oven (220°C/425°F, Gas Mark 7) for 20 minutes. Cool on a wire rack.
Makes 8

Chocolate Chews

METRIC/IMPERIAL
50 g/2 oz caster sugar
2 tablespoons golden syrup
75 g/3 oz butter
225 g/½ lb quick cook oats
3 tablespoons cocoa powder
1 teaspoon vanilla or rum essence
25 g/1 oz walnuts, chopped
50 g/2 oz seedless raisins,
chopped

AMERICAN
¼ cup sugar
2 tablespoons light or dark corn
syrup
⅓ cup butter
½ lb quick cook oats
3 tablespoons unsweetened cocoa
1 teaspoon vanilla or rum extract
¼ cup chopped walnuts
⅓ cup seedless raisins, chopped

Place the sugar, syrup and butter in a saucepan. Stir over gentle heat until the sugar has dissolved. Bring the mixture to the boil, remove from the heat and stir in the oats, cocoa, vanilla or rum essence (extract), chopped walnuts and chopped raisins.

Mix very thoroughly and spread in a buttered 20 cm/8 inch square cake tin. Chill in the refrigerator until firm then cut into 5 cm/2 inch squares. Remove from the tin with a palette knife and store in an airtight container.
Makes 16

Scones

METRIC/IMPERIAL
225 g/8 oz self-raising flour
½ teaspoon salt
50 g/2 oz butter
150 ml/¼ pint milk
extra milk for brushing

AMERICAN
2 cups self-rising flour
½ teaspoon salt
¼ cup butter
¾ cup milk
extra milk for brushing

Sift the flour and salt into a bowl. Rub in the butter finely. Add the milk and mix to a soft dough using a knife. Put onto a lightly floured board and knead quickly until smooth.

Roll out to 1 cm/½ inch thick and cut out 9 to 12 rounds using a 6 cm/2½ inch biscuit (cookie) cutter. Place on a lightly buttered baking sheet. Brush with milk. Bake in a preheated hot oven (230°C/450°F, Gas Mark 8) for 7 to 12 minutes. Cool on a wire rack. Serve with butter.
Makes 9 to 12

VARIATIONS:
Cheese Scones – make as above, adding 1 teaspoon dry mustard and a pinch of cayenne pepper with the flour, and 50 g/2 oz (½ cup) finely grated Cheddar cheese after the butter.
Ham and Parsley Scones – make as above, adding ½ teaspoon dry mustard with the flour, and 25 g/1 oz (3 tablespoons) diced cooked ham and 1 teaspoon finely chopped parsley after the butter.

Soured Cream Scones

METRIC/IMPERIAL
225 g/8 oz self-raising flour
½ teaspoon salt
40 g/1½ oz butter
4 tablespoons soured cream
4 tablespoons milk
extra milk for brushing

AMERICAN
2 cups self-rising flour
½ teaspoon salt
3 tablespoons butter
¼ cup sour cream
¼ cup milk
extra milk for brushing

Sift the flour and salt into a bowl. Rub in the butter well. Add the soured cream and milk and mix to a soft dough. Put on a lightly floured board and knead quickly until smooth.

Roll out to 1 cm/½ inch thick and cut out 9 to 12 rounds using a 6 cm/2½ inch biscuit (cookie) cutter. Brush with milk and put on a lightly buttered baking sheet. Bake in a preheated hot oven (230°C/450°F, Gas Mark 8) for 7 to 12 minutes. Cool on a wire rack.
Makes 9 to 12

VARIATION:
Buttermilk Scones – make as above, using 150 ml/¼ pint (⅔ cup) buttermilk instead of the milk and soured cream.

Tea Scones

METRIC/IMPERIAL	AMERICAN
225 g/8 oz self-raising flour	*2 cups self-rising flour*
½ teaspoon salt	*½ teaspoon salt*
50 g/2 oz butter	*¼ cup butter*
25 g/1 oz caster sugar	*2 tablespoons sugar*
150 ml/¼ pint milk	*¾ cup milk*
extra milk for brushing	*extra milk for brushing*

Sift the flour and salt into a bowl. Rub in the butter. Stir in the sugar. Add the milk and mix to a soft dough using a knife. Put onto a floured board and knead quickly until smooth.

Roll out to 1 cm/½ inch thick and cut into 9 to 12 rounds using a 6 cm/ 2½ inch biscuit (cookie) cutter. Put onto a lightly buttered baking sheet and brush with milk. Bake in a preheated hot oven (230°C/450°F, Gas Mark 8) for 7 to 10 minutes. Cool on a wire rack, and serve with butter.
Makes 9 to 12

VARIATIONS:
Fruity Scones – make as above, adding to 25 to 50 g/1 to 2 oz (3 to 5 tablespoons) currants or sultanas (golden raisins) with the sugar.
Date and Walnut Scones – make as above, adding 2 tablespoons each finely chopped dates and walnuts with the sugar.
Lemon and Raisin Scones – make as above, adding ½ teaspoon finely grated lemon rind and 50 g/2 oz (⅓ cup) raisins with the sugar.
Orange and Cherry Scones – make as above, adding ½ teaspoon finely grated orange rind and 40 g/1½ oz (¼ cup) chopped glacé cherries with the sugar.
Spice Scones – make as above, adding 1 teaspoon mixed spice (apple pie spice) or ground cinnamon with the flour.
Honey Scones – make as above, adding 1 tablespoon honey with the milk.
Syrup and Ginger Scones – make as above, adding ½ teaspoon ground ginger with the flour, and 1 tablespoon golden syrup (light corn or maple syrup) with the milk.

Dropped Scones

These scones are also called Scotch or American pancakes.

METRIC/IMPERIAL	AMERICAN
225 g/8 oz self-raising flour	2 cups self-rising flour
½ teaspoon salt	½ teaspoon salt
1 tablespoon caster sugar	1 tablespoon sugar
1 egg	1 egg
300 ml/½ pint milk	1½ cups milk
25–50 g/1–2 oz butter, melted	2–4 tablespoons butter, melted

Sift the flour and salt into a bowl. Stir in the sugar. Add the egg and half the milk and mix to a creamy batter. Stir in the rest of the milk.

Brush a large heavy frying pan or griddle with the melted butter and heat. Drop small piles of the scone batter into the frying pan, and cook until bubbles come to the top. Turn over carefully and cook for another 2 to 4 minutes.

Put the scones, in a pile, in a clean folded tea (dish) towel to keep warm. Serve as soon as possible.

Makes about 20

VARIATIONS:

Dropped Scones with Ham – make as above, omitting the sugar, and adding 1 teaspoon dry mustard with the flour, and 50 g/2 oz (¼ cup) diced cooked ham to the batter.

Dropped Scones with Spice – make as above, using brown sugar instead of white, and adding 1 teaspoon mixed spice (apple pie spice) with the flour.

Raspberry Shortcakes

METRIC/IMPERIAL	AMERICAN
1 quantity tea scone dough (page 204)	1 quantity tea scone dough (page 204)
milk for brushing	milk for brushing
50–75 g/2–3 oz butter	¼–⅓ cup butter
4 tablespoons double cream, whipped	¼ cup heavy cream, whipped
225 g/8 oz raspberries	½ lb raspberries
50 g/2 oz icing sugar, sifted	½ cup confectioners' sugar, sifted

Roll out the scone dough to 2.5 cm/1 inch thick. Cut into four rounds with a 7.5 cm/3 inch biscuit (cookie) cutter. Place on a lightly buttered baking sheet and brush with milk. Bake in a preheated hot oven (220°C/425°F, Gas Mark 7) for 15 to 20 minutes. Cool on a wire rack.

Pull open the scones with your fingers and butter both sides thickly. Sandwich together with the whipped cream, and raspberries mixed with the sugar.

Wholemeal Treacle Scones

METRIC/IMPERIAL
100 g/4 oz flour
100 g/4 oz wholemeal flour
25 g/1 oz sugar
½ teaspoon cream of tartar
½ teaspoon bicarbonate of soda
1 teaspoon ground mixed spice
50 g/2 oz butter
2 tablespoons black treacle,
   warmed
7 tablespoons milk

AMERICAN
1 cup flour
1 cup wholemeal flour
2 tablespoons sugar
½ teaspoon cream or tartar
½ teaspoon baking soda
1 teaspoon ground apple pie spice
¼ cup butter
2 tablespoons molasses, warmed
7 tablespoons milk

Put the dry ingredients into a bowl and stir until thoroughly mixed. Rub in the butter then stir in the treacle (molasses) and 6 tablespoons of the milk.

Turn the dough out on a floured surface and knead lightly. Roll out gently until about 1 cm/½ inch thick and stamp out about 10 rounds with a 5 cm/2 inch cutter.

Place the scones on a greased and floured baking sheet and brush with remaining milk. Bake in a fairly hot oven (190°C/375°F, Gas Mark 5) for 20 minutes.
Makes 10 to 12

Welsh Cakes

METRIC/IMPERIAL
225 g/8 oz self-raising flour
pinch of salt
100 g/4 oz butter
50 g/2 oz sugar
50 g/2 oz currants
25 g/1 oz chopped nuts
1 egg
2 tablespoons milk
vegetable oil or fat for greasing the
   griddle

AMERICAN
2 cups self-rising flour
pinch of salt
½ cup butter
¼ cup sugar
⅓ cup currants
¼ cup chopped nuts
1 egg
2 tablespoons milk
vegetable oil or fat for greasing the
   griddle

Sift the flour and salt together into a bowl. Rub (cut) in the butter until the mixture resembles fine breadcrumbs. Add the sugar, currants and chopped nuts and mix to a fairly stiff dough with the egg and the milk. Knead the dough lightly on a floured surface and roll out until about 5 mm/¼ inch thick. Cut into 5 cm/2 inch rounds with a cutter.

Grease and warm a griddle or heavy-based frying pan (skillet). The griddle is hot enough when a piece of the mixture placed on it turns golden-brown underneath in 30 seconds.

Cook the cakes for 2 to 3 minutes on each side. Serve warm with butter.
Makes 8 to 10

Sugar and Spice Rings

METRIC/IMPERIAL
225 g/8 oz self-raising flour
½ teaspoon salt
40 g/1½ oz butter
150 ml/¼ pint milk
FILLING:
25 g/1 oz butter, melted
50 g/2 oz caster sugar
40 g/1½ oz currants
1 teaspoon ground cinnamon

AMERICAN
2 cups self-rising flour
½ teaspoon salt
3 tablespoons butter
¾ cup milk
FILLING:
2 tablespoons butter, melted
¼ cup sugar
¼ cup currants
1 teaspoon ground cinnamon

Sift the flour and salt into a bowl. Rub in the butter well. Add the milk and mix to a soft dough using a knife. Put on a lightly floured board and knead quickly until smooth.

Roll out to an oblong 20 x 30 cm/8 x 12 inches. Brush with the melted butter to within 1 cm/½ inch of the edge. Mix the sugar with the currants and cinnamon and sprinkle over the butter. Dampen the edges and roll up like a Swiss (jelly) roll. Cut into slices and arrange, cut sides downwards, in a well-buttered 20 cm/8 inch round cake pan.

Bake in a preheated hot oven (220°C/425°F, Gas Mark 7) for 15 to 20 minutes. Place on a wire rack and leave until lukewarm, then gently pull apart to separate the rings.
Makes 16 to 20

Basic Brown or White Bread

METRIC/IMPERIAL
15 g/½ oz dried yeast
2 tablespoons soft brown sugar
900 ml/1½ pints water
1 tablespoon salt
1½ kg/3 lb strong white or
    wholewheat flour
25 g/1 oz butter
1 egg, beaten with a pinch of salt

AMERICAN
4 teaspoons active dry yeast
2 tablespoons firmly packed light
    brown sugar
3¾ cups water
1 tablespoon salt
12 cups strong white or
    wholewheat flour
2 tablespoons butter
1 egg, beaten with a pinch of salt

Put the dried yeast into a small basin with 1 teaspoon of the sugar. Heat the water to 50°C/110°F. (If the water is too cool, the dough will not rise properly.) Whisk 300 ml/½ pint (1¼ cups) of the warm water into the dried yeast and sugar. Leave in a warm place for 10 to 15 minutes, until the surface is covered with bubbles. Add the salt and the remaining sugar to the rest of the warm water.

Any of the following three methods can be used for mixing the dough:

1. Put the flour into a large mixing bowl and rub (cut) in the butter. Pour in both the salt water and the yeast liquid. Quickly work the flour and liquid together to a dough with the fingertips. If the mixture seems dry, add a little more water. Knead the dough for 5 minutes until smooth, pulling the outside dough into the centre.

2. Put the flour into a pile on a clean working surface and rub (cut) in the butter. Make a large well in the centre of the flour and carefully pour in both the salt water and yeast liquid. Using a round-bladed knife, flick the flour from the sides into the liquid in the centre, mixing with the fingertips as you go. When the liquid has absorbed enough flour to become sticky, work in the rest of the flour. Knead for 5 minutes.

3. Using an electric mixer, put the flour into the mixer bowl with the butter, salt water and yeast liquid. Mix on a slow speed, using the dough

208

hook attachment, until the liquid is absorbed. Continue mixing for 2 minutes, instead of kneading by hand.

Put the kneaded dough into a greased mixing bowl and cover with a damp cloth. Leave in a warm place for about 45 minutes. The dough should double in size.

Turn out the risen dough on a floured working surface and knead lightly, using as little flour as possible. The dough is now ready for shaping.

VARIATIONS:

Loaves – divide the dough in half and keep one half warm. Knead the other portion of dough into a smooth ball and punch into shape to fit a 1 kg/2 lb loaf tin (9 x 5 inch loaf pan). Put into the warmed and greased tin.

Divide the remaining dough into 2 and shape for 2 500 g/1 lb loaf tins (7 x 3 inch loaf pans). Put into the warmed and greased tins. Brush the loaves with the beaten egg mixture. If using a wholewheat dough, sprinkle with a little cracked wheat or bran.

Put the loaves in a warm, draught-free place and cover with polythene bags. Leave to rise for 20 minutes until the dough reaches the top of the tins. Bake the loaves in a very hot oven (230°C/450°F, Gas Mark 8) for 20 minutes, then reduce the heat to fairly hot (200°C/400°F, Gas Mark 6) for a further 20 minutes for the large loaf, and 10 minutes for the smaller loaves. Tip the loaves out of their tins and tap them on the bottom – the loaves should sound hollow if they are cooked. Cool on a wire rack.

Rolls – divide the dough into 50 g/2 oz portions, and roll under a cupped hand on a lightly floured surface until round and smooth. Arrange on greased baking sheets and brush with a little beaten egg mixture. The rolls can be sprinkled with sesame, poppy or caraway seeds, or bran. Cover with polythene bags and leave in a warm place to rise for 10 to 15 minutes. Bake in a very hot oven (230°C/450°F, Gas Mark 8) for 10 to 15 minutes.
Makes about 40 rolls

Cottage Loaf – cut off about one quarter of the dough for the 'knob' of the cottage loaf. Knead the larger piece of dough into a smooth, even round and put it on a greased baking sheet. Form the smaller piece of dough into a smooth even ball. Brush the top of the larger piece of dough with water and put the 'knob' centrally on top. Fix in position by pressing the floured handle of a wooden spoon right through the centre to the base of the bottom piece of dough, pulling the spoon handle out carefully.

Cover the shaped loaf with a large polythene bag and leave in a warm place for about 30 minutes until it has risen. The dough should seem light and spongy.

Dredge the top very lightly with flour. Bake in a very hot oven (230°C/450°F, Gas Mark 8) for 15 minutes, then reduce the heat to moderate (180°C/350°F, Gas Mark 4) for a further 20 minutes. Cool on a wire rack.
Individual Cottage Loaves – use 75 g/3 oz risen dough for each loaf, breaking off a portion for the knob. Mould as above, but only bake for the first 15 minutes.
NOTE: Fresh yeast can be used in place of dried. 25 g/1 oz (1 cake) fresh (compressed) yeast is equivalent to 15 g/½ oz (4 teaspoons) dried yeast.

Quick Brown Bread

METRIC/IMPERIAL
225 g/8 oz wholemeal flour
225 g/8 oz plain white flour
2 teaspoons salt
2 teaspoons sugar
15 g/½ oz butter
15 g/½ oz fresh yeast
150 ml/¼ pint lukewarm water
150 ml/¼ pint lukewarm milk
salted water
1–2 tablespoons cracked wheat or cornflakes

AMERICAN
2 cups wholewheat flour
2 cups white bread flour
2 teaspoons salt
2 teaspoons sugar
1 tablespoon butter
½ oz cake compressed yeast
¾ cup lukewarm water
¾ cup lukewarm milk
salted water
1–2 tablespoons cracked wheat or cornflakes

Sift the flours, salt and sugar into a mixing bowl. Rub in the butter finely. Mix the yeast to a smooth, creamy liquid with a little of the warm water, then mix in the rest of the water and the milk. Add to the flour mixture and mix to a soft dough that leaves the sides of the bowl clean. Turn out onto a floured board and knead for 10 minutes or until smooth and elastic.

Cut the dough in half and shape each piece to fit a 500 g/1 lb (7 x 3 inch) loaf pan. Brush the pans with a little melted butter, then put the dough in. Brush the tops with salted water and sprinkle with the cracked wheat or cornflakes. Cover and leave to rise until doubled in bulk.

Bake in a preheated hot oven (230°C/450°F, Gas Mark 8) for 30 to 40 minutes. Turn out onto a wire rack and leave to cool.
Makes 2 loaves

VARIATION:
Crusty Brown Rolls – make the dough as above, then divide into 12 equal pieces and shape into balls. Place 2.5 cm/1 inch apart on a lightly buttered and floured baking sheet and leave to rise. Bake as above, allowing 20 to 30 minutes.
Makes 12

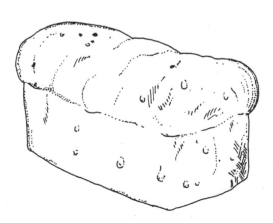

Quick White Bread

METRIC/IMPERIAL	AMERICAN
25 g/1 oz fresh yeast	1 oz cake compressed yeast
400 ml/⅔ pint lukewarm water	2 cups lukewarm water
25 g tablet ascorbic acid	25 g tablet ascorbic acid
675 g/1½ lb flour	6 cups flour
1 teaspoon sugar	1 teaspoon sugar
15 g/½ oz salt	1 tablespoon salt
15 g/½ oz butter	1 tablespoon butter
milk for brushing	milk for brushing

Mix the yeast and warm water together. Crush the ascorbic acid tablet and add to the yeast mixture. Sift the flour, sugar and salt into a large mixing bowl. Rub in the butter. Add the yeast mixture and mix to a stiff dough that leaves the sides of the bowl clean.

Turn out onto a lightly floured board and knead for 10 minutes. Shape to fit a 1 kg/2 lb (9 x 5 inch) loaf pan. Brush the pan with a little melted butter and place the dough in the pan. Put the pan into a greased plastic bag and leave in a warm place until the dough has nearly doubled in bulk.

Remove from the bag. Brush with milk and bake in a preheated hot oven (230°C/450°F, Gas Mark 8) for 30 to 35 minutes. Cool on a wire rack.

Wholemeal (Wholewheat) Bread

METRIC/IMPERIAL	AMERICAN
1.25 kg/3 lb wholemeal flour	3 lb (12 cups) wholewheat flour
2 teaspoons caster sugar	2 teaspoons sugar
2 teaspoons salt	2 teaspoons salt
25 g/1 oz butter	2 tablespoons butter
50 g/2 oz fresh yeast	2 oz cake compressed yeast
600 ml/1 pint lukewarm water	2¾ cups lukewarm water
300 ml/½ pint lukewarm milk	1½ cups lukewarm milk
salted water	salted water

Sift the flour, sugar and salt into a mixing bowl. Rub in the butter. Mix the yeast to a creamy liquid with a little of the warm water. Add to the flour mixture with the milk and the rest of the water and mix to a stiff dough.

Turn out onto a lightly floured board and knead until smooth and elastic. Cover and leave to rise until nearly double in size.

Knead the dough well and cut in half. Shape each piece to fit a 1 kg/2 lb (9 x 5 inch) loaf pan. Brush the pans with a little melted butter and put the dough in. Brush the tops with salted water, cover and leave until risen to the tops of the pans.

Bake in a preheated hot oven (230°C/450°F, Gas Mark 8) for 45 to 50 minutes. Cool on a wire rack.
Makes 2 loaves

Currant Bread

METRIC/IMPERIAL
450 g/1 lb flour
1 teaspoon salt
25 g/1 oz butter
100 g/4 oz currants
25 g/1 oz caster sugar
25 g/1 oz fresh yeast
150 ml/¼ pint lukewarm water
150 ml/¼ pint lukewarm milk
clear honey

AMERICAN
4 cups flour
1 teaspoon salt
2 tablespoons butter
⅔ cup currants
2 tablespoons sugar
1 oz cake compressed yeast
¾ cup lukewarm water
¾ cup lukewarm milk
clear honey

Sift the flour and salt into a mixing bowl. Rub in the butter. Add the currants and sugar and toss lightly to mix. Mix the yeast to a smooth and creamy liquid with a little of the warm water, then mix in the rest of the water and the milk. Add to the flour mixture and mix to a firm dough, adding more flour if necessary, until the dough comes away cleanly from the sides of the bowl.

Turn out onto a floured board and knead for 10 minutes or until smooth and elastic. Cut the dough in half and shape each piece to fit a 500 g/1 lb (7 x 3 inch) loaf pan. Brush the pans with a little melted butter and put in the dough. Cover and leave until the dough rises to the tops of the pans.

Bake in a preheated hot oven (220°C/425°F, Gas Mark 7) for 40 to 45 minutes. Turn out onto a wire rack and glaze the tops with a wet brush dipped in honey. Cool completely before cutting.
Makes 2 loaves

Baps

METRIC/IMPERIAL
*ingredients as for basic white bread
    dough (page 208)*
1 teaspoon dried yeast

AMERICAN
*ingredients as for basic white bread
    dough (page 208)*
1 teaspoon active dry yeast

Make up the basic bread dough as on page 208, using the extra dried yeast, and leave to rise.

Divide the risen dough into 75 g/3 oz portions. Form each piece into a smooth ball and roll it into a flat round on a lightly floured surface. Arrange the shaped baps on floured baking sheets, leaving space between each one to allow for spreading.

Cover with a large polythene bag and leave in a warm place for about 20 minutes until risen. The baps should be light and fluffy. Press the floured handle of a wooden spoon into the centre of each bap, and then dredge the tops lightly with flour. Bake in a hot oven (220°C/425°F, Gas Mark 7) for 10 minutes. Cool the cooked baps between folded clean tea towels so that they keep a soft, spongy texture.
Makes about 30

Milk Loaf

METRIC/IMPERIAL
450 g/1 lb flour
15 g/½ oz fresh yeast
200 ml/⅓ pint lukewarm milk
1 teaspoon sugar
1 teaspoon salt
50 g/2 oz butter
1 egg, beaten
extra milk for brushing

AMERICAN
4 cups flour
½ oz cake compressed yeast
1 cup lukewarm milk
1 teaspoon sugar
1 teaspoon salt
¼ cup butter
1 egg, beaten
extra milk for brushing

Sift one-third of the flour into a large mixing bowl. Add the yeast, milk and sugar and mix well. Leave in a warm place for 20 minutes or until frothy.

Sift the rest of the flour and the salt into another bowl. Rub in the butter. Add the egg and yeast mixture and mix well to a soft dough.

Turn out onto a floured board and knead for 10 minutes or until smooth and elastic. Cover and leave to rise until doubled in bulk.

Knead the dough lightly, then shape to fit a 500 g/1 lb (7 x 3 inch) loaf pan. Brush the pan with a little melted butter and put in the dough. Cover and leave until the dough has risen to the top of the pan.

Brush with milk. Bake in a preheated moderately hot oven (190°C/375°F, Gas Mark 5) for 45 to 50 minutes. Cool on a wire rack.
Makes 2 loaves

VARIATION:
Poppy Seed Plaits (Braids) – make the dough as above and leave to rise. Knead lightly, then divide into six equal pieces. Shape each piece into a long thin strip. Plait (braid) into two loaves. Place on a buttered and floured baking sheet and brush with a little beaten egg. Sprinkle each loaf with poppy seeds. Cover and leave to rise until doubled in bulk. Bake as above.

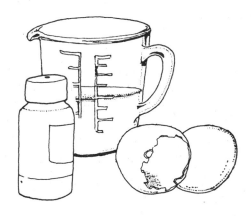

Malt Loaves

METRIC/IMPERIAL	AMERICAN
25 g/1 oz butter	2 tablespoons butter
75 g/3 oz malt extract	¼ cup malt extract
2 tablespoons black treacle	2 tablespoons molasses
450 g/1 lb flour	4 cups flour
1 teaspoon salt	1 teaspoon salt
225 g/8 oz sultanas	1⅓ cups golden raisins
25 g/1 oz fresh yeast	1 oz cake compressed yeast
175 ml/6 fl oz lukewarm water	¾ cup lukewarm water
clear honey	clear honey

Put the butter, malt extract and treacle (molasses) into a saucepan and heat gently until the butter melts. Leave to cool.

Sift the flour and salt into a mixing bowl, add the sultanas (raisins) and toss gently to mix. Mix the yeast to a creamy liquid with a little of the water, then mix in the rest of the water. Add to the flour mixture with the cooled malt mixture and work to a soft dough.

Turn out onto a floured board and knead for 10 minutes or until smooth and elastic. Cut the dough in half and shape each piece to fit a 500 g/1 lb (7 x 3 inch) loaf pan. Brush the pans with melted butter and put in the dough. Cover and leave to rise until the dough reaches the tops of the pans.

Bake in a preheated moderately hot oven (200°C/400°F, Gas Mark 6) for 40 to 45 minutes. Turn out onto a wire rack and glaze the tops with a wet brush dipped in honey. Cool completely before cutting.
Makes 2 loaves

Cheese and Poppy Seed Pinwheels

METRIC/IMPERIAL	AMERICAN
500 g/1 lb risen bread dough	1 lb risen bread dough
1 egg, beaten with a pinch of salt	1 egg, beaten with a pinch of salt
25 g/1 oz grated Parmesan cheese	¼ cup grated Parmesan cheese
poppy seeds	poppy seeds

Divide the risen bread dough into 12 even-sized portions. Roll each piece into a long thin sausage shape, and flatten lightly with the palm of the hand. Brush each strip of dough with the beaten egg mixture and sprinkle with a little grated Parmesan cheese. Roll up each strip of dough tightly, pressing the ends of the dough to seal.

Stand the pinwheels on greased baking sheets, leaving space for spreading. Brush each pinwheel with the beaten egg mixture and sprinkle the tops with poppy seeds.

Cover with a large polythene bag and leave in a warm place for about 20 minutes until risen. Bake in a hot oven (220°C/425°F, Gas Mark 7) for 15 minutes.
Makes 12

Rye Bread

METRIC/IMPERIAL
25 g/1 oz dried yeast
2 tablespoons black treacle
900 ml/1½ pints water
1 tablespoon salt
1 kg/2 lb wholewheat flour
½ kg/1 lb rye flour
25 g/1 oz butter
1 egg, beaten with a pinch of salt
cracked wheat or bran

AMERICAN
8 teaspoons active dried yeast
2 tablespoons molasses
3¾ cups water
1 tablespoon salt
8 cups wholewheat flour
4 cups rye flour
2 tablespoons butter
1 egg, beaten with a pinch of salt
cracked wheat or bran

Make the rye bread dough as for the basic white bread dough (see page 208), using the mixed wholewheat and rye flours, and the black treacle (molasses) in place of sugar. Allow the dough to rise for 45 minutes and then knead lightly.

Divide the risen dough into 2 equal portions. Shape each one into a long, oval loaf. Put the shaped loaves on greased baking sheets, brush the surface with the beaten egg mixture and sprinkle with cracked wheat or bran.

Make several diagonal cuts in the surface of the loaves with a sharp knife. These cuts allow the loaves to rise or 'bloom' well, hence the name 'bloomer'. Bake in a very hot oven (230°C/450°F, Gas Mark 8) for 20 minutes, then reduce the heat to fairly hot (200°C/400°F, Gas Mark 6) for a further 20 minutes.

Wholewheat Popover Rolls

METRIC/IMPERIAL
500 g/1 lb risen wholewheat bread
    dough
1 egg, beaten with a pinch of salt
cracked wheat or bran

AMERICAN
1 lb risen wholewheat bread dough
1 egg, beaten with a pinch of salt
cracked wheat or bran

Brush the insides of 12 small dariole moulds or castle pudding tins with melted butter. Divide the risen wholewheat bread dough into 12 even-sized portions and drop into the prepared tins.

Cover with a large polythene bag and leave in a warm place for about 20 minutes until risen. Brush the tops of the popovers with the beaten egg mixture and sprinkle with a little cracked wheat or bran. Bake in a hot oven (220°C/425°F, Gas Mark 7) for 15 to 20 minutes until well risen and golden-brown. Turn the popover rolls out of their tins and tap the bottoms to see that they are cooked. Cool on a wire rack.
Makes 12

Brioches

METRIC/IMPERIAL
225 g/8 oz flour
15 g/½ oz caster sugar
½ teaspoon salt
15 g/½ oz fresh yeast
2 tablespoons lukewarm water
2 eggs, beaten
50 g/2 oz butter, melted and cooled
beaten egg for brushing

AMERICAN
2 cups flour
1 tablespoon sugar
½ teaspoon salt
½ oz cake compressed yeast
2 tablespoons lukewarm water
2 eggs, beaten
¼ cup butter, melted and cooled
beaten egg for brushing

Sift the flour, sugar and salt into a mixing bowl. Mix the yeast to a creamy liquid with the water. Add to the flour mixture with the eggs and butter and mix to a soft dough. Turn out onto a floured board and knead for 5 minutes or until the dough is no longer sticky. Cover and leave to rise until almost doubled in bulk.

Knead lightly again and divide three-quarters of the dough into 12 pieces. Shape into balls and put into well-buttered deep bun (muffin) tins. Press a deep hole in each. Divide the rest of the dough into 12 pieces. Roll into small balls and place on top of the holes. Cover and leave to rise (about 1 hour).

Brush with beaten egg. Bake in a preheated hot oven (230°C/450°F, Gas Mark 8) for 10 minutes. Cool on a wire rack, and serve with butter.
Makes 12

Sugared Bun Cluster

METRIC/IMPERIAL
500 g/1 lb risen bread dough
demerara sugar
milk
4 tablespoons honey, melted
25 g/1 oz chopped or flaked nuts

AMERICAN
1 lb risen bread dough
brown or raw sugar
milk
¼ cup honey, melted
¼ cup chopped or slivered nuts

Divide the bread dough into 8 even-sized portions. Work a little sugar into each portion of dough, kneading it gently on a very lightly floured surface, to form a smooth ball. Arrange the shaped pieces of dough in a greased 20 cm/8 inch sandwich tin, so that they just touch.

Cover the tin with a large polythene bag and leave in a warm place for about 20 minutes until risen.

Brush the top of the bun cluster with milk. Spoon over the melted honey and sprinkle the surface with extra sugar and the nuts. Bake in a very hot oven (230°C/450°F, Gas Mark 8) for 15 minutes, then reduce the heat to fairly hot (200°C/400°F, Gas Mark 6) for a further 10 minutes. Carefully turn out the bun cluster on a wire rack and allow to cool.
Makes 8

Doughnuts

METRIC/IMPERIAL
225 g/8 oz flour
½ teaspoon caster sugar
15 g/½ oz fresh yeast
6 tablespoons lukewarm milk
¼ teaspoon salt
15 g/½ oz butter, melted and
  cooled
1 egg, beaten
8 teaspoons red jam
oil for deep frying
COATING:
4 tablespoons caster sugar
1 teaspoon ground cinnamon

AMERICAN
2 cups flour
½ teaspoon sugar
½ oz cake compressed yeast
6 tablespoons lukewarm milk
¼ teaspoon salt
1 tablespoon butter, melted and
  cooled
1 egg, beaten
8 teaspoons red jam
oil for deep frying
COATING:
¼ cup sugar
1 teaspoon ground cinnamon

Sift 50 g/2 oz (½ cup) of the flour with the sugar into a bowl. Mix the yeast to a smooth cream with the milk. Add to the flour mixture and mix well together. Leave for 30 minutes or until frothy.

Sift the rest of the flour and the salt together. Add to the yeast mixture with the butter and egg. Mix to a soft dough that leaves the sides of the bowl clean. Put onto a floured board and knead for 5 minutes or until the dough has lost its stickiness. Cover and leave to rise until doubled in bulk.

Knead lightly and divide into eight pieces. Shape into balls and leave to rise for 30 minutes.

Make a hole in each ball using your finger or thumb. Put a teaspoon of jam in each hole and pinch the hole closed again.

Deep fry the doughnuts in hot oil for 5 minutes. Drain on paper towels and roll in a mixture of the sugar and cinnamon.

Makes 8

Hot Cross Buns

METRIC/IMPERIAL
450 g/1 lb flour
50 g/2 oz caster sugar
25 g/1 oz fresh yeast
150 ml/¼ pint lukewarm milk
4 tablespoons lukewarm water
1 teaspoon mixed spice
½ teaspoon ground cinnamon
1 teaspoon salt
50 g/2 oz chopped mixed peel
100 g/4 oz currants
50 g/2 oz butter, melted and cooled
1 egg, beaten
GLAZE:
50 g/2 oz granulated sugar
3 tablespoons milk

AMERICAN
4 cups flour
¼ cup sugar
1 oz cake compressed yeast
¾ cup lukewarm milk
¼ cup lukewarm water
1 teaspoon apple pie spice
½ teaspoon ground cinnamon
1 teaspoon salt
*⅓ cup chopped mixed candied
  peel*
⅔ cup currants
¼ cup butter, melted and cooled
1 egg, beaten
GLAZE:
¼ cup sugar
3 tablespoons milk

Sift 100 g/4 oz (1 cup) of the flour into a bowl and add 1 teaspoon of the sugar. Mix the yeast to a smooth cream with the milk and water and add to the flour. Mix well and leave until frothy.

Sift the rest of the flour, the spices and salt into another bowl. Add the remaining sugar, the peel and currants and toss lightly to mix. Add to the yeast mixture with the butter and egg. Mix to a stiff dough that leaves the sides of the bowl clean. Put onto a floured board and knead for 5 minutes. Cover and leave to rise until doubled in bulk.

Knead again and divide into 12 pieces. Shape each into a bun. Place, well apart, on a lightly buttered baking sheet. Cover and leave to rise for 30 minutes.

Cut a cross on the top of each bun using a sharp knife. Bake in a preheated hot oven (220°C/425°F, Gas Mark 7) for 25 to 35 minutes. Place on a wire rack.

For the glaze, dissolve the sugar in the milk and boil for 2 minutes. Brush thickly over the buns twice and leave to cool.
Makes 12

Yorkshire Tea Cakes

METRIC/IMPERIAL
450 g/1 lb flour
25 g/1 oz caster sugar
1 teaspoon salt
25 g/1 oz butter
50 g/2 oz currants
15 g/½ oz fresh yeast
300 ml/½ pint lukewarm water
milk for brushing

AMERICAN
4 cups flour
2 tablespoons sugar
1 teaspoon salt
2 tablespoons butter
⅓ cup currants
½ oz cake compressed yeast
1½ cups lukewarm water
milk for brushing

Sift the flour, sugar and salt into a mixing bowl. Rub in the butter. Add the currants and toss lightly to mix. Mix the yeast with the milk and add to the flour mixture. Mix to a firm dough that leaves the sides of the bowl clean. Turn out onto a floured board and knead until smooth and elastic. Cover and leave to rise until doubled in bulk.

Knead for 5 minutes. Divide into six pieces and roll each out to a 15 cm/6 inch round. Put on a lightly buttered baking sheet. Brush the tops with milk. Cover and leave to rise until doubled in size.

Bake in a preheated moderately hot oven (200°C/400°F, Gas Mark 6) for 20 to 25 minutes. Cool on a wire rack.
Makes 6

Sally Lunns

METRIC/IMPERIAL
50 g/2 oz butter
1 teaspoon caster sugar
200 ml/⅓ pint milk
2 eggs, beaten
15 g/½ oz fresh yeast
450 g/1 lb strong plain flour
1 teaspoon salt
GLAZE:
1 tablespoon water
1 tablespoon sugar

AMERICAN
¼ cup butter
1 teaspoon sugar
1 cup milk
2 eggs, beaten
½ oz cake compressed yeast
4 cups white bread flour
1 teaspoon salt
GLAZE:
1 tablespoon water
1 tablespoon sugar

Melt the butter in a saucepan. Remove from the heat and stir in the sugar and milk. Add the eggs and yeast and mix well. Sift the flour and salt into a mixing bowl. Add the yeast mixture and knead lightly.

Divide the dough in half and place in two well-greased 13 cm/5 inch cake pans. Leave to rise in a warm place for about 45 minutes to 1 hour.

Bake in a preheated hot oven (230°C/450°F, Gas Mark 8) for 15 to 20 minutes. Turn onto a wire rack.

Heat the water and sugar for the glaze in a saucepan until the mixture boils and boil for 2 minutes. Glaze the Sally Lunns while still hot.
Makes 2

Rum Babas

METRIC/IMPERIAL
25 g/1 oz fresh yeast
6 tablespoons lukewarm milk
225 g/8 oz flour
4 eggs, beaten
100 g/4 oz currants
½ teaspoon salt
100 g/4 oz butter, softened
25 g/1 oz caster sugar
300 ml/½ pint double cream,
    whipped, to decorate
SYRUP:
4 tablespoons rum
4 tablespoons golden syrup
4 tablespoons water
GLAZE:
3 tablespoons apricot jam
2 tablespoons water

AMERICAN
1 oz cake compressed yeast
6 tablespoons lukewarm milk
2 cups flour
4 eggs, beaten
⅔ cup currants
½ teaspoon salt
½ cup butter, softened
2 tablespoons sugar
1¼ cups heavy cream, whipped, to
    decorate
SYRUP:
¼ cup rum
¼ cup light corn syrup
¼ cup water
GLAZE:
3 tablespoons apricot jam
2 tablespoons water

Mix the yeast with the milk and 50 g/2 oz (½ cup) of the flour. Leave for 20 to 30 minutes or until frothy, then mix with the rest of the flour, the eggs, currants, salt, butter and sugar. Beat well for about 5 minutes.

Brush 16 dariole moulds with melted butter and fill halfway with the mixture. Cover and leave to rise until two-thirds full.

Bake in a preheated moderately hot oven (200°C/400°F, Gas Mark 6) for 15 to 20 minutes. Cool for 5 minutes, then turn onto a wire rack.

Heat the rum, syrup and water together. Pour enough over the babas to soak them well.

Heat the jam slowly with the water. Strain and brush thickly over the babas. Leave to cool completely.

Put onto a serving dish and pile whipped cream into the middles.
Makes 16

VARIATIONS:
Cherry Savarin – make the dough as above, omitting the currants. Use to half fill a well-buttered 20 cm/8 inch ring mould. Leave to rise, then bake as above. Prick, then soak with a syrup made from 2 to 3 tablespoons rum, 4 tablespoons sugar or golden syrup (light corn syrup) and 150 ml/¼ pint (¾ cup) water. Fill the centre of the ring with 225 g (8 oz) of stoned fresh cherries. Serve hot.
Cream Savarin – make as for Cherry Savarin, omitting the cherries. Fill the centre of the soaked cake with whipped cream and sprinkle with sugar.
Fruit Savarin – make as for Cherry Savarin, omitting the cherries. Drain a can of fruit cocktail, or fruit of your choice, and use the syrup to soak the cake. Fill the centre of the cake with fruit.

Bath Buns

METRIC/IMPERIAL
450 g/1 lb flour
25 g/1 oz caster sugar
25 g/1 oz fresh yeast
150 ml/¼ pint lukewarm milk
4 tablespoons lukewarm water
1 teaspoon salt
50 g/2 oz chopped mixed peel
175 g/6 oz sultanas
1 egg, beaten
50 g/2 oz butter, melted and cooled
GLAZE:
beaten egg mixed with a little water
crushed cube sugar

AMERICAN
4 cups flour
2 tablespoons sugar
1 oz cake compressed yeast
¾ cup lukewarm milk
¼ cup lukewarm water
1 teaspoon salt
⅓ cup chopped mixed candied
  peel
1 cup golden raisins
1 egg, beaten
¼ cup butter, melted and cooled
GLAZE:
beaten egg mixed with a little water
crushed cube sugar

Sift 100 g/4 oz (1 cup) of the flour into a mixing bowl. Add 1 teaspoon of the sugar. Mix the yeast with the milk and water and add to the flour and sugar. Mix well and leave until frothy (20 to 30 minutes).

Sift the rest of the flour and the salt into another bowl. Add the remaining sugar, the peel and sultanas (raisins) and toss lightly to mix. Add to the yeast mixture with the egg and butter. Mix to a stiff dough that leaves the bowl clean.

Turn out onto a floured board and knead until smooth and no longer sticky. Cover and leave to rise until nearly doubled in bulk. Knead lightly again. Drop in 14 tablespoons onto a lightly buttered and floured baking sheet. Cover and leave to rise for a further 20 minutes.

Brush with the beaten egg and water mixture and sprinkle with crushed cube sugar. Bake in a preheated hot oven (220°C/425°F, Gas Mark 7) for 20 to 25 minutes. Cool on a wire rack.
Makes 14

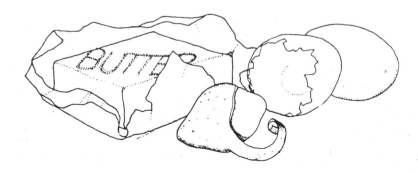

Devon Splits

METRIC/IMPERIAL
450 g/1 lb flour
50 g/2 oz caster sugar
25 g/1 oz fresh yeast
150 ml/¼ pint lukewarm milk
150 ml/¼ pint lukewarm water
1 teaspoon salt
50 g/2 oz butter, melted and cooled

AMERICAN
4 cups flour
¼ cup sugar
1 oz cake compressed yeast
¾ cup lukewarm milk
¾ cup lukewarm water
1 teaspoon salt
¼ cup butter, melted and cooled

Sift 100 g/4 oz (1 cup) of the flour into a bowl. Add 1 teaspoon of the sugar. Mix the yeast to a smooth cream with the milk and water and add to the flour and sugar. Mix well and leave for 30 minutes.

Sift the rest of the flour and the salt into another bowl. Add the rest of the sugar, the yeast mixture and butter and mix to a dough that leaves the sides of the bowl clean. Put onto a floured board and knead for 5 to 10 minutes. Cover and leave to rise until doubled in bulk.

Knead lightly again. Divide into 14 pieces and shape into balls. Place well apart on a buttered and floured baking sheet. Cover and leave to rise until doubled again (about 30 minutes).

Bake in a preheated hot oven (220°C/425°F, Gas Mark 7) for 20 to 25 minutes. Cool on a wire rack.

If wished, when the rolls are cold, they can be split open and filled with jam and whipped cream.

Makes 14

BUDGET

Preserves

MEALS

Tomato Pickle

METRIC/IMPERIAL
2 kg/4 lb green tomatoes, cut into
    5 mm/¼ inch slices
4 medium onions, sliced
175 g/6 oz salt
1 green pepper, cored, seeded and
    chopped
500 g/1 lb sugar
2 tablespoons plus 1 teaspoon
    mustard seeds
2 tablespoons celery seeds
600 ml/1 pint vinegar
1 teaspoon whole cloves
2 x 7.5 cm/3 inch cinnamon sticks
1 teaspoon black peppercorns
1 teaspoon allspice berries

AMERICAN
4 lb green tomatoes, cut into
    ¼ inch slices
4 medium-size onions, sliced
¾ cup salt
1 green pepper, seeded and
    chopped
2 cups sugar
2 tablespoons plus 1 teaspoon
    mustard seeds
2 tablespoons celery seeds
2½ cups vinegar
1 teaspoon whole cloves
2 x 3 inch cinnamon sticks
1 teaspoon black peppercorns
1 teaspoon allspice berries

Place the tomatoes in a bowl in layers with the onions, sprinkling each
layer with salt. Leave to stand overnight.

Drain the tomatoes and onions and rinse in cold water. Put in a large
saucepan and add the green peppers, sugar, 2 tablespoons of the
mustard seeds, the celery seeds and vinegar. Tie the cloves, cinnamon
and peppercorns together in a muslin (cheesecloth) bag and add to the
pan. Bring to the boil and simmer, stirring, for about 20 minutes or until
thickened.

Remove and discard the spice bag. Pour the pickle into 4 hot, dry,
600 ml/1 pint jars. To each jar add ½ teaspoon salt, ¼ teaspoon mustard
seeds and ¼ teaspoon allspice berries. Seal.
Makes about 2.4 litres/4 pints

Mustard Pickle

METRIC/IMPERIAL
3.3 litres/5½ pints water
350 g/12 oz salt
750 g/1½ lb cucumbers, sliced
4 very small onions, peeled
500 g/1 lb cauliflower, broken into florets
175 g/6 oz tender carrots, sliced
500 g/1 lb small green tomatoes, quartered
3 green peppers, cored, seeded and chopped
500 g/1 lb green beans, cut into 2.5 cm/1 inch pieces
900 ml/1½ pints strong white vinegar
MUSTARD DRESSING:
9 tablespoons flour
5 tablespoons dry mustard
2½ teaspoons turmeric
1½ teaspoons celery seeds
1.2 litres/2 pints strong white vinegar
275 g/10 oz sugar

AMERICAN
13¾ cups water
1½ cups salt
1½ lb cucumbers, sliced
4 very small onions, peeled
1 lb cauliflower, broken into florets
½ lb tender carrots, sliced
1 lb small green tomatoes, quartered
3 green peppers, seeded and chopped
1 lb green beans, cut into 1 inch pieces
3¾ cups strong white vinegar
MUSTARD DRESSING:
9 tablespoons flour
5 tablespoons dry mustard
2½ teaspoons turmeric
1½ teaspoons celery seed
5 cups strong white vinegar
1¼ cups sugar

Mix 2.4 litres/4 pints (10 cups) of the water with the salt. Put all the vegetables in a large bowl and pour the salt water over, making sure that all the vegetables are covered. Leave to soak overnight.

Drain the vegetables and rinse twice in fresh water. Shake off the extra moisture. Place the vegetables in a large saucepan (or two smaller ones) and cover with the vinegar and remaining water. Leave to stand for 1 hour.

Meanwhile make the mustard dressing. Sift the flour into a bowl and add the mustard, turmeric and celery seeds. Slowly add the vinegar, stirring well, then stir in the sugar. Pour into a saucepan and cook over a very low heat, stirring until thick.

Bring the vegetables to the boil. Drain off the vinegar, then add the mustard dressing. Simmer for 5 minutes. Pour into hot, clean jars and seal.

Makes about 3 litres/5 pints

Pickled Peppers

METRIC/IMPERIAL
6 red peppers
6 green peppers
600 ml/1 pint vinegar
600 ml/1 pint water
100 g/4 oz sugar
salt
2 teaspoons mustard seeds
2 teaspoons allspice berries

AMERICAN
6 red peppers
6 green peppers
2½ cups vinegar
2½ cups water
½ cup sugar
salt
2 teaspoons mustard seeds
2 teaspoons allspice berries

Cut the peppers into quarters lengthways, core and seed them. Mix the vinegar, water, sugar and 2 teaspoons salt in a saucepan and bring to the boil. Add the peppers and heat through slowly.

Pack into 4 hot, dry, 600 ml/1 pint jars. To each jar add ½ teaspoon salt, ½ teaspoon mustard seeds and ½ teaspoon allspice. Cover with the hot vinegar liquid and seal.
Makes 2.4 litres/4 pints

Sweet Cucumbers

METRIC/IMPERIAL
2 kg/4 lb cucumbers, sliced
175 g/6 oz salt
350–500 g/12–16 oz sugar
1.2 litres/2 pints vinegar
1 teaspoon allspice berries
1 teaspoon whole cloves
2 cinnamon sticks, broken
1 teaspoon white mustard seeds

AMERICAN
4 lb cucumbers, sliced
¾ cup salt
1½–2 cups sugar
5 cups vinegar
1 teaspoon allspice berries
1 teaspoon whole cloves
2 cinnamon sticks, broken
1 teaspoon white mustard seeds

Place the cucumbers in an earthenware or glass dish and sprinkle with the salt. Leave to stand for 3 hours.

While the cucumbers are salting, put the sugar and vinegar in a saucepan. Put the spices in a muslin (cheesecloth) bag and add to the vinegar. Bring to the boil and boil for 10 minutes. Remove from the heat, cover and leave to stand for 3 hours.

Drain the cucumbers and squeeze out any excess moisture. Remove the spice bag from the vinegar mixture. Add the cucumber and bring to a simmer; do not boil. Pack into clean, dry jars and seal.
Makes about 3 litres/5 pints

Pickled Green Beans

METRIC/IMPERIAL
2–3 kg/4–6 lb green beans
salt
600 ml/1 pint vinegar
600 ml/1 pint water
350 g/12 oz sugar
4 tablespoons lemon juice

AMERICAN
4–6 lb green beans
salt
2½ cups vinegar
2½ cups water
1½ cups sugar
¼ cup lemon juice

Cook the beans in boiling salted water until tender. Drain well and pack into warm, dry jars.

Mix the vinegar, water, sugar and lemon juice together in a saucepan. Bring to the boil and simmer for 5 minutes. Pour over the beans and seal.
Makes about 5.5 litres (8 pints)

Pickled Beetroot (Beets)

METRIC/IMPERIAL
1 teaspoon whole cloves
2 teaspoons mustard seeds
2 teaspoons celery seeds
2 cinnamon sticks
4 teaspoons salt
1.2 litres/2 pints strong vinegar
225 g/8 oz sugar
2.25 kg/4½ lb beetroot, cooked, peeled and sliced
5 small onions, peeled

AMERICAN
1 teaspoon whole cloves
2 teaspoons mustard seeds
2 teaspoons celery seeds
2 cinnamon sticks
4 teaspoons salt
5 cups strong vinegar
1 cup sugar
4½ lb beets, cooked, peeled and sliced
5 small onions, peeled

Tie the spices together in a muslin (cheesecloth) bag. Put the bag of spices with the salt, vinegar and sugar in a large saucepan and bring to the boil. Add the beetroot (beets) and onions and return to the boil.

Remove the spice bag. Pack the vegetables into hot, dry jars and pour the hot liquid over. Seal tightly.
Makes about 3 litres/6 pints

Redcurrant Jelly

METRIC/IMPERIAL
1.5 kg/3 lb redcurrants
sugar

AMERICAN
3 lb red currants
sugar

String the redcurrants and place in a saucepan without any water. Heat very slowly and gently until the redcurrants are softened (about 45 minutes). Mash well and strain through a scalded jelly bag.

Measure the liquid obtained, and to every 600 ml/1 pint (2¼ cups), use 600 g/1¼ lb (2½ cups) sugar. Put the liquid and sugar in a saucepan. Bring to the boil, stirring until the sugar has dissolved. Boil for 1 minute without stirring. Skim and quickly pour into warm, dry jars. Seal.

Apple Jelly

METRIC/IMPERIAL
2 kg/4 lb cooking apples
1 teaspoon finely grated lemon rind
sugar

AMERICAN
4 lb cooking apples
1 teaspoon finely grated lemon rind
sugar

Wash the apples and cut up without peeling or coring. Cut off any discoloured bits. Place in a saucepan and just about cover with water – about 1.2 to 1.5 litres/2 to 3 pints (1 to 1½ quarts). Add the lemon rind and bring to the boil. Simmer until just tender, about 1 hour.

Strain through a scalded jelly bag. Measure the liquid and for each 600 ml/1 pint (2½ cups) use 500 g/1 lb (2 cups) sugar. Pour the liquid and sugar into a clean pan and bring to the boil. Test for setting by placing a small quantity of jelly on a plate. Cool, then push the jelly gently with your fingertip. If the surface wrinkles, the jelly is ready. Pour the jelly into hot, dry jars and seal.

Blackberry and Apple Jelly

METRIC/IMPERIAL
2 kg/4 lb blackberries
2 kg/4 lb cooking apples, chopped
1.2 litres/2 pints water
sugar

AMERICAN
4 lb blackberries
4 lb cooking apples, chopped
5 cups water
sugar

Place the blackberries and apples in separate saucepans and add half the water to each. Simmer gently for 1 hour or until tender.

Mash the fruit well, then strain together through a scalded jelly bag. Measure the liquid and for each 600 ml/1 pint (2½ cups) use 500 g/1 lb (2 cups) sugar. Put the liquid and sugar in a pan and bring to the boil, stirring to dissolve the sugar. Boil until setting point is reached. Pour into warm, dry jars and seal.

Mint Jelly

METRIC/IMPERIAL
2.5 kg/5 lb green apples, quartered
670 ml/1⅛ pints water
small bunch of fresh mint
670 ml/1⅛ pints vinegar
sugar
3 tablespoons chopped fresh mint
few drops of green food colouring

AMERICAN
5 lb green apples, quartered
2¾ cups water
small bunch of fresh mint
2¾ cups vinegar
sugar
3 tablespoons chopped fresh mint
few drops of green food coloring

Place the apples in a saucepan with the water and bunch of mint. Simmer until the apples are soft and mushy. Stir in the vinegar and boil for 5 minutes.

Strain through a scalded jelly bag. Measure the liquid and to each 600 ml/1 pint (2½ cups) obtained, use 500 g/1 lb (2 cups) sugar. Put the liquid with the sugar in a pan and bring to the boil, stirring until the sugar has dissolved. Boil rapidly until setting point is nearly reached. Add the chopped mint and food colouring and continue boiling until setting point is reached. Pour into warm, dry jars and seal.

Gooseberry Jelly

METRIC/IMPERIAL
2 kg/4 lb green gooseberries
1.2–1.5 litres/2–3 pints water
sugar

AMERICAN
4 lb green gooseberries
1¼–1½ quarts water
sugar

Place the gooseberries in a large pan. Add the water. Cook gently until the fruit is tender and has broken.

Strain through a scalded jelly bag. To each 600 ml/1 pint (2½ cups) use 350 to 500 g/12 oz to 1 lb (1½ to 2 cups) sugar. Place the juice and sugar in a saucepan and bring to the boil, stirring to dissolve the sugar. Boil rapidly until setting point has been reached. Pour into warm, dry jars and seal.

Blackcurrant Jam

METRIC/IMPERIAL
1 kg/2 lb blackcurrants, stemmed
900 ml/1½ pints water
1.5 kg/3 lb sugar
15 g/½ oz butter

AMERICAN
2 lb blackcurrants, stemmed
1 quart water
3 lb (6 cups) sugar
1 tablespoon butter

Put the blackcurrants into a saucepan. Add the water and bring to the boil. Cover and simmer for 45 to 55 minutes.

Add the sugar and stir until it has dissolved. Bring back to the boil and boil for 5 to 10 minutes or until setting point is reached.

Remove from the heat and stir in the butter (this will get rid of the scum). Pot and cover as usual.

Strawberry and Rhubarb Jam

METRIC/IMPERIAL
1 kg/2 lb rhubarb, leaves and base
   trimmed from the stalks
150 ml/¼ pint water
3 tablespoons lemon juice
1 kg/2 lb strawberries, hulled
2 kg/4 lb preserving sugar
15 g/½ oz butter
1 bottle liquid pectin

AMERICAN
2 lb rhubarb, leaves and base
   trimmed from the stalks
⅔ cup water
3 tablespoons lemon juice
2 lb strawberries, hulled
4 lb preserving sugar
1 tablespoon butter
1 bottle liquid pectin

Cut the rhubarb stalks into 2.5 cm/1 inch lengths. Place in a preserving pan with the water and lemon juice. Bring slowly to the boil, simmer for 5 minutes, allow to cool. Add the strawberries, cutting the larger fruit in half. Add the sugar. Allow to stand for 1 hour, stirring occasionally. Place over a low heat and stir continuously until the sugar has dissolved. Add the butter to reduce foaming, bring to a full rolling boil, and boil rapidly for 5 minutes. Remove from the heat, add the pectin and stir well.

Allow to cool for 20 minutes before potting to prevent the fruit from rising to the top of the jars. Have ready sufficient warm, dry sterilized jars on a board, and pour in the jam. Allow to get completely cold, cover with waxed paper discs and plastic wrap covers. Label the jars.
Makes 3 kg/6-7 lb jam

VARIATION:
Jam can be made in the same way with raspberries instead of strawberries, but as they have a better setting power than strawberries, reduce both the lemon juice and liquid pectin in proportion. You can also use diced marrow (squash) flesh or pumpkin flesh to make mixed fruit jams, but make sure the diced flesh is sufficiently tender before adding the berry fruit and sugar.

Damson Jam

METRIC/IMPERIAL
1 kg/2 lb damsons
450 ml/¾ pint water
1.5 kg/3 lb sugar
15 g/½ oz butter

AMERICAN
2 lb damsons or other plums
2 cups water
3 lb (6 cups) sugar
1 tablespoon butter

Put the damsons into a saucepan. Add the water and bring to the boil. Cover and simmer for 45 to 55 minutes.

Add the sugar and stir until it has dissolved. Bring back to the boil and boil for 10 to 15 minutes or until setting point is reached. Skim off the damson stones (pits) as they appear on the surface.

Remove from the heat and stir in the butter (this will get rid of the scum). Pot and cover as usual.

VARIATION:
Gooseberry Jam – make as above, using gooseberries instead of damsons.

Apple and Blackberry Jam

METRIC/IMPERIAL
500 g/1 lb apples, peeled, cored
    and thinly sliced
1 kg/2 lb blackberries
150 ml/¼ pint water
1.5 kg/3 lb sugar
15 g/½ oz butter

AMERICAN
1 lb apples, peeled, cored and
    thinly sliced
2 lb blackberries
¾ cup water
3 lb (6 cups) sugar
1 tablespoon butter

Put the apples into a saucepan with the blackberries and water and bring to the boil. Lower the heat, cover and simmer for 10 to 15 minutes. Crush the fruit against the sides of the saucepan until it is soft and pulpy.

Add the sugar and heat gently, stirring until the sugar dissolves. Bring to the boil and boil for 10 to 15 minutes or until setting point is reached.

Remove from the heat and stir in the butter (this will get rid of the scum). Pot and cover as usual.

VARIATION:
Mixed Fruit Jam – make as above, using 1.5 kg/3 lb mixed soft fruit instead of apples and blackberries.

Apple and Plum Butter

METRIC/IMPERIAL
*1.5 kg/3 lb apples, peeled, cored
and sliced
water
500 g/1 lb plums, stoned
sugar*

AMERICAN
*3 lb apples, peeled, cored and
sliced
water
1 lb plums, pitted
sugar*

Place the apples in a saucepan with just enough water to cover the bottom of the pan. Cook gently until soft and pulpy. Add the plums and continue cooking until the plums are tender.

Sieve the pulp and measure, then return it to the saucepan. To each 500 g/1 lb (2 cups) of pulp, add 350 g/12 oz (1½ cups) sugar. Stir until the sugar has dissolved, then boil until thick and creamy. Pour into hot, dry jars and cover.

Makes about 900 ml/1½ pints (1 quart)

Spiced Apple Butter

METRIC/IMPERIAL
*1.8 litres/3 pints medium sweet
cider
1 kg/2 lb ripe apples, cored and
quartered
100 g/4 oz light brown sugar
¾ teaspoon ground cinnamon
⅛ teaspoon ground allspice
¼ teaspoon ground cloves
⅛ teaspoon salt*

AMERICAN
*7½ cups medium sweet apple cider
2 lb ripe apples, cored and
quartered
½ cup firmly packed light brown
sugar
¾ teaspoon ground cinnamon
⅛ teaspoon ground allspice
¼ teaspoon ground cloves
⅛ teaspoon salt*

Boil the cider for 30 to 45 minutes or until it has been reduced by half. Add the apples and cook until they are soft and pulpy.

Using a slotted spoon, remove the apples, then sieve them back into the hot cider. Stir in the sugar, spices and salt and simmer until the mixture is dark and stiff. Pour into hot, dry jars and cover.

Makes about 900 ml/1½ pints (1 quart)

BUDGET

Sauces,
Pastries,
Fillings
and Icings

MEALS

Simple Sweet White Sauce

METRIC/IMPERIAL
600 ml/1 pint milk
2 tablespoons caster sugar
25 g/1 oz cornflour

AMERICAN
2½ cups milk
2 tablespoons sugar
¼ cup cornstarch

Place the milk, sugar and cornflour (cornstarch) in a saucepan. Whisk over moderate heat until the sauce comes to the boil. Simmer for 2 minutes until smooth and thickened, stirring all the time. To make a basic vanilla sauce, add ½ teaspoon vanilla essence (extract) and stir well.

VARIATION:
Chocolate Sauce – add 1 tablespoon cocoa with the cornflour (cornstarch) when making up the basic sauce. To make a nutty-flavoured chocolate sauce add half an 85 g/3 oz bar of hazelnut or peanut chocolate, broken into squares. Stir into the hot sauce until melted.

Sherried Custard Sauce

METRIC/IMPERIAL
300 ml/½ pint milk
2 egg yolks, beaten
2 tablespoons caster sugar
2 tablespoons sweet sherry

AMERICAN
1¼ cups milk
2 egg yolks, beaten
2 tablespoons sugar
2 tablespoons sweet sherry

Place the milk in a saucepan and bring just to boiling point. Beat together the egg yolks and sugar, then add a little of the scalded milk and beat well. Add this mixture to the rest of the milk and cook over a pan of simmering water until the sauce will coat the back of a wooden spoon, stirring all the time. Do not boil. Remove from the heat, cover the surface with a circle of greaseproof (parchment) paper and allow to cool.

When the sauce is cold, stir in the sherry.

Rich Lemon Sauce

METRIC/IMPERIAL
300 ml/½ pint water
1 chicken stock cube, crumbled
thinly pared rind of ½ lemon
25 g/1 oz butter
20 g/¾ oz flour
3 tablespoons lemon juice
1 egg yolk
2 tablespoons single cream or
  evaporated milk
salt and freshly ground white
  pepper

AMERICAN
1¼ cups water
1 chicken bouillon cube, crumbled
thinly pared rind of ½ lemon
2 tablespoons butter
3 tablespoons flour
3 tablespoons lemon juice
1 egg yolk
2 tablespoons light cream or
  evaporated milk
salt and freshly ground white
  pepper

Place the water, crumbled stock (bouillon) cube, lemon rind, butter and flour into a saucepan. Place over a moderate heat and whisk constantly until the sauce comes to the boil. Cook gently for 2 minutes until thickened and smooth, stirring frequently.

Beat together the lemon juice and egg yolk in a bowl, beat in a little of the hot sauce then return this mixture to the pan and reheat without boiling. Stir in the cream or evaporated milk and season to taste.
Makes 450 ml/¾ pint (2 cups)

Fudge Sauce

METRIC/IMPERIAL
25 g/1 oz plain chocolate
15 g/½ oz butter
2 tablespoons warm milk
1 tablespoon golden syrup
100 g/4 oz soft brown sugar
½ teaspoon vanilla essence

AMERICAN
1 square (1 oz) semisweet
  chocolate
1 tablespoon butter
2 tablespoons warm milk
1 tablespoon light corn syrup
⅔ cup firmly packed brown sugar
½ teaspoon vanilla extract

Break up the chocolate and put it in a heatproof bowl standing over a saucepan of hot water or in a double boiler. Add the butter. Leave until melted, stirring occasionally. Blend in the milk and pour into a saucepan. Add the syrup and sugar. Heat gently, stirring, until the sugar has dissolved, then bring to the boil and boil for 5 minutes without stirring. Remove from the heat and stir in the vanilla essence (extract). Serve hot.
Makes about 250 ml/8 fl oz (1 cup)

VARIATION:
Coffee Fudge Sauce – add 1 teaspoon instant coffee powder with the butter.

Coffee Cream Sauce

METRIC/IMPERIAL
2 eggs
6 tablespoons hot strong black
  coffee
pinch of salt
50 g/2 oz caster sugar
150 ml/¼ pint double cream

AMERICAN
2 eggs
6 tablespoons hot strong black
  coffee
pinch of salt
¼ cup sugar
¾ cup heavy cream

Beat the eggs well in a heatproof bowl standing over a saucepan of simmering water or in a double boiler, then slowly beat in the coffee. Add the salt and sugar and cook without boiling until the sauce is thick enough to coat the back of a spoon. Stir frequently. Remove from the heat and chill.

Just before serving, whip the cream until thick and gently fold into the coffee sauce. Serve with hot gingerbread, ice cream, Christmas puddings and mince pies.
Makes about 250 ml/8 fl oz (1 cup)

Brandy Sauce

METRIC/IMPERIAL
15 g/½ oz cornflour
300 ml/½ pint milk
15 g/½ oz butter
1 tablespoon caster sugar
1–2 tablespoons brandy

AMERICAN
2 tablespoons cornstarch
1¼ cups milk
1 tablespoon butter
1 tablespoon sugar
1–2 tablespoons brandy

Mix the cornflour (cornstarch) to a smooth paste with a little of the cold milk. Warm the remaining milk in a saucepan, pour over the cornflour (cornstarch) paste and mix well together. Return to the saucepan and cook, stirring, until the sauce comes to the boil and thickens. Simmer for 2 minutes, then remove from the heat and stir in the butter, sugar and brandy. Serve with Christmas pudding and other baked and steamed fruit puddings.
Makes about 300 ml/½ pint (1½ cups)

VARIATION:
Vanilla Sauce – make as above, using ½ to 1 teaspoon vanilla essence (extract) instead of brandy.

Custard Sauce

METRIC/IMPERIAL
2 eggs
2 teaspoons caster sugar
300 ml/½ pint milk
¼ teaspoon vanilla essence

AMERICAN
2 eggs
2 teaspoons sugar
1¼ cups milk
¼ teaspoon vanilla extract

Beat the eggs with the sugar and 3 tablespoons of the milk in a heatproof bowl standing over a pan of simmering water or in a double boiler. Heat the rest of the milk until just lukewarm, then beat into the eggs. Cook without boiling until the custard thickens enough to coat the back of a spoon thinly, stirring frequently. Pour into a jug and stir in the vanilla essence (extract). Serve hot or cold with steamed and baked puddings, fruit and mince pies and stewed fruit.
Makes about 300 ml/½ pint (1½ cups)

VARIATIONS:
Lemon or Orange Custard Sauce – add ½ teaspoon finely grated lemon or orange rind to the milk before heating.

Apricot Jam Sauce

METRIC/IMPERIAL
2 teaspoons cornflour
150 ml/¼ pint cold water
2 teaspoons lemon juice
4 tablespoons apricot jam
1 teaspoon caster sugar

AMERICAN
2 teaspoons cornstarch
¾ cup cold water
2 teaspoons lemon juice
¼ cup apricot jam
1 teaspoon sugar

Mix the cornflour (cornstarch) to a smooth paste with a little of the cold water. Put the rest of the water into a saucepan and add the lemon juice, jam and sugar. Heat slowly, stirring, until the sugar has dissolved. Add the cornflour (cornstarch) paste and cook, stirring all the time, until the sauce thickens and comes to the boil. Simmer for 2 minutes. Serve hot or warm with steamed and baked puddings.
Makes about 250 ml/8 fl oz (1 cup)

VARIATIONS:
Marmalade Sauce – use orange marmalade instead of apricot jam, and increase the sugar to 1 tablespoon.
Red Jam Sauce – use raspberry, strawberry, blackcurrant or plum jam instead of apricot jam.

Syrup Sauce

METRIC/IMPERIAL
2 teaspoons cornflour
4 tablespoons cold water
finely grated rind and juice of
  1 lemon
4 tablespoons golden syrup

AMERICAN
2 teaspoons cornstarch
¼ cup cold water
finely grated rind and juice of
  1 lemon
¼ cup light corn or maple syrup

Mix the cornflour (cornstarch) to a smooth paste with the cold water and put into a saucepan with the lemon rind and juice and syrup. Heat gently, stirring, until the sauce comes to the boil and thickens. Simmer for 2 minutes. Serve hot.
Makes about 150 ml/¼ pint (¾ cup)

Apple Sauce

METRIC/IMPERIAL
500 g/1 lb cooking apples, peeled,
  cored and sliced
3 tablespoons water
large pinch of salt
2 teaspoons caster sugar
15 g/½ oz butter

AMERICAN
1 lb tart apples, peeled, cored and
  sliced
3 tablespoons water
large pinch of salt
2 teaspoons sugar
1 tablespoon butter

Place the apples in a saucepan with the water. Cook gently until pulpy and soft, then beat to a thickish purée. Add the salt, sugar and butter. Reheat gently, stirring all the time. Serve hot or cold, with pork, duck and goose.
Makes 150–300 ml/¼–½ pint (⅔–1¼ cups)

Butterscotch Sauce

METRIC/IMPERIAL
1 tablespoon cornflour
150 ml/¼ pint milk
25 g/1 oz butter
100 g/4 oz soft brown sugar
½–1 teaspoon vanilla essence

AMERICAN
1 tablespoon cornstarch
¾ cup milk
2 tablespoons butter
⅔ cup firmly packed brown sugar
½–1 teaspoon vanilla extract

Mix the cornflour (cornstarch) to a smooth paste with a little of the cold milk. Put the rest of the milk into a saucepan with the butter and sugar. Cook over a low heat, stirring, until the sugar has dissolved.
  Add the cornflour (cornstarch) paste and cook, stirring, until the sauce comes to the boil and thickens. Add the vanilla essence (extract). Simmer for 3 minutes. Serve hot with steamed puddings, or cold over ice cream.
Makes about 350 ml/12 fl oz (1½ cups)

Brandy Fudge Sauce

METRIC/IMPERIAL
25 g/1 oz plain chocolate
15 g/½ oz butter
2 tablespoons warm milk
1 tablespoon golden syrup
100 g/4 oz soft brown sugar
2 teaspoons brandy

AMERICAN
1 square (1 oz) semisweet
  chocolate
1 tablespoon butter
2 tablespoons warm milk
1 tablespoon light corn syrup
⅔ cup firmly packed brown sugar
2 teaspoons brandy

Break up the chocolate and put it in a heatproof bowl standing over a saucepan of hot water or in a double boiler. Add the butter and stir occasionally until melted. Blend in the milk, then pour into a saucepan. Add the syrup and sugar. Heat gently, stirring, until the sugar has dissolved. Bring to the boil and boil for 5 minutes without stirring. Remove from the heat and stir in the brandy. Serve hot with steamed and baked puddings.
Makes about 250 ml/8 fl oz (1 cup)

Brandy Hard Sauce

METRIC/IMPERIAL
100 g/4 oz butter, softened
100 g/4 oz caster sugar
100 g/4 oz icing sugar, sifted
1 tablespoon milk
1 tablespoon brandy
50 g/2 oz ground almonds
ground cinnamon

AMERICAN
½ cup butter, softened
½ cup granulated sugar
1 cup confectioners' sugar, sifted
1 tablespoon milk
1 tablespoon brandy
½ cup ground almonds
ground cinnamon

Beat the butter until creamy, then slowly beat in the sugars, alternately with the milk and brandy. Beat until light and fluffy. Add the almonds and mix well. Put into a small dish and sprinkle lightly with cinnamon. Serve with Christmas puddings and other baked and steamed puddings.
Makes 150 to 300 ml/¼ to ½ pint (⅔ to 1¼ cups)

VARIATION:
Rum Hard Sauce – make as above, using rum instead of brandy.

Béchamel Sauce

METRIC/IMPERIAL
300 ml/½ pint milk
1 small onion, quartered
½ small celery stalk, chopped
2 whole cloves
1 small carrot, sliced
6 white peppercorns
1 mace blade
1 parsley sprig
25 g/1 oz butter
25 g/1 oz flour
large pinch of grated nutmeg
salt and white pepper

AMERICAN
1½ cups milk
1 small onion, quartered
½ small celery stalk, chopped
2 whole cloves
1 small carrot, sliced
6 white peppercorns
1 mace blade
1 parsley sprig
2 tablespoons butter
4 tablespoons flour
large pinch of grated nutmeg
salt and white pepper

Put the milk in a saucepan. Add the onion, celery, cloves, carrot, peppercorns, mace and parsley. Slowly bring to just under boiling point, then remove from the heat and cover. Leave to infuse for 30 minutes.

Strain the milk and set aside. Melt the butter in a clean saucepan, add the flour and cook for 2 minutes, stirring. Be sure that the mixture does not brown. Gradually stir in the flavoured milk and cook, stirring, until the sauce comes to the boil and thickens. Simmer very gently for 3 minutes. Remove from the heat and stir in the nutmeg and salt and pepper to taste.
Makes about 300 ml/½ pint (1½ cups)

VARIATIONS:
Cucumber Sauce – add 4 tablespoons finely grated peeled cucumber and 2 tablespoons double (heavy) cream to the finished sauce.
Mornay Sauce – add 50 g/2 oz finely grated Cheddar cheese mixed with 1 egg and 2 tablespoons double (heavy) cream to the finished sauce.
Hot Horseradish Sauce – add 2 tablespoons grated horseradish, ½ teaspoon sugar and 1 teaspoon vinegar to the finished sauce.

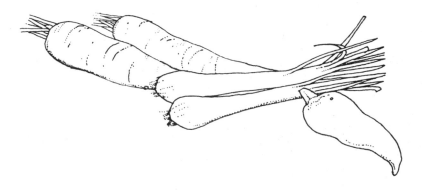

Chocolate Sauce

METRIC/IMPERIAL
1 tablespoon cornflour
300 ml/½ pint milk
50 g/2 oz plain chocolate, grated
½ teaspoon vanilla essence
1–1½ tablespoons caster sugar
15 g/½ oz butter

AMERICAN
1 tablespoon cornstarch
1¼ cups milk
2 squares (1 oz each) semisweet
 chocolate, grated
½ teaspoon vanilla extract
1–1½ tablespoons sugar
1 tablespoon butter

Mix the cornflour (cornstarch) to a smooth paste with a little of the cold milk. Put the rest of the milk into a saucepan with the grated chocolate and heat very slowly until the chocolate melts. Pour onto the cornflour (cornstarch) paste and mix well together. Return to the saucepan and cook slowly, stirring, until the sauce comes to the boil and thickens. Add the vanilla, sugar and butter and simmer for 3 minutes. Serve hot.
Makes about 350 ml/12 fl oz (1½ cups)

Curry Sauce

METRIC/IMPERIAL
2 teaspoons olive oil
50 g/2 oz butter
2 large onions, finely chopped
2 tablespoons curry powder
1 tablespoon flour
2 whole cloves
¼ teaspoon ground ginger
¼ teaspoon ground cinnamon
2 tablespoons sweet pickle
1 tablespoon sugar
1 tablespoon lemon juice
1 tablespoon tomato purée
450 ml/¾ pint stock or water
salt and pepper

AMERICAN
2 teaspoons olive oil
¼ cup butter
2 large onions, finely chopped
2 tablespoons curry powder
1 tablespoon flour
2 whole cloves
¼ teaspoon ground ginger
¼ teaspoon ground cinnamon
2 tablespoons pickle relish
1 tablespoon sugar
1 tablespoon lemon juice
1 tablespoon tomato paste
2 cups broth or water
salt and pepper

Heat the oil and butter in a saucepan. Add the onions and fry gently until pale gold. Stir in the curry powder and flour, then add the cloves, ginger, cinnamon, sweet pickle (relish), sugar, lemon juice and tomato purée (paste). Slowly blend in the stock (broth) or water and bring to the boil, stirring. Lower the heat, season to taste with salt and pepper, cover and simmer gently for 45 minutes to 1 hour.
Makes 600–900 ml/1–1½ pints (2½–3¾ cups)

French Dressing

METRIC/IMPERIAL
¼ teaspoon Worcestershire sauce
½ teaspoon dry mustard
2 tablespoons wine vinegar
½ teaspoon caster sugar
salt and pepper
4 tablespoons olive oil

AMERICAN
¼ teaspoon Worcestershire sauce
½ teaspoon dry mustard
2 tablespoons wine vinegar
½ teaspoon sugar
salt and pepper
¼ cup olive oil

Place the Worcestershire sauce, mustard, vinegar, sugar and salt and pepper to taste in a bowl and beat until smooth. Slowly beat in the oil and continue to beat until thick and creamy. Store in a covered container.
Makes about 75 ml/3 fl oz (⅓ cup)

Brown Sauce

METRIC/IMPERIAL
1 teaspoon olive oil
25 g/1 oz butter
25 g/1 oz lean cooked ham or
    bacon, chopped
½ small celery stalk, chopped
25 g/1 oz mushrooms, chopped
½ small carrot, sliced
½ small onion, chopped
25 g/1 oz flour
450 ml/¾ pint beef stock
1 small tomato, chopped
2 parsley sprigs
1 small bay leaf
salt and pepper

AMERICAN
1 teaspoon olive oil
2 tablespoons butter
2 tablespoons chopped lean
    cooked ham or bacon
½ small celery stalk, chopped
¼ cup chopped mushrooms
½ small carrot, sliced
½ small onion, chopped
¼ cup flour
2 cups beef broth
1 small tomato, chopped
2 parsley sprigs
1 small bay leaf
salt and pepper

Heat the oil and butter in a saucepan. Add the ham or bacon, celery, mushrooms, carrot and onion. Fry gently for 7 to 10 minutes or until golden.
 Add the flour and cook, stirring, until it turns light brown. Slowly stir in the stock (broth) and cook, stirring, until the sauce comes to the boil and thickens. Add the tomato, parsley and bay leaf. Cover the pan and simmer gently for 30 minutes.
 Strain and season to taste with salt and pepper. Reheat gently.
Makes about 300 ml/½ pint (1¼ cups)

VARIATIONS:
Brown Onion Sauce – make the sauce as above. Fry a large chopped onion in butter until golden brown and stir into the strained sauce.
Madeira Sauce – make the sauce as above, then stir in 3 tablespoons Madeira wine after straining.

Bread Sauce

METRIC/IMPERIAL	AMERICAN
4 whole cloves	4 whole cloves
1 small onion	1 small onion
6 white peppercorns	6 white peppercorns
large pinch of grated nutmeg	large pinch of grated nutmeg
300 ml/½ pint milk	1¼ cups milk
½ small bay leaf	½ small bay leaf
50 g/2 oz fresh white breadcrumbs	1 cup soft white bread crumbs
2 tablespoons single cream	2 tablespoons light cream
25 g/1 oz butter	2 tablespoons butter
salt and pepper	salt and pepper

Press the cloves into the onion. Place in a saucepan and add the peppercorns, nutmeg, milk and bay leaf. Slowly bring to the boil, then reduce the heat, cover and simmer for 15 minutes.

Strain and return to the pan. Add the breadcrumbs, cream and butter and season to taste with salt and pepper. Reheat gently just before serving.

Makes about 350 ml/12 fl oz (1½ cups)

Sweet and Sour Sauce

METRIC/IMPERIAL	AMERICAN
50 g/2 oz butter	¼ cup butter
2 medium onions, finely chopped	2 medium-size onions, finely chopped
2 lean bacon rashers, derinded and finely chopped	2 lean Canadian bacon slices, finely chopped
300 ml/½ pint cider	1¼ cups apple cider
150 ml/¼ pint + 2 tablespoons water	⅔ cup + 2 tablespoons water
2 tablespoons tomato purée	2 tablespoons tomato paste
1 tablespoon demerara sugar	1 tablespoon raw brown sugar
2 tablespoons Worcestershire sauce	2 tablespoons Worcestershire sauce
2 tablespoons mango chutney	2 tablespoons mango chutney
salt and pepper	salt and pepper
1 tablespoon arrowroot	1 tablespoon arrowroot

Melt the butter in a saucepan. Add the onions and bacon and fry until they are soft but not brown. Add all the rest of the ingredients except for the arrowroot and 2 tablespoons of the water. Bring to the boil, stirring, and simmer for 15 to 20 minutes.

Mix the arrowroot to a smooth paste with the reserved water. Add to the sauce and cook, stirring, for 1 minute. Serve hot or cold.

White Pouring Sauce

METRIC/IMPERIAL
15 g/½ oz butter
15 g/½ oz flour
300 ml/½ pint milk
salt and pepper

AMERICAN
1 tablespoon butter
2 tablespoons flour
1½ cups milk
salt and pepper

Melt the butter in a saucepan. Add the flour and cook over a low heat, stirring, for 2 minutes. Do not let it brown. Slowly stir in the milk and cook, stirring, until the sauce comes to the boil and thickens. Simmer very gently for 3 minutes, then season to taste with salt and pepper.
Makes 300 ml/½ pint (1½ cups)

VARIATIONS:
White Coating Sauce – make as above, using 25 g/1 oz (2 tablespoons) butter and 25 g/1 oz (¼ cup) flour.
Caper Sauce – make as above, adding 2 tablespoons chopped capers and 2 teaspoons vinegar from the caper jar after the sauce has come to the boil.
Cheese Sauce – make as above, then add 50 g/2 oz (½ cup) finely grated Cheddar cheese, ½ to 1 teaspoon made mustard and a pinch of cayenne.
Egg Sauce – make as above, then stir in 1 finely chopped large hard-boiled (hard-cooked) egg.
Lemon Sauce – make as above, then stir in the finely grated rind and juice of 1 small lemon.
Mustard Sauce – make as above, then stir in 2 teaspoons each dry mustard and vinegar.
Onion Sauce – make as above, then stir in 1 boiled and finely chopped large onion.
Parsley Sauce – make as above, then stir in 1 to 2 tablespoons finely chopped parsley.
Mushroom Sauce – make as above, then stir in 50 to 75 g/2 to 3 oz (½ to ¾ cup) chopped mushrooms that have been lightly fried in butter.

Cream Cheese Dressing

METRIC/IMPERIAL
100 g/4 oz cream cheese
1 tablespoon single cream
1 tablespoon lemon juice or vinegar
1 teaspoon caster sugar
salt and pepper

AMERICAN
½ x ½ lb package cream cheese
1 tablespoon light cream
1 tablespoon lemon juice or vinegar
1 teaspoon sugar
salt and pepper

Place the cream cheese in a mixing bowl and beat until softened. Beat in the remaining ingredients with salt and pepper to taste. Chill in the refrigerator for at least 15 minutes before using.
Makes about 175 ml/6 fl oz (¾ cup)

Cream Cheese and Nut Dressing

METRIC/IMPERIAL
1 tablespoon lemon juice
225 g/8 oz cream cheese
4 tablespoons single cream
50 g/2 oz Cheddar cheese, finely
    grated
1 teaspoon caster sugar
2 tablespoons finely chopped
    salted cashew nuts
salt and pepper

AMERICAN
1 tablespoon lemon juice
1 x ½ lb package cream cheese
¼ cup light cream
½ cup grated Cheddar cheese
1 teaspoon sugar
2 tablespoons finely chopped
    salted cashew nuts
salt and pepper

Beat the lemon juice, cream cheese and cream together until smooth. Stir in the grated cheese, sugar and chopped nuts. Season to taste with salt and pepper and thin with a little extra cream or some milk if necessary. Use as required.
Makes about 300 ml/½ pint (1¼ cups)

Cranberry Sauce

METRIC/IMPERIAL
175 g/6 oz sugar
300 ml/½ pint water
225 g/8 oz cranberries

AMERICAN
¾ cup sugar
1¼ cups water
½ lb cranberries

Put the sugar and water in a saucepan and heat slowly until the sugar dissolves. Add the cranberries and cook fairly quickly for 2 to 3 minutes or until the skins pop open. Reduce the heat and simmer very gently for a further 10 minutes. Serve hot or cold.
Makes about 450 ml/¾ pint (2 cups)

Mint Sauce

METRIC/IMPERIAL
4 tablespoons finely chopped fresh
    mint
3 tablespoons boiling water
¼ teaspoon salt
1 tablespoon caster sugar
3 tablespoons vinegar

AMERICAN
¼ cup finely chopped fresh mint
3 tablespoons boiling water
¼ teaspoon salt
1 tablespoon sugar
3 tablespoons vinegar

Stir the mint into the boiling water, then add the salt and sugar. Leave until cold. Stir in the vinegar and serve.
Makes about 120 ml/4 fl oz (½ cup)

Meat or Poultry Gravy

METRIC/IMPERIAL
meat or poultry dripping
1 tablespoon cornflour
300 ml/½ pint stock or water
salt and pepper

AMERICAN
meat or poultry drippings
1 tablespoon cornstarch
1¼ cups broth or water
salt and pepper

Pour off all dripping from the roasting pan except for about 1 tablespoon. Add the cornflour (cornstarch) and mix well together. Place the roasting pan over a very low heat on top of the stove and slowly stir in the stock (broth) or water. Cook, stirring, until the gravy comes to the boil and thickens. Lower the heat and simmer for 3 minutes, then season to taste with salt and pepper.
Makes 300 ml/½ pint (1¼ cups)

Hollandaise Sauce

METRIC/IMPERIAL
1 tablespoon cold water
1 teaspoon lemon juice
3 white peppercorns
1 teaspoon wine vinegar
½ small bay leaf
4 egg yolks
225 g/8 oz butter, softened
salt and white pepper

AMERICAN
1 tablespoon cold water
1 teaspoon lemon juice
3 white peppercorns
1 teaspoon wine vinegar
½ small bay leaf
4 egg yolks
1 cup butter, softened
salt and white pepper

Put the water, lemon juice, peppercorns, vinegar and bay leaf in a saucepan and boil gently until the liquid is reduced by half. Leave until cold, then strain.

Place the strained liquid and egg yolks in a heatproof bowl standing over a saucepan of gently simmering water, or a double boiler, and whisk until creamy and thick. Slowly add the butter, a small piece at a time. Keep whisking until all the butter has been melted and absorbed into the sauce, and the sauce has become like mayonnaise. Season to taste with salt and pepper and serve immediately.
Makes about 300 ml/½ pint (1¼ cups)

Basic Choux Pastry

METRIC/IMPERIAL
65 g/2½ oz plain flour
pinch of salt
50 g/2 oz butter
150 ml/¼ pint water
2 large eggs, lightly beaten

AMERICAN
10 tablespoons all-purpose flour
pinch of salt
¼ cup butter
⅔ cup water
2 large eggs, lightly beaten

Sift the flour and salt together. Put the butter into a saucepan with the water, and bring just to boiling point over a moderate heat, until the butter has melted. Remove the pan from the heat and beat in the sifted flour immediately, until the choux paste forms a smooth ball and leaves the sides of the pan clean. Allow to cool, and then gradually beat in the beaten eggs. If the choux paste is too hot the eggs will curdle.

Éclairs – follow the instructions for piping and baking Chocolate Éclairs on page 200. When the éclairs are cooked, remove them to a wire rack and make a slit in the side of each one to allow the steam to escape. Once cold, fill the éclairs with Crème pâtissière (see page 249) and coat with coffee, chocolate or vanilla glacé icing.
Makes 10 to 12

Cream Buns – put the choux pastry into a piping bag fitted with a large star nozzle. Pipe small round, raised shapes on to greased and floured baking sheets, leaving space for spreading. Each round of choux should be about 5 cm/2 inches in diameter. Bake as for éclairs, and make a small hole in the base of each cooked bun, to allow the steam to escape. Once cold, fill the buns with whipped cream and dust with sifted icing (confectioners') sugar.
Makes 10 to 12

Profiteroles – put the choux pastry into a piping bag fitted with a 1 cm/ ½ inch plain nozzle. Pipe very small raised mounds, no more than 2.5 cm/1 inch in diameter, on to greased and floured baking sheets, leaving space for spreading. Bake as for éclairs, but for only 20 minutes, and make a small hole in the base of each cooked profiterole to allow the steam to escape. Once cold, fill with whipped cream. Arrange the profiteroles in a pyramid on a serving dish, and either dust with sifted icing (confectioners') sugar or top with a chocolate sauce.
Serves 4

NOTE: For a party snack the baked profiteroles can be served hot with a savoury filling – try cream cheese flavoured with anchovy essence and mixed with chopped prawns (shrimp); white sauce mixed with flaked tuna and chopped hard-boiled (hard-cooked) egg; or minced (ground) ham and chutney.

Shortcrust (Pie) Pastry

METRIC/IMPERIAL
225 g/8 oz flour
¼ teaspoon salt
100 g/4 oz butter

AMERICAN
2 cups flour
¼ teaspoon salt
½ cup butter

Sift the flour and salt into a mixing bowl. Add the butter and cut into the flour with a knife, then rub in with the fingertips until the mixture looks like fine breadcrumbs. Add enough cold water to bind to a dough.

Turn out onto a lightly floured board. Knead quickly until crack-free and smooth. Roll out and use as required.

Makes 225 g/8 oz (2 cup) quantity

VARIATIONS:

Rich Shortcrust Pastry – make as above, increasing the butter to 150 g/ 5 oz (10 tablespoons). Cover and chill for 30 minutes before using.

Lemon Pastry – make as above, adding 1 teaspoon very finely grated lemon rind before the water.

Nut Pastry – make as above, adding 25 to 40 g/1 to 1½ oz (¼ to ⅓ cup) very finely chopped walnuts before the water.

Puff Pastry

METRIC/IMPERIAL
225 g/8 oz butter
225 g/8 oz flour
¼ teaspoon salt
1 teaspoon lemon juice

AMERICAN
1 cup butter
2 cups flour
¼ teaspoon salt
1 teaspoon lemon juice

Put the butter in a clean tea (dish) towel and squeeze well to remove any surplus moisture, and to make it soft and pliable. Shape into a 7.5 cm/ 3 inch brick.

Sift the flour and salt into a mixing bowl. Add the lemon juice and enough chilled water to bind to a soft dough. Turn out onto a lightly floured board and knead well.

Roll out into an oblong about 30 x 15 cm/12 x 6 inches. Place the butter on the lower half of the oblong and cover with the top half. Press the open edges together with a rolling pin. Place in a plastic bag or cover with foil, and chill for 15 minutes.

Remove from the bag or foil and with the fold on your right, roll out into a 45 x 15 cm/18 x 6 inch oblong. Fold in three, envelope-style, by bringing the bottom third over the middle and then the top third over on top. Seal the edges, replace in the foil or plastic bag and chill. Repeat until the dough has been rolled, folded and chilled seven times.

Replace in the plastic bag or foil and chill for at least 30 minutes before rolling out to 6 mm/¼ inch thickness and using as required.

Makes 225 g/8 oz (2 cup) quantity

Hot Water Crust Pastry

METRIC/IMPERIAL
350 g/12 oz flour
½ teaspoon salt
1 egg yolk
4 tablespoons milk
4 tablespoons water
25 g/1 oz butter
75 g/3 oz lard

AMERICAN
3 cups flour
½ teaspoon salt
1 egg yolk
⅓ cup milk
⅓ cup water
2 tablespoons butter
6 tablespoons lard or shortening

Sift the flour and salt into a mixing bowl and warm slightly in a cool oven. Make a well in the centre. Beat the egg yolk with 1 tablespoon of the milk and pour into the well.

Put the rest of the milk with the water in a saucepan, add the butter and lard and heat slowly until the butter and lard melt. Bring to the boil and pour into the well in the flour. Mix together with a wooden spoon until well blended. Turn out onto a lightly floured board and knead quickly until smooth.

Place in a heatproof bowl standing over a saucepan of hot water. Cover with a tea (dish) towel and leave to rest for 30 minutes.

Roll out the warm dough to 6 mm/¼ inch thick and use as required.
Makes 350 g/12 oz (3 cup) quantity

Rough Puff Pastry

METRIC/IMPERIAL
225 g/8 oz flour
¼ teaspoon salt
150 ml/¼ pint chilled water
1 teaspoon lemon juice
175 g/6 oz butter, diced

AMERICAN
2 cups flour
¼ teaspoon salt
¾ cup chilled water
1 teaspoon lemon juice
¾ cup butter, diced

Sift the flour and salt into a mixing bowl. Mix together the water and lemon juice. Add the butter to the flour with the liquid and, using a knife, mix to a fairly soft dough, making sure that you do not break down the butter any smaller.

Turn out onto a lightly floured board and shape into a block. Roll out into a 6 mm/¼ inch thick oblong, about 45 x 15 cm/18 x 6 inches. Fold in three, by bringing the bottom third up over the middle and then the top third down on top. Seal the open edges together well by pressing down firmly with a rolling pin.

Give the dough a quarter turn, so that the edges are to the left and right. Roll out and turn three more times.

Place the folded dough in a plastic bag or wrap in foil and chill for at least 15 minutes before using as required.
Makes 225 g/8 oz (2 cup) quantity

Sweet Flan Pastry

METRIC/IMPERIAL
1 egg yolk
2 teaspoons sifted icing sugar
100 g/4 oz flour
pinch of salt
65 g/2½ oz butter
1–2 teaspoons cold water

AMERICAN
1 egg yolk
2 teaspoons confectioners' sugar
1 cup flour
pinch of salt
5 tablespoons butter
1–2 teaspoons cold water

Mix the egg yolk and sugar well together. Sift the flour and salt into a mixing bowl. Add the butter and cut into the flour with a knife, then rub in with the fingertips.

Add the egg yolk mixture and water and mix to a very stiff paste. Turn out onto a lightly floured board and knead quickly until smooth. Place in a plastic bag or wrap in foil and chill for at least 30 minutes before using.
Makes 100 g/4 oz (1 cup) quantity

Suet Crust Pastry

METRIC/IMPERIAL
225 g/8 oz self-raising flour
½ teaspoon salt
1 teaspoon baking powder
100 g/4 oz finely grated or
  shredded beef suet
150 ml/¼ pint cold water

AMERICAN
2 cups self-rising flour
½ teaspoon salt
1 teaspoon baking powder
½ cup finely grated or shredded
  beef suet
¾ cup cold water

Sift the flour, salt and baking powder into a mixing bowl, add the suet and toss lightly together. Mix to a soft paste with the water.

Turn out onto a lightly floured board and knead until smooth. Roll out to about 3 mm/⅛ inch thickness. Use immediately, as required.
Makes 225 g/8 oz (2 cup) quantity

Milk Puff Pastry

METRIC/IMPERIAL
225 g/8 oz self-raising flour
¼ teaspoon salt
175 g/6 oz butter
4–5 tablespoons cold milk

AMERICAN
2 cups self-rising flour
¼ teaspoon salt
¾ cup butter
4–5 tablespoons cold milk

Sift the flour and salt into a mixing bowl. Add the butter and cut into the flour until the pieces are no bigger than peas. Mix to a dough with the milk.

Quickly shape into a ball and place in a plastic bag or wrap in foil. Chill for 1 hour before using as required.
Makes 225 g/8 oz (2 cup) quantity

Flaky Pastry

METRIC/IMPERIAL
175 g/6 oz butter
225 g/8 oz flour
¼ teaspoon salt
150 ml/¼ pint chilled water
1 teaspoon lemon juice

AMERICAN
¾ cup butter
2 cups flour
¼ teaspoon salt
¾ cup chilled water
1 teaspoon lemon juice

Divide the butter into four equal parts and chill three of the portions. Sift the flour and salt into a mixing bowl and add the remaining portion of butter. Rub in well together. Mix to a dough with the water and lemon juice.

Turn out onto a lightly floured board and knead thoroughly. Place in a plastic bag or wrap in foil and chill for at least 30 minutes.

Roll out into an oblong about 45 x 15 cm/18 x 6 inches, and 6 mm/ ¼ inch thick. Using the tip of the knife, flake a portion of chilled butter over the top and middle third of the dough oblong, to within 2.5 cm/1 inch of the edges. Dust very lightly with flour, then fold up envelope-style, by bringing the bottom third over the middle and then the top third over on top. Seal the edges by pressing together with a rolling pin. Put back in the plastic bag or foil and chill for a further 15 minutes.

Remove from the bag or foil and with folded edges to the left and right, roll out again to an oblong as before. Cover with another portion of chilled butter as before, then again fold, seal and chill for 15 minutes.

Repeat with the last portion of butter, and chill for 15 minutes.

Roll out, fold, seal and chill for at least 30 minutes before using.
Makes 225 g/8 oz (2 cup) quantity

Crème Pâtissière (Pastry Cream)

METRIC/IMPERIAL
2 tablespoons cornflour
300 ml/½ pint milk
1 tablespoon caster sugar
few drops of vanilla essence
2 egg yolks
4 tablespoons whipped cream

AMERICAN
2 tablespoons cornstarch
1¼ cups milk
1 tablespoon sugar
few drops of vanilla extract
2 egg yolks
¼ cup whipped cream

Blend the cornflour (cornstarch) with a little of the milk. Put the remaining milk into a saucepan with the sugar and the vanilla. Bring the milk to the boil and stir into the blended cornflour (cornstarch). Return the mixture to the saucepan and cook, stirring constantly, until the mixture thickens.

Remove from the heat and beat in the egg yolks. Stir over gentle heat for a few minutes to cook the egg but do not allow to boil. Cover the pastry cream with a circle of dampened greaseproof (waxed) paper until you are ready to use it, to prevent a skin forming, and cool. Fold in the whipped cream and any chosen additional flavouring or food colouring.
Makes about 450 ml/¾ pint (2 cups)

Meringue Topping

METRIC/IMPERIAL
2 egg whites
50–75 g/2–3 oz caster sugar
1 tablespoon granulated sugar

AMERICAN
2 egg whites
¼–⅓ cup superfine sugar
1 tablespoon granulated sugar

Place the egg whites in a large dry bowl. Beat until very stiff and peaky. Fold in the caster (superfine) sugar using a large metal spoon. Spoon the mixture over the pie or pudding and sprinkle the granulated sugar on top.

Buttercream

METRIC/IMPERIAL
100 g/4 oz butter, softened
225 g/8 oz icing sugar, sifted
2 tablespoons cold milk

AMERICAN
½ cup butter, softened
2 cups confectioners' sugar, sifted
2 tablespoons cold milk

Beat the butter until really soft and creamy. Slowly beat in the icing (confectioners') sugar, alternately with the milk. Continue beating until fluffy and light.

VARIATIONS:
Chocolate Buttercream – make as above, then add 50 g/2 oz (2 squares) melted and cooled plain (sweet or semisweet) chocolate.
Coffee Buttercream – make as above, adding 3 to 4 teaspoons instant coffee powder with the sugar.
Lemon or Orange Buttercream – make as above, adding 1 teaspoon grated lemon or orange rind to the butter before the sugar.
Vanilla Buttercream – make as above, adding ½ to 1 teaspoon vanilla essence (extract) with the milk.

Coffee Fudge Icing

METRIC/IMPERIAL
1 tablespoon single cream
50 g/2 oz butter
3 tablespoons coffee essence
100 g/4 oz soft brown sugar
450 g/1 lb icing sugar, sifted

AMERICAN
1 tablespoon light cream
¼ cup butter
3 tablespoons strong black coffee
⅔ cup firmly packed brown sugar
4 cups confectioners' sugar, sifted

Put the cream, butter, coffee essence (black coffee) and brown sugar into a saucepan. Heat gently until the butter has melted and the sugar dissolved. Bring to the boil and boil for 3 minutes. Remove from the heat and stir in the icing (confectioners') sugar. Beat until smooth and shiny, then continue beating for 5 minutes or until the icing has cooled.

Crème Chantilly

METRIC/IMPERIAL
6 tablespoons double cream
1 egg white
2 teaspoons caster sugar
½ teaspoon vanilla essence

AMERICAN
6 tablespoons heavy cream
1 egg white
2 teaspoons sugar
½ teaspoon vanilla

Whip the cream until if forms soft peaks. Wash and dry the beaters carefully then beat the egg white until stiff. Add the sugar and vanilla essence and continue beating until glossy. Lightly fold the meringue into the cream until well blended.

Glacé Icing

METRIC/IMPERIAL
225 g/8 oz icing sugar, sifted
2 tablespoons hot water

AMERICAN
2 cups confectioners' sugar, sifted
2 tablespoons hot water

Put the sugar in a bowl. Slowly add the water and beat until smooth and thick enough to coat the back of the spoon. If too thin, add more sugar; if too thick, add more hot water.

VARIATIONS:
Coffee Glacé Icing – make as above, adding 2 teaspoons instant coffee powder dissolved in the water.
Chocolate Glacé Icing – make as above, adding 2 teaspoons cocoa powder dissolved in the water.
Orange or Lemon Glacé Icing – make as above, adding 1 teaspoon finely grated orange or lemon rind to the sugar.

Coffee Velvet Icing

METRIC/IMPERIAL
2 tablespoons coffee essence
25 g/1 oz butter, melted
175 g/6 oz icing sugar, sifted

AMERICAN
2 tablespoons strong black coffee
2 tablespoons butter, melted
1½ cups confectioners' sugar, sifted

Mix the coffee essence (black coffee) well into the butter. Slowly stir in the sugar and beat until fairly thick and creamy.

VARIATIONS:
Lemon or Orange Velvet Icing – make as above, using undiluted lemon or orange squash (concentrated lemon or orange juice) instead of coffee.
Lime Velvet Icing – make as above, using undiluted lime cordial or juice instead of coffee.

Whipped Cream Icing

METRIC/IMPERIAL
150 ml/¼ pint double cream
1 tablespoon milk
1 tablespoon caster sugar

AMERICAN
¾ cup heavy cream
1 tablespoon milk
1 tablespoon sugar

Whip the cream and milk together until light and thick, then whip in the sugar. Use as required.

VARIATION:
Coffee Cream Icing – add 1 teaspoon instant coffee powder with the sugar.

Caramel Cream Frosting

METRIC/IMPERIAL
25 g/1 oz caster sugar
2 teaspoons water
300 ml/½ pint chilled double cream

AMERICAN
2 tablespoons sugar
2 teaspoons water
1¼ cups chilled heavy cream

Place the sugar and water in a saucepan and heat, stirring, until the sugar dissolves. Bring to the boil, then cover and boil for 30 seconds. Remove the lid and keep boiling until the syrup has turned a light caramel colour. Remove from the heat and quickly stir in 2 teaspoons of the cream. Leave to cool completely.
   Add the rest of the cream and whip until thick and creamy.

Mocha Icing

METRIC/IMPERIAL
50 g/2 oz plain chocolate
2 teaspoons instant coffee powder
2 tablespoons warm water
15 g/½ oz butter
½ teaspoon vanilla essence
175 g/6 oz icing sugar, sifted

AMERICAN
2 squares (1 oz each) semisweet
   chocolate
2 teaspoons instant coffee powder
2 tablespoons warm water
1 tablespoon butter
½ teaspoon vanilla extract
1½ cups confectioners' sugar,
   sifted

Break up the chocolate and put it in a heatproof bowl placed over a saucepan of simmering water (or use a double boiler). Add the coffee powder, water and butter and heat until melted, stirring just once or twice.
   Remove from the heat. Add the vanilla and slowly beat in the sugar. Use immediately

VARIATION:
Chocolate Icing – make as above, omitting the coffee powder.

American Boiled Frosting

METRIC/IMPERIAL
450 g/1 lb sugar
150 ml/¼ pint water
2 egg whites
pinch of cream of tartar
1 teaspoon vanilla essence

AMERICAN
2 cups sugar
¾ cup water
2 egg whites
pinch of cream of tartar
1 teaspoon vanilla extract

Put the sugar and water into a saucepan and heat gently, stirring, until the sugar dissolves. Bring to the boil, then cover and boil for 1 minute. Uncover and boil for a further 5 minutes without stirring.

Beat the egg whites and cream of tartar together to a peaky snow. Gradually pour the sugar syrup onto the egg whites, beating constantly. Add the vanilla and continue beating until cool enough to use.

Sweet Fritter Batter

METRIC/IMPERIAL
50 g/2 oz flour
pinch of salt
1 teaspoon sifted icing sugar
4 teaspoons lukewarm water
2 teaspoons melted butter
1 egg white

AMERICAN
½ cup flour
pinch of salt
1 teaspoon sifted confectioners'
* sugar*
4 teaspoons lukewarm water
2 teaspoons melted butter
1 egg white

Sift the flour and salt into a bowl. Add the sugar, then gradually beat in the water and melted butter and beat until smooth and thick.

Whisk the egg white to stiff snow. Fold into the batter, using a metal spoon, just before using.

Pork Sage Stuffing

METRIC/IMPERIAL
225 g/8 oz pork sausagemeat
100 g/4 oz fresh white
* breadcrumbs*
2 teaspoons chopped parsley
1 teaspoon crumbled dried sage
½ teaspoon dried thyme
¾ teaspoon grated nutmeg
½ teaspoon salt
3 tablespoons milk

AMERICAN
½ lb bulk pork sausagemeat
2 cups soft white bread crumbs
2 teaspoons chopped parsley
1 teaspoon crumbled dried sage
½ teaspoon dried thyme
¼ teaspoon grated nutmeg
½ teaspoon salt
3 tablespoons milk

Place all the ingredients in a bowl and mix well together for 2 to 3 minutes. Use as required.

Index